THE WORLD OF
Drafting

THE WORLD OF
Drafting

STAN ROSS

Downey, California

An introductory mission for you in the
use of 2-dimensional space for the
development of 3-dimensional space.

McKNIGHT & McKNIGHT PUBLISHING COMPANY · BLOOMINGTON, ILLINOIS

Preface

Drafting is said to be the language of industry. As a means of communicating ideas and details, it is second only in importance to your native language. Drafting provides an efficient means for people to plan, specify, and evaluate their ideas.

The learning experiences provided in this book are for the beginning or the introductory study level of drafting. The book covers a wide range of drafting experiences for the purpose of developing an ability to plan, express, and interpret ideas efficiently. In order to accomplish this purpose, the students should plan on spending a minimum 30 hours (6 week course) of study. There are enough experiences provided in this book for a study involving at least 90 hours (18 week course) and can be used for a one year course. A teacher can select the subjects to be emphasized in a short course. The author suggests that the students become acquainted with the first six chapters in depth. Students should do as many drawing problems as possible in the available drawing time.

The material in this publication represents many new concepts in the teaching and learning of drafting. These concepts have been developed and presented through a careful analysis of the following questions:

1. What abilities help people succeed in life?
2. What are the interests and abilities of people beginning the study of drafting?
3. What is drafting?

All of the learning experiences in this book have direct application to your educational and life experiences. The drawings represent useful projects that may be made in the school or at home. The variety of drawings offer you experiences in other areas of industrial expression such as *woodworking, metalworking, plastics, electricity-electronics, mechanics,* and the *graphic arts.*

Stan Ross

Acknowledgments

The author wishes to express his sincere appreciation to the many people, companies and associations that have been of assistance during the preparation of this book.

Allis Chalmers
846 South 70th Street
Milwaukee, Wisconsin 53201

A.W. Faber—
  Castell Pencil Company
Newark, New Jersey 07103

Black and Decker Manufacturing
  Company
701 East Joppa Road
Towson, Maryland 21204

Blu-Ray Incorporated
6426 Westbrook Road
Essex, Connecticut 06426

Boeing
7755 East Marginal Way
Seattle, Washington 98124

Charles Bruning Company
1800 West Central Road
Mount Prospect, Illinois 60058

Cincinnati Milling Machine
4701 Narbury Avenue
Cincinnati, Ohio 45209

Dazor Manufacturing Corporation
4455 Duncan Avenue
St. Louis, Missouri 63110

Diamond Chain Company
402 Kentucky Avenue
Indianapolis, Indiana 46207

Eagle Pencil Corporation
Danbury, Connecticut

Eastman Kodak
Rochester, New York 14650

Eberhard-Faber Incorporated
Crestwood Street
Wilkes-Barre, Pennsylvania 18703

Eugene Dietzgen Company
2425 North Sheffield Avenue
Chicago, Illinois 60614

Ewald Manufacturing Company
1143 Norman Avenue
Thousand Oaks, California

Fluid Power Society
P.O. Box 43
Thiensville, Wisconsin 53092

Frederick Post Company
3646 North Avondale Avenue
Chicago, Illinois

Fullerton Engineering Sales Company
811 Milford Street
Glendale, California 91203

Graymark Enterprises Incorporated
3211 Pico Boulevard
Santa Monica, California 90405

Itek Business Products
1001 Jefferson Road
Rochester, New York 14603

Keuffel and Esser Company
300 Adams Street
Hoboken, New Jersey 07030

Koh-I-Noor, Incorporated
103 North Street
Bloomsbury, New Jersey 08804

Lietz Company
1224 South Hope Street
Los Angeles, California 90015

North American Rockwell
12214 South Lakewood Boulevard
Downey, California 90241

Plan-A-Room
Paul MacAlister and Associates,
  Incorporated
Lake Bluff, Illinois 60044

Plant Layout Materials,
  Incorporated
24 Eastview Road
Latham, New York 12110

Prestape, Incorporated
136 West 21st Street
New York, New York 10011

Los Angeles Times
Times-Mirror Square
Los Angeles, California 90053

Rapidesign
P.O. Box 429
Burbank, California 91503

Stacor Corporation
285 Emmet Street
Newark, New Jersey 07144

United States Steel Corporation
445 South Figueroa Street
Los Angeles, California 90017

V and E Manufacturing Company
766 South Fair Oaks
Pasadena, California

Wheelabrator Corporation
400 South Byrkit Street
Mishawaka, Indiana 46544

X-Acto Incorporated
48 VanOam Street
Long Island City, New York 11101

vi

Table of Contents

List of Tables

Introduction

THE WORLD OF DRAFTING is an introduction to various kinds of drawings that express ideas for others to understand. You will learn to make and read drawings by using the two dimensional area of flat surfaces. The drawings will be plans for products and activities to be used in the development of three dimensional objects. The three dimensional space used by man is of three types: (1) gas (air or outer space), (2) liquid (water or oceans), and (3) solid (land or planets).

THE WORLD OF DRAFTING is a refreshingly new approach for you to use in developing your abilities to make and understand drawings. The *what, why, and how* in every learning activity is explained to you. These instructional procedures reflect the most effective techniques of learning and have been developed with students by the author. The learning activities have been selected to represent the use of drafting in *life experiences*. This is accomplished through a concise use of words and an abundant use of more than 600 illustrations. Material is arranged in a systematic order according to function or need. Every drawing is of a *useful* product or activity that can be made or used. There is a wide range of interest applications of drafting shown such as wood, metal, plastic, paper, and fabric products, as well as activities dealing with manufacturing, marketing, servicing, designing, sports, electronics, data processing, music, and transportation. In all learning activities there are more problems provided than are needed to develop your abilities. This gives you the opportunity to make choices according to interests and abilities.

You begin to understand THE WORLD OF DRAFTING with the "big picture" in the first chapter entitled "Drafting Is." It includes the purpose, organization, jobs, drawings, and fields of drafting. The process and elements used in making drawings are explained. The education needed by a draftsman is described. Chapter 1 gives you a complete preview of your book with a brief explanation of what you will learn in each chapter.

The author's experiences with drafting began as a young boy in a family workshop. He has personally experienced employment in many of the drafting occupations described in the first chapter. You will benefit from his long experience as an educator through the use of new learning techniques. The encouragement of his wife Connie and their children, Lori, Stacy, Kendall, and Randy, and the talents of many students and the publisher combine with the author's experiences to provide you with the opportunity to learn THE WORLD OF DRAFTING.

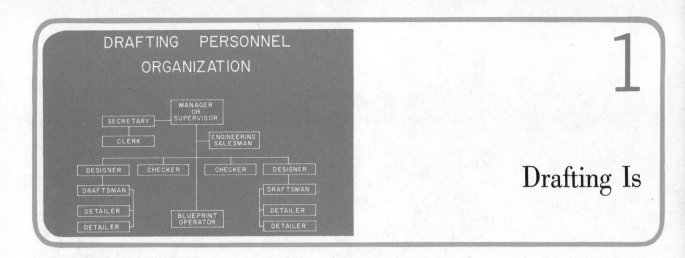

DRAFTING PERSONNEL ORGANIZATION

Drafting Is

Why Study This Chapter?

Your school building, your desk, your ball-point pen all began as ideas. Certain people, who knew how these objects should work and how they should look, drew plans for their construction. The plans were studied and understood by other people who then built the objects.

You can learn to communicate your ideas in this way and to understand drawings. This chapter explains what skills and knowledge are needed. It introduces to you the exciting subject of what DRAFTING IS.

Everyone has ideas!

Boys . . Girls . . Business People . . Industrial Workers . . Farmers . . Artists . . Housewives . . Professional People

Ideas are expressed in many ways.

Words . . Numbers . . Drawings . . Models . . Music . . Symbols

Some ideas are expressed best with *words*,

GO   OUCH   CUT THE BOARD   CLEAR LACQUER FINISH

numbers,

$3 + 5 = 8$ $5 \times 9 = 45$ $3.25 \times 2 = 6.5$

or *symbols.*

SYMBOLS

" , ! ? X + = %

Other ideas are best shown with a *picture,*

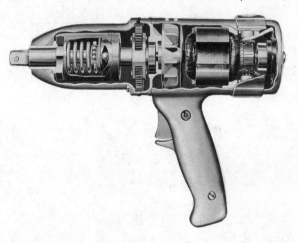

working drawings,

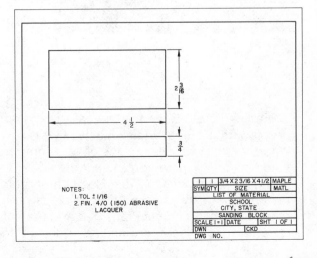

NOTES:
1. TOL ± 1/16
2. FIN. 4/0 (150) ABRASIVE
   LACQUER

| | | 3/4 X 2 3/16 X 4 1/2 | MAPLE |
| SYM | QTY | SIZE | MATL |
| LIST OF MATERIAL |
| SCHOOL |
| CITY, STATE |
| SANDING BLOCK |
| SCALE 1 = 1 | DATE | | SHT 1 OF 1 |
| DWN | | CKD |
| DWG NO. |

or charts.

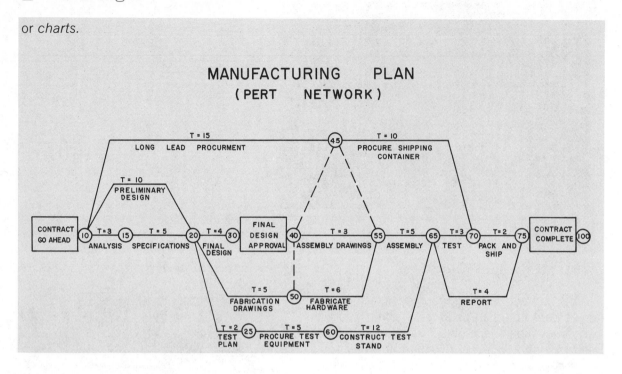

MANUFACTURING   PLAN
(PERT   NETWORK)

Drafting deals with expressing ideas in the form of drawings such as pictures, working drawings, and charts. The drawings are supported with symbols, numbers, words, and colors so that the meaning cannot be misunderstood.

What is Drafting?

Drafting is preparing drawings for things that are to be made or done. Such drawings can be drawn and used in any of several forms by most everyone in their daily life. People who earn their living by drafting are known as draftsmen, engineers, or architects.

Drafting is said to be the language of industry and serves many useful purposes. It provides people with accurate and economical ways of developing, recording, and explaining their ideas. With drawings, complete plans of very complex machines, buildings, and organizations can be made by one or more draftsmen.

Copies of drawings may be used in a distant location by a builder or several builders to make the object exactly as desired. Building can be done using drawings as the only means of communication between the draftsman and the builder. In drafting, the most effective methods are used to express ideas for building or doing things.

DRAFTSMAN

DRAWING PRINTS

BUILDER

Usually, plans are drawn with pencil or ink, but they may be put together with various types of printed materials and tape. In drafting, such elements as lines, symbols, numbers, colors, shades, and words are used to make pictorial, orthographic, and systems drawings. The airplane drawing is an example of pictorial drawing. The sanding block gauge is an example of orthographic projection. The transistor receiver on page 4 is an example of a systems drawing.

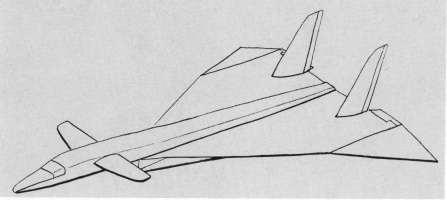

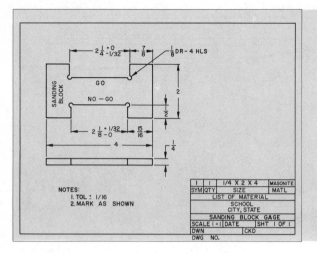

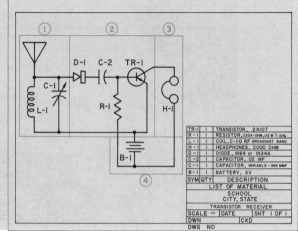

People in Drafting

People employed in a drafting occupation usually work in small groups, and each individual may have different areas or levels of responsibility. A typical drafting group is organized as shown in this chart.

DRAFTING PERSONNEL

ORGANIZATION

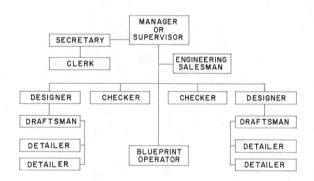

At work, the organization might look like the drafting group shown in these pictures.

Each of the jobs done in this organization is explained in the following job descriptions.

Supervisor and Designer

Supervisors (chief; leader; head; senior) *of Drafting or Engineering* coordinate activities of a group of workers chiefly engaged in one type of drafting. They determine the work procedures. They give written and oral instruction. They assign duties to workers and examine their work. They maintain teamwork among their employees. They adjust errors and complaints. They may also employ, train, and discharge workers.

Designers (engineering) draw preliminary sketches and apply mathematical, scientific, and fundamental information to develop and change designs. They select a standard for ready-made parts. They draft complete layout or design drawings. They also work with sales people to fulfill customer needs.

Checker

Checkers examine engineering drawings to correct errors in computing and recording dimensions and specifications. They compare figures on production layout drawings with detail drawings by examining the angles, tolerances, bend allowances, and dimensions for accuracy. They determine the suitability of designs, materials, tooling, and fabrication sequences, as guided by their knowledge of techniques and methods of manufacture. They confer with design personnel to resolve design problems. They also note corrections on drawing prints.

Draftsman

Draftsmen prepare clear, complete, and accurate working plans and detail drawings from layouts, sketches, or notes. They use their knowledge of machines, materials, mathematics, and science to complete the drawings. They also exercise skill in the use of drafting tools.

Detailer

Detailers make detailed drawings of parts for machines or structures from a general design or rough drawings. They record the dimensions and materials to be used as well as the other information necessary to make an idea or plan clear and complete. They have skill in making finished drawings on tracing paper.

Printing Machine Operator

Printing machine operators (blueprint) make copies (whiteprints also called blueprints) of printed materials such as documents. They examine the original drawing surface for its ability to allow light to pass through it and select sensitized paper for printing. The machine controls must be regulated for proper

Apprentice Draftsman

Apprentice draftsmen, according to written or oral agreement, learn to be draftsmen during two or more years of *on-the-job training*. They may be considered qualified workers after thorough job experience which is supplemented by related instruction. Both men and women can become draftsmen.

exposure (time and light intensity) according to the translucency of the original and the type of sensitized paper. The original and the sensitized paper are put into the machine to expose and develop the print. The supply of chemicals for developing the print must be regulated. The finished print is examined for specified color, intensity, and printed line quality. The prints are then folded and packaged. The operator's job title may be designated according to the trade name of the machine, such as Copyflex[R] machine operator or Ozalid[R] operator.

Sales Engineer

Sales engineers sell drafting or engineering services to manufacturing and building companies. They are capable of discussing engineering problems and economic alternates with their customers when selling products or services. They prepare financial and operational estimates for work to be done.

Secretary

Secretaries answer telephones, schedule appointments, greet visitors, take dictation, and transcribe notes on a typewriter, read and route incoming mail, and compose and type routine letters. They may arrange travel schedules, supervise clerical workers, keep personnel records, and order supplies.

Office Clerk

Office clerks type bills, receipts, correspondence, and transfer information from one record to another. They sort and file records, drawings, correspondence, and catalogs. They answer telephones, take messages, run errands, and operate office duplicating equipment.

Making and Using Drawings

Making a drawing involves the use of: tools, elements, media, and reproduction equipment.

Tools commonly used to make drawings are the pencil, eraser, scale, drawing board, T-square or parallel straight edge, triangles, a protractor, a compass, and templates.

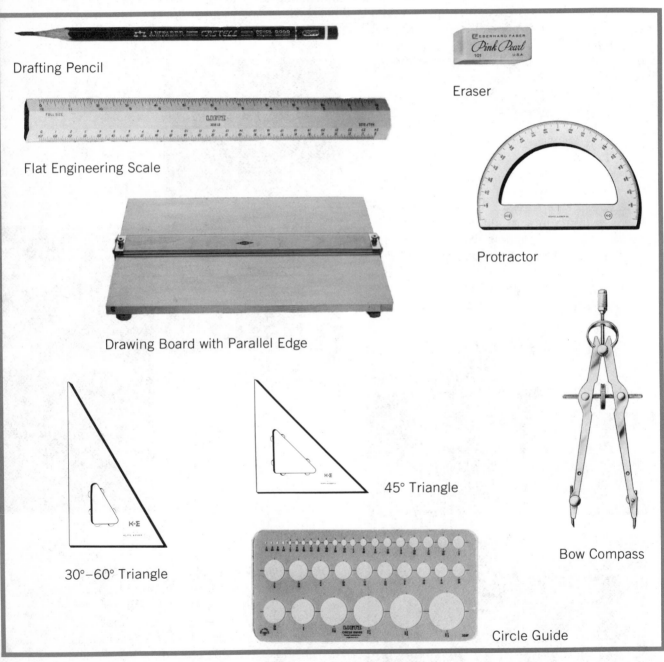

Drafting Pencil

Eraser

Flat Engineering Scale

Protractor

Drawing Board with Parallel Edge

45° Triangle

Bow Compass

30°–60° Triangle

Circle Guide

Common Drafting Tools

Elements or building blocks used to make drawings are lines, symbols, numbers, words, shades, and colors.

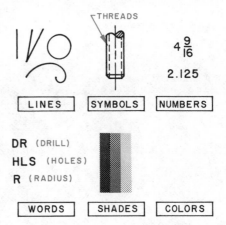

MAP OF DRAFTING PRODUCTION

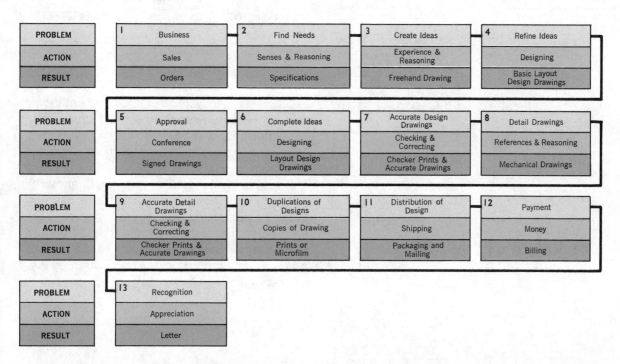

Media includes the surface materials and the tools used for marking the surface. In drafting, marks are made with lead, ink, tape, and printed adhesive-backed materials. Paper and plastic are the surfaces most often used for drawing.

Reproduction methods used in copying or printing drawings are the photographic or copy machine processes. The photographic process is used to enlarge or reduce the size of drawings while the copy process is used to make same-size reproductions. Some copy process machines are capable of reducing the size of a drawing in making copies.

The "Map for Making Drawings" will help you understand how drawings are developed in a business.

Drawings Express

Parts

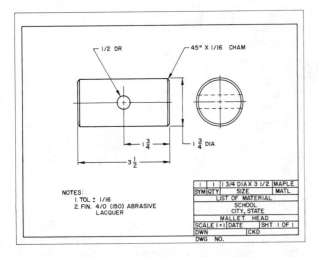

In drafting, drawings express ideas by showing the exact forms of parts, assemblies, or systems. *Parts* are individual pieces and carry out a complete function themselves or are combined with other parts to form an assembly.

Assemblies

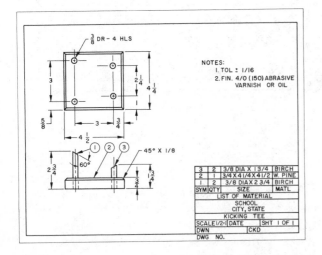

Assemblies perform intended functions through the use of several parts. An assembly drawing shows the relationship of one part to another and how the parts fit together.

Parts and assembly drawings show the exact appearance of the form or structure. They are used as a quick and accurate way of creating and evaluating products.

Systems

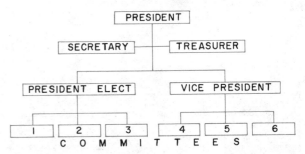

Drawings of Systems are representations that do not show exact size and shape. They give information in symbolic form. Some types of system drawings are called schematics. Drawings of systems provide a graphic method for expressing, organizing, and evaluating information. Drawings of this type are used in planning and expressing various systems such as a personnel organization, a football play, a radio diagram, a hydraulic jack (fluid power), a bus route, sheet music, and a data processing sequence.

Drawings Control

There is no way to control the exact shape, organization, size, or quality of a product. However, these can be controlled within limits. *Limits* mean the most and the least that is acceptable to satisfy a particular need. These limits are called tolerances.

SIZE   TOLERANCE

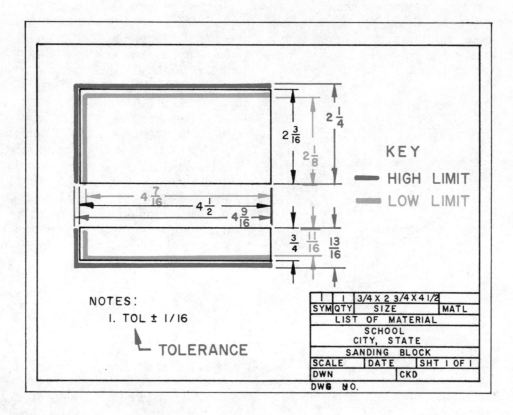

NOTES:
1. TOL ± 1/16

⌐ TOLERANCE

KEY

━━ HIGH LIMIT
━━ LOW LIMIT

		3/4 X 2 3/4 X 4 1/2	
SYM	QTY	SIZE	MATL
LIST OF MATERIAL			
SCHOOL CITY, STATE			
SANDING BLOCK			
SCALE	DATE	SHT I OF I	
DWN		CKD	
DWG NO.			

Tolerances are used on drawings to control the shape, organization, size, and quality of a design within acceptable limits. *Shape* means the form or appearance of an article. *Organization* is the arrangement of the parts. *Size* means the bulk dimensions, volume, or largeness. *Quality* is the degree of fineness or excellence. It deals with the kind of materials and the results of manufacturing processes.

Types of Drawings

The three basic types of drawings used are the orthographic projection, pictorial, and schematic.

Orthographic Projection

Orthographic projection is a way to draw an object using its various views in an organized manner. Drawings of the orthographic projection type are very good for showing accurate detail and dimensions. This type of drawing generally requires special training in order to draw and understand.

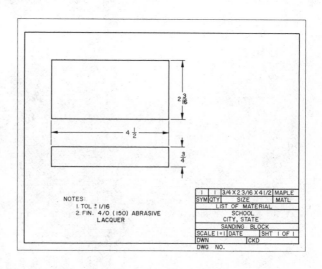

NOTES:
1. TOL ± 1/16
2. FIN. 4/0 (150) ABRASIVE
   LACQUER

		3/4 X 2 3/16 X 4 1/2	MAPLE
SYM	QTY	SIZE	MATL
LIST OF MATERIAL			
SCHOOL CITY, STATE			
SANDING BLOCK			
SCALE I=I	DATE	SHT I OF I	
DWN		CKD	
DWG NO.			

Pictorial

Pictorial drawings generally show three adjacent faces of the object in one view. It is the easiest drawing to understand; however, it is not the best for planning detail or showing dimensions accurately.

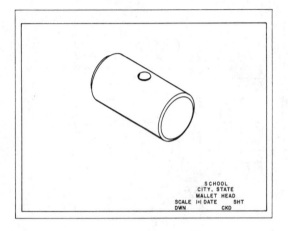

Schematic

Schematic drawings are not drawn to scale but are used to show the flow of activity, energy, or work. Electronic and fluid power drawings are types of schematic drawings.

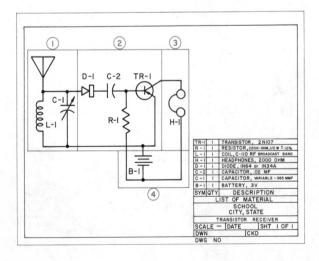

Types of Drafting

There are many specialized types of drafting. Some of the most common are engineering, tooling industrial design, technical illustration, electrical-electronic, architectural, and civil drafting. Many aspects of drafting are common to all fields; but because of the wide differences in the things to be drawn, specialized fields have developed. It would be very difficult for anyone to know all fields of drafting very well. However, good draftsmen are usually able to work in more than one drafting field. It is best that you become acquainted with several fields of drafting before you select the most meaningful fields to you for further study. Study the following information for a brief explanation of the major fields in drafting.

Engineering Drafting

Engineering drafting deals with designing useful products for use by the public. These consumer products are usually movable, rather than such things as buildings and roads. Machines, appliances, engines, transmissions, automobiles, and airplanes are drafted in engineering drawings.

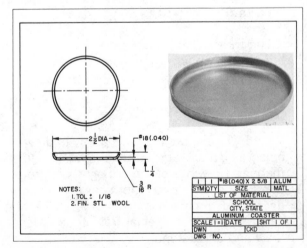

Tooling

Tooling involves designing devices such as jigs, fixtures, cutters, dies, and inspection gages which are used when making, checking, or assembling parts, machines, or structures.

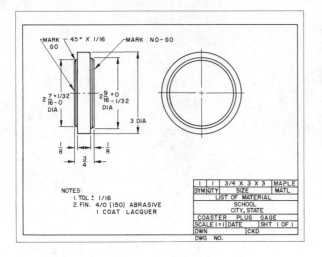

Industrial Design

Industrial design is the creating of attractive designs for industrial products. The design is a result of giving special attention to customer appeal, function, materials, and manufacturing processes.

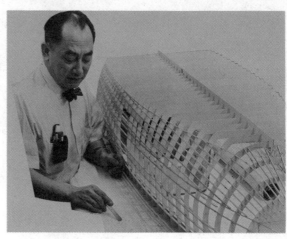

Technical Illustration

Technical illustration is the designing and preparing of visual materials, often in a pictorial form which are used with advertising, and in instructions for assembling, installing, operating, maintaining, or repairing industrial products.

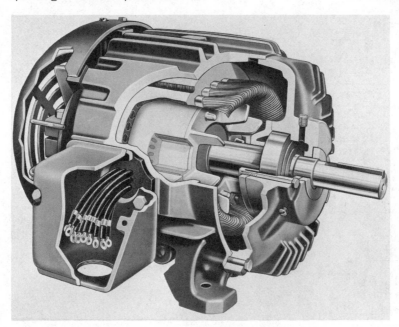

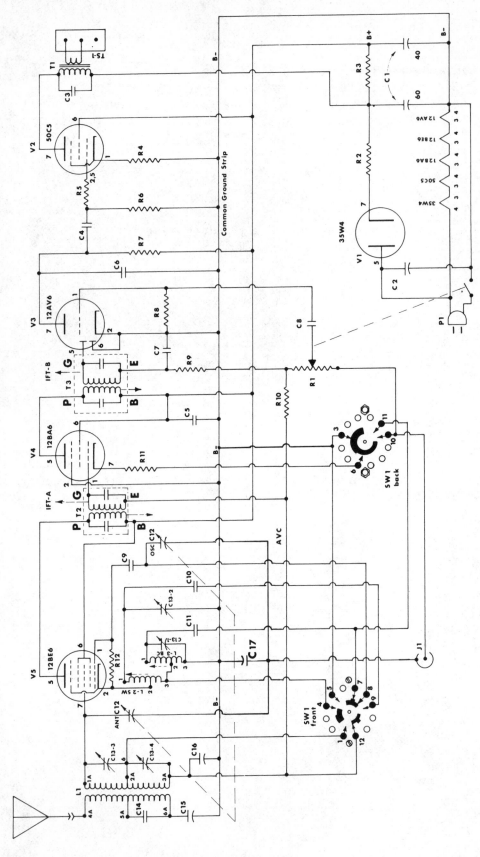

TWO BAND RECEIVER

Electrical Drafting

Electrical-electronic drafting deals with designing and drawing electrical or electronic circuits. The drawings do not show the detail of size and shape of the electronic parts.

Architectural Drafting

Architectural drafting involves the planning of buildings—their function, location, materials, processes, and beauty. Houses, stores, offices, factories, and ships are drafted in architectural drawings.

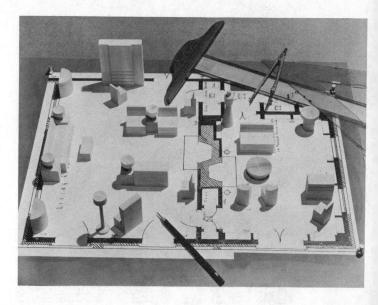

Civil Drafting

Civil drafting is the designing of cities and municipal projects such as roads, harbors, dams, levees, railroads, bridges, or parks.

Reproduction Services

Reproduction services deal with making copies of drawings in quantities from one to thousands through the use of cameras, copy machines, and printing presses.

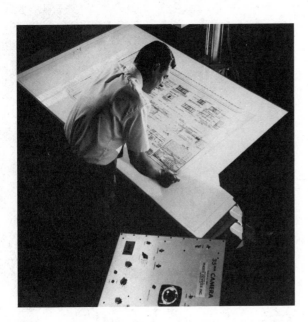

Levels of Drafting

There are four levels of occupations in progressing from beginning to higher levels of drafting. The levels are: (1) beginning, (2) detailer draftsman, (3) designer-checker, (4) manager or sales. There are also four levels of learning if you are interested in a career in drafting.

The *beginning level* is general learning about drafting that can help you in your life regardless of your interests or occupational goals. This book provides the material for you to learn the beginning level of drafting. In it, you have the opportunity to learn what drafting is and how to express and understand ideas dealing with planning and building things. These learnings can be used with your hobbies, at home, in the community and in almost any job you will be doing.

The *detailer-draftsman level* is the second level of learning. It is the one you will need to complete if you want to enter an occupation or field of study that deals directly with drafting. In the detailer-draftsman level you should learn to do the things required of the detail-draftsman. Requirements are: speed, skill and understanding in the fundamentals of drawing plans for parts using as a primary source of information design layout assembly drawings made by the designer-draftsman.

The *designer-draftsman and checker level* of drafting requires creative ability and a thorough understanding of technology. You can learn about technology by taking industrial education classes in school, touring manufacturing plants, building things as a hobby or job, and studying technical literature. If you want or are interested in a technical occupation you should gain these experiences.

The *manager-sales level* of drafting requires a thorough understanding of drafting design and the ability to get along well with or lead people and to organize. You will have plenty of opportunity in school and in work for gaining experiences in these activities. With superior ability you may become a manager or engineering salesman.

Education for Drafting

The education needed by the prospective draftsman usually involves learning experiences with drafting in junior high school and high school and very often in some college-level courses. The program of study often includes 30 to 90 or more hours in general drafting during the junior high school. This is followed by 180 or more hours of general drafting. Drafting students can often qualify for beginning drafting jobs after completing 180 to 360 or more hours of study in school for a special field of drafting. It is recommended that students interested in becoming draftsmen or engineers gain knowledge of the characteristics and uses of materials and manufacturing processes by taking classes in several fields of industrial education. Fundamental learnings in mathematics, physical sciences, and art are also helpful.

Junior High School

Grade 7	Industrial Education	Minimum of 180* hours with
Grade 8	Industrial Education	30–90 hours of drafting

High School

Grade 9	Drafting	180 hours
Grade 10	Enroll in subjects dealing with manufacturing and services such as metals, plastics, electronics, and/or mechanics	360 hours
Grade 11	Drafting	180 hours
Grade 12	Drafting	180 hours

ELECTIVES: Mathematics, Art, Physical Sciences, Typing, and General Business.

---

* School year—one hour per day.

Job and/or Trade School or College

Additional experience gained from employment that is related to your school experience is valuable. Also, continued study in trade school or college should result in satisfying employment.

Preview of Your Book

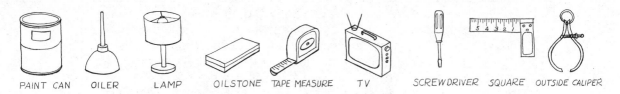

PAINT CAN   OILER   LAMP   OILSTONE   TAPE MEASURE   TV   SCREWDRIVER   SQUARE   OUTSIDE CALIPER

Chapter 2

Even before you started school, you were drawing freehand with crayon, chalk or pencil. Your pictures, crude as they may have been, expressed your ideas.

Improving your freehand drawing is not difficult once you learn how to use a pencil and paper; how to make straight, curved, and circular lines; and the step-by-step procedure for drawing round, square, and flat objects. You will progress from drawing such simple objects as boxes to more complex ones, such as cars.

During these experiences, you will learn to put your ideas on paper, evaluate them, develop and alter them until the ideas have become truly functional. You will find this skill useful in describing your ideas to others.

TYPES OF DIMENSIONS

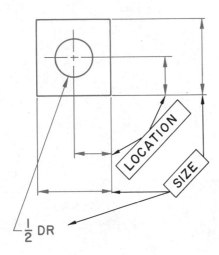

LOCATION

SIZE

½ DR

Chapter 3

Drawing plans and blueprints can be understood by people working in different industries or located in different places, such as California, New York, Texas, Illinois, or even in other countries. This is because certain rules and regulations of drawing are used worldwide in the system of drafting. By learning these CONVENTIONAL PRACTICES, you will be able to communicate with other people.

This chapter will prove a valuable reference when you are seeking the correct procedure for making your drawings, or when you need help in understanding the various conventional practices used by draftsmen. Here you will learn how to (1) select a drawing size; (2) layout the border, title block, and list of materials; (3) select views; (4) draw lines and dimension orthographic projections; (5) make special views; and (6) check finished drawings accurately.

Chapter 4

Like the carpenter who needs different kinds of hammers and saws, nails and screws, and many materials to construct a house, the draftsman also uses many different things in order to get his job done. This includes a variety of TOOLS, BOOKS, SUPPLIES, AND EQUIPMENT. This chapter introduces you to each of these and the function they serve.

Tools of special kinds are used for making lines, pointing or sharpening pencils, measuring distances, drawing different line shapes, drawing symbols or standard object outlines, and cutting supplies.

Books are important sources of information for the draftsman. You will learn to depend on books for "hard-to-remember" information.

Supplies of various kinds are needed as drawing surfaces, for marking lines, erasing, coating and protecting drawing surfaces. Supplies are necessary for holding, cleaning, and duplicating drawings.

Equipment is important to the draftsman in having a comfortable and functional place in which to work. Drawing equipment is designed to increase the rate of a draftsman's output.

As you become familiar with these, you will be able to select tools, supplies, books, and equipment which will improve your drawing skill.

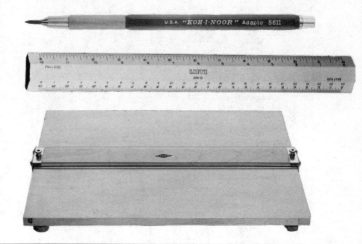

Chapter 5

There are *tricks in every trade*. More properly expressed, these are the "know-how" or skills that are acquired with time and practice. When you learn what they are and how to use them, the work becomes easier and the results more professional.

To achieve skill in DRAWING MECHANICALLY, you will learn how to hold the tools you studied about in Chapter 4, and how to use them in a variety of ways. This, also, will be your opportunity to work with the conventional practices studied in Chapter 3.

As you practice mechanical drawing, this chapter will help you develop the know-how so that you can:

1. Measure distance and locate specific points.
2. Make scale drawings.
3. Prepare and use a pencil.
4. Draw various types of horizontal, vertical, and angular straight lines.
5. Draw circles and arcs with templates or compasses.
6. Draw irregularly curved lines with irregularly curved tools.
7. Erase lines and keep drawings clean.
8. Letter, make arrowheads, and place dimensions on drawings.
9. Make simple geometric drawings.

After a new skill or technique is explained, *you will be given a drawing problem*. What you learn in this chapter will help you meet successfully the assignments in the next six chapters.

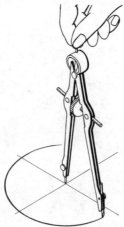

Chapter 6

The knowledge and skill you have acquired so far will be challenged in this chapter as you make progressively more difficult drawings. The drawing problems begin with simple square or round shapes and advance to different assembly drawings.

DRAWING ORTHOGRAPHIC PROJECTIONS can be learned quickly and accurately by *using a six-step drawing procedure.* As you follow it, you will be applying the knowledge already gained in Chapters 3, 4, and 5.

The products you draw in this chapter's assignments can be constructed in your industrial arts class or your home workshop. This will help you to see the relationship between the drawing and the actual construction of the object. You will have a choice of drawing problems so that you can select the one most appealing to you for later construction. These projects represent several areas of industrial education — *woodworking, metalworking, graphic arts,* and *plastics.*

These problems will help you to draw ideas which others can understand. With practice, you can learn to draw orthographic projections, use the conventional practices, and draw quickly and accurately.

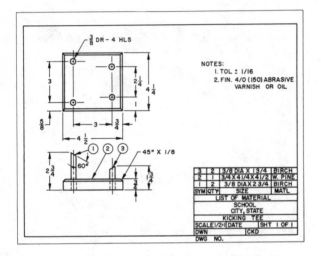

PICTORIAL DRAWINGS

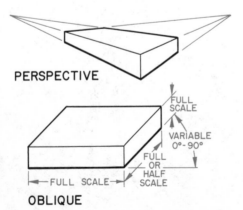

ISOMETRIC

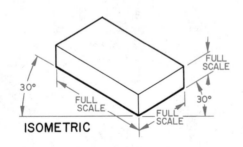

PERSPECTIVE

OBLIQUE

Chapter 7

Another way of giving form to objects can be learned by DRAWING PICTORIALLY. Pictorial drawings show objects somewhat as they would appear in a photograph. They include isometric, perspective, and oblique views. Of these, the isometric drawing is the easiest and most widely used.

Before you are ready to make pictorial drawings of simple objects, you will need to study diagrams and illustrations included in this chapter. Here is also the opportunity to use another mechanical drawing tool as you learn to make circles with elipse guides.

Chapter 8

The chassis for a car and the cone for a space capsule first take shape on the drawing board when the draftsman shows how such objects are to be cut, bent, folded, or assembled from sheet materials.

In DRAWING DEVELOPMENTS, you will learn to communicate this kind of information by developing layout forms for simple objects as a file folder, envelope, box, cylinder, and cone. You will understand how useful a development drawing is when you plan the cutting, folding, bending, or assembly of containers to be made from a flat piece of material, such as paper, metal, plastic, or fabric.

Skill you have already gained in drawing orthographic projection will help you learn to describe these products which can be constructed in your other industrial arts classes.

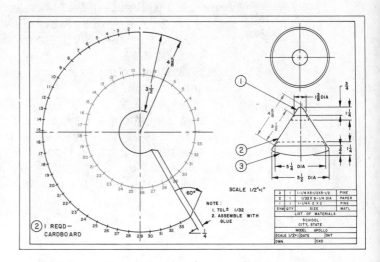

Chapter 9

All sizes and shapes from molecules to monuments can be drawn on paper. It is a matter of enlarging or reducing the object's size. This is done by DRAWING WITH GRIDS.

In this chapter you can learn how to use grid paper to draw irregularly shaped objects, such as animals, boats, cars, and airplanes. This is also your opportunity to learn the grid drawing method for making *patterns and templates* which duplicate shapes.

Your grid drawing ability will be challenged in this chapter as you progress from simple curved objects to complex ones, such as model sailboats.

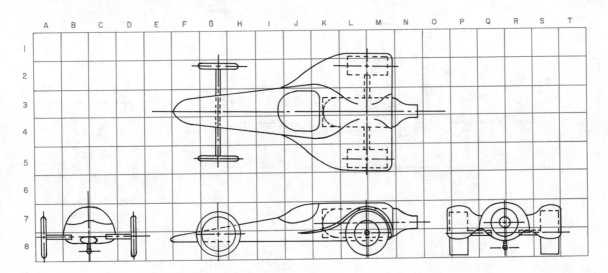

Chapter 10

Your home, the restaurants, movie theaters, and shops you visit all began on a drawing board as plans. The size of the building, the location of rooms, the purpose of each was decided on paper before construction.

As you study DRAWING A BUILDING, you will learn:

1. How to plan floor layouts and how to place windows, walls, doors, and furniture.
2. How the floor plan can serve your needs and how to communicate with an architect.
3. How to use scale models (two-dimensional cutouts) of furniture and equipment in developing a floor plan.
4. How to read an architect's scale and the fundamentals of dimensioning architectural plans.

Knowing how to communicate this information can prove valuable to you throughout your lifetime as you use buildings.

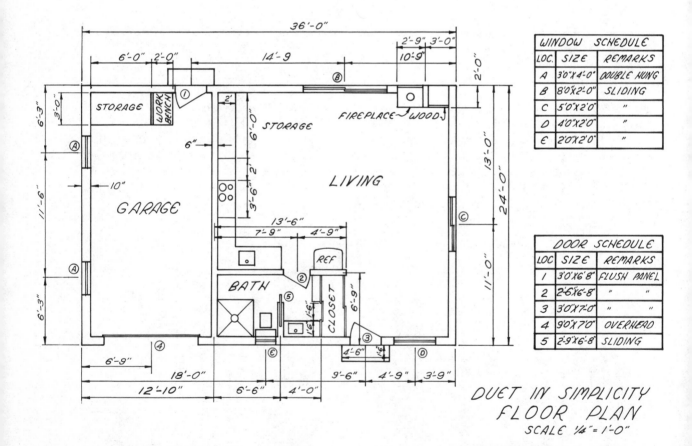

WINDOW	SCHEDULE	
LOC.	SIZE	REMARKS
A	3'0"X4'-0"	DOUBLE HUNG
B	8'0"X2'-0"	SLIDING
C	5'0"X2'0"	"
D	4'0"X2'0"	"
E	2'0"X2'0"	"

DOOR	SCHEDULE	
LOC	SIZE	REMARKS
1	3'0"X6'8"	FLUSH PANEL
2	2'-6"X6'-8"	" "
3	3'0"X7'-0"	" "
4	9'0"X7'0"	OVERHEAD
5	2'-9"X6'-8"	SLIDING

DUET IN SIMPLICITY
FLOOR PLAN
SCALE ¼"=1'-0"

Chapter 11

The plays in a football game, the song by your school chorus, and the electrical devices in your home all have systems. Each can be described by symbols.

Many other systems exist as a result of the activities, movement, and performance of men and machines. In this chapter you will learn how these actions can be planned and described by DRAWING SYSTEMS.

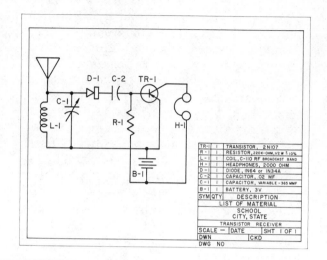

You will study how symbols are used to describe such systems as maps, production plans, games, electronic circuits, the working relationships of people, data processing systems, and fluid power systems.

When you have learned to represent the activities of man or devices with symbols in a drawing, you will have a better understanding of the importance of planning and recording the action to take place.

Chapter 12

A finished drawing deserves proper care because it is often copied numerous times and then stored for later use. It represents time, effort, and materials which are costly.

In studying the REPRODUCTION AND CARE OF DRAWINGS, you will learn how to fold, store, and repair drawings. This chapter also introduces you to methods of making copies of the original drawings.

Chapter 13

The skills you have gained in drawing and using various tools and techniques have lead you to the point where you can now learn about drawing for industry. As you study DRAFTING DESIGN, you will discover that industry challenges your creative thinking.

Drafting design is reaching out, or extending your thoughts, to describe a new or better way of constructing products and tools. It invites new ideas. Early man had ideas which helped him to get along better in his world. He learned to shape things with his hands or teeth, and later refined this idea when he used a stone and then a knife. In the beginning he carried things in his arms. Through the centuries, however, his thinking and efforts continued to reach out creatively until his better ways of carrying objects have developed from carts and wagons to such vehicles as trains and forklift trucks.

To serve industry as a draftsman, you must gain an understanding of how industry serves the people around you by the use of various standards, materials, and practices. By extending your thinking, as early man did in developing ways of handling materials, you can learn how to draw your ideas on paper and how to refine them. In this way your original idea is improved.

You will need to know the following fundamentals of drafting design:

1. The creative process.
2. Common objectives of design.
3. Standard parts.
4. Standard materials.
5. Basic manufacturing practices.

By learning these fundamentals of drafting design and using your ability to record, refine, and express ideas with drawings, you can begin designing parts and assemblies for products.

MATERIAL HANDLING

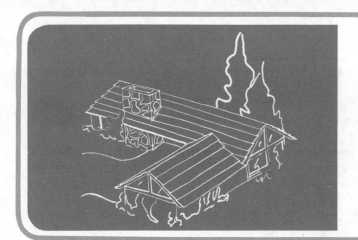

2

Drawing Freehand

Why Study This Chapter?

DRAWING FREEHAND will show you how to:

1. Improve your freehand drawing skill.
2. Use pencil and paper so that you can make better drawings.
3. Make straight, circular, and curved lines.
4. Use a step-by-step procedure for drawing round, square, and flat objects.
5. Record your ideas on paper and evaluate them, then alter and develop them until they are functional.

You will begin by drawing simple objects and advance to more complicated objects such as cars, houses, and airplanes.

Freehand drawing is a widely used method of drawing because it is a relatively quick and easy way to show your ideas. Freehand drawings are formed without the use of guides or tools other than a pencil and plain paper. This type of drawing is quickly developed because accurate measurements are not required when you are recording your ideas. You need only two things to make a freehand drawing: (1) a tool to make marks, and (2) a surface to record the marks. Examples of these two requirements are:

1. A pencil and paper, or
2. A stick and sand, or
3. Chalk and pavement or similar tools and materials.

Freehand Drawing is Easy to Do

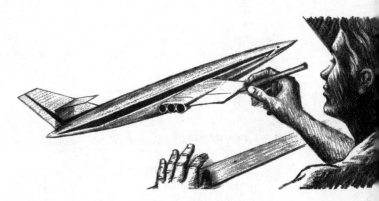

The basic fundamentals for drawing freehand are shown in this chapter. By studying and practicing them, you can make good freehand pictorial and working drawings. While you are learning to draw, *it is better to practice drawing many different objects rather than to draw the same thing over and over.*

The Order of Learning

There are four levels of learning in developing drawing skill. If you are to gain the ability to do freehand drawing, it will be helpful to understand and follow the order of learning as described below.

Copying is the First Skill to Develop

Start by using the proven methods shown in this chapter to copy good freehand drawing practices.

Analyzing Pictures is the Second Skill to Develop

Pictures in this book should be used as a source of ideas. Pictures found in newspapers, magazines, books, and catalogs also work well for this purpose. It is important that you analyze the picture so you understand what you see and draw.

Using Objects as Models is the Third Skill to Develop

Drawing abilities are further developed by using objects or models as a source of ideas.

Creating Ideas is the Fourth Skill to Develop

Creating drawings from your thoughts or the "mind's eye" is the final goal in developing the ability to do freehand drawings.

A few people have the natural ability to express themselves with drawings without much practice. Most people need practice to develop skill in this important method of communicating ideas. With proper practice, nearly everyone can express his thoughts in drawings. The amount of effort needed to learn how to draw will vary with individuals; however, everyone can benefit by following a few basic procedures.

Basic Procedures

Basic procedures for freehand drawing are easy to follow. They are much like the procedures used in good handwriting.

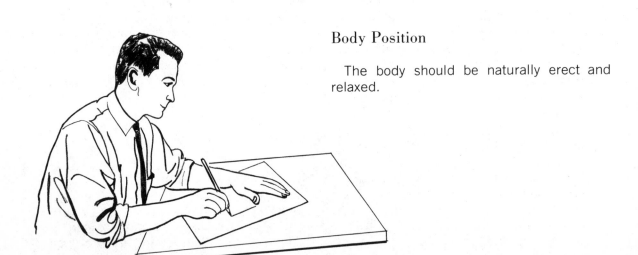

Body Position

The body should be naturally erect and relaxed.

Paper Position

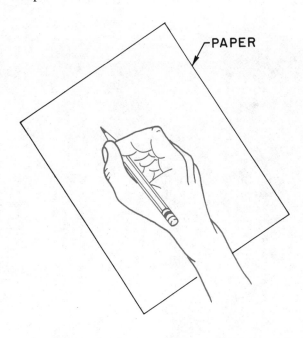

The paper is slanted along the natural angle of the drawing arm and should be kept in that position. Plain paper without lines is the best to use.

Pencil in Hand

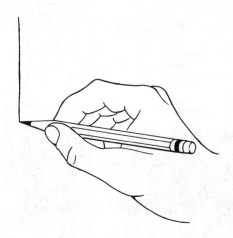

The pencil should be held near the point, just as in writing. The pencil should lay on the hand next to the thumb, between the thumb and the first finger.

Arm Motion

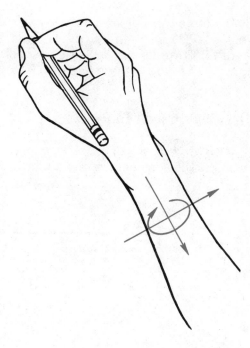

Use arm motion rather than wrist or finger movements. Only when very small details are drawn is the hand planted on the drawing surface and the fingers moved. Normally, the hand holding the pencil glides over the paper with the relaxed arm motion.

Single-Stroke Lines

Lines should be drawn with single strokes. The single-stroke method should be used. The colored area shows the poor results obtained when a line is drawn with several short strokes.

Directions for Drawing Lines

The three types of lines used to make drawings are (1) straight, (2) circles and arcs, and (3) irregular curves. They should be drawn according to these directions:

Drawing Straight Lines

Straight lines are drawn at various angles with a single stroke in the direction shown.

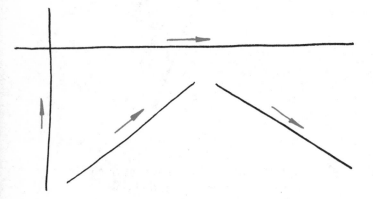

Drawing Circles

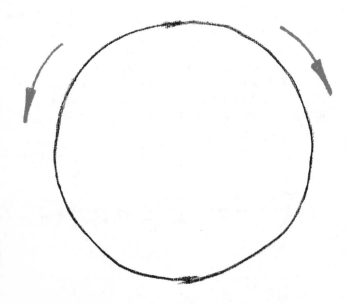

Circles and *arcs* are drawn with strokes in the directions shown.

Drawing Oval Lines

Pictorial circles are called *ovals* or *ellipses*. They are drawn with a single stroke.

Drawing Curved Lines

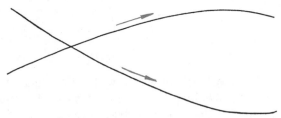

Irregular lines are not uniform in shape. These lines should be drawn in long, sweeping strokes.

Alignment

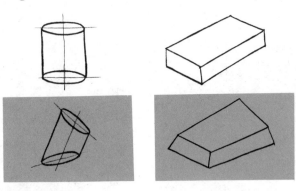

Drawings are usually made of several sets of parallel lines. It is very important to keep these lines parallel to each other. The colored area is an exaggerated example of poor layout of parallel lines.

Proportion

Proportion is the size relationship of various parts of a drawing. The relationship of the height, width, and length should be maintained on a freehand drawing. The colored area shows poor size relationships.

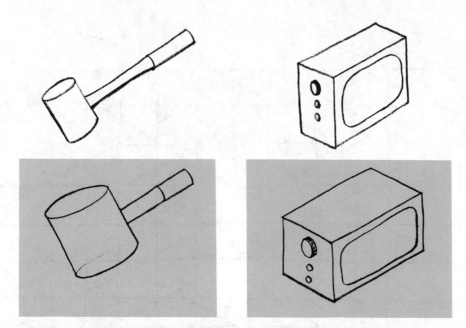

These basic techniques for drawing freehand should be learned through practice. To make improved freehand drawings, the lines should be made very light until the desired results are gained. The acceptable lines are then drawn darker.

Draw Lines

It is advisable to practice drawing lines before beginning to draw objects. Remember:

1. Your body should be naturally erect and relaxed.
2. The pencil is held near the tip as in writing.
3. Arm motion is used rather than wrist or finger movement.
4. Corners and line intersections need not meet exactly.
5. Paper is kept in one position.

RELAX!

Avoid repeating errors. The colored area shows how it is possible to repeat·errors.

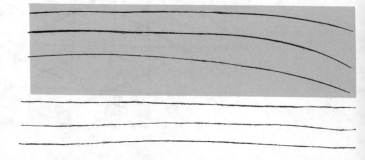

On a full sheet of plain white paper, draw a series of four sets of lines in the order shown: (1) horizontal, (2) vertical, (3) 30° slanted to the upper right, and (4) 30° slanted from the upper left.

Pictorials

Freehand *pictorial drawing* is the use of one view to show two or three faces of an object. This is the easiest type of drawing to understand. It is a good technique for expressing the general shape of the object, but it is not an accurate way of showing details and measurements. Freehand pictorial drawing is a very good method of exchanging ideas with people because it is easily understood.

Basic Procedures For Pictorials

When a freehand pictorial drawing is made, the first step is to form the largest portion or mass of the object. After the mass has been drawn with good alignment and proportion, the detail is added. Large detail is completed before small detail.

First the Mass

The *mass* or overall shape of the object should be studied to determine the basic shape. The basic shape in this example is the outline of a house. Observe that the large mass of the house is represented by the mass of a rectangular box.

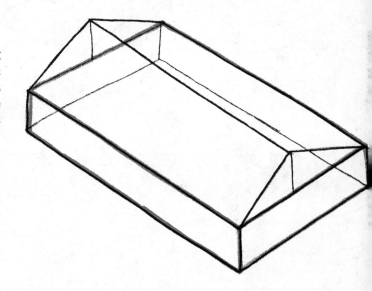

Last the Detail

Detail is added last when drawing an object. After the large mass has been drawn, add the details in proportion to their size as related to the mass. Detail should be added to the mass in the sequence of the various sizes. Add large detail first and progress until the smallest detail is added. In this example, the door is added before the doorknob. In this sequence (large to small), the door is added in proportion to the house and the doorknob is added in proportion to the door.

Round, Square, and Flat Objects

The *basic shape* of the mass should be identified. There are three basic shapes: round, square, and flat.

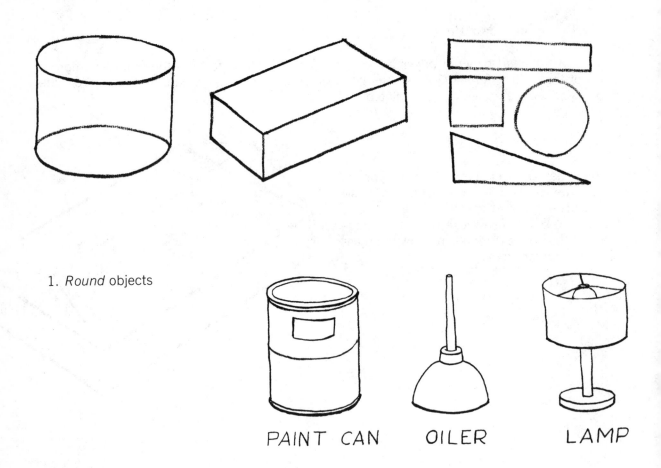

1. *Round* objects

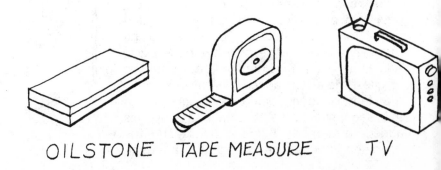

PAINT CAN   OILER   LAMP

2. *Square* objects

OILSTONE   TAPE MEASURE   TV

3. *Flat* objects

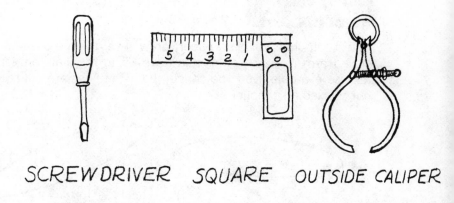

SCREWDRIVER   SQUARE   OUTSIDE CALIPER

Step-by-step instruction for drawing these basic shapes are shown in the following pages. You should practice and learn to draw these shapes.

Drawing Pictorials of Round Objects Freehand

Start by drawing the ovals of the round objects first. Draw the top oval first and work from the top down, drawing just ovals. This has been shown in the example above. The ovals are drawn with single line strokes, starting at the top as shown.

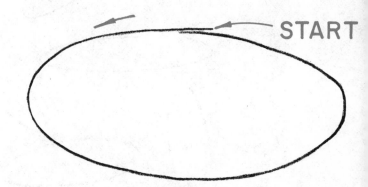

Pictorials of round or cylindrical-shaped objects should be drawn in a position so that the front, top, and side are shown. After studying the mass of several round objects, a series of ovals should become apparent to you.

Learn to draw the basic shape of a cylinder. These basic shapes will help you when draw-the mass of round objects.

┌─ REMEMBER! ────────────────────┐

Body should be naturally erect and relaxed. Pencil is held near the tip.

└──────────────────────────────┘

On a full sheet of plain paper, draw several large ovals at various angles and sizes using a relaxed arm motion. You should have 15 to 20 ovals on your work sheet similar to the *Oval Exercise* example. Don't be concerned if the lines are not connected perfectly. Concentrate on your relaxed arm motion.

The mass of round or cylindrical objects is drawn in three steps as shown in the following procedure:

Step 1: Draw the top oval.

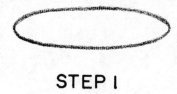

STEP 1

Step 2: Draw the bottom oval.

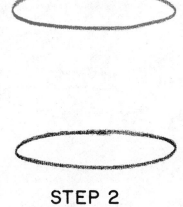

STEP 2

Step 3: Draw the straight line to connect the ovals and form the cylinder.

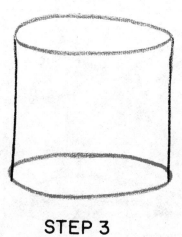

STEP 3

Using the three-step procedure, draw about six large cylinders at various angles on a sheet of paper. Use a relaxed arm motion.

On another piece of paper, draw several different objects with slanted or curved lines. Use a relaxed arm motion.

Using the proper procedures, draw at least six of the round objects of the following pages. Draw large enough that no more than four drawings fill a sheet. By making large drawings, you can practice using a relaxed arm motion. Do not practice drawing with hand, finger, or wrist motion. (Note—it is not necessary to draw the small examples that are used to show the drawing procedure.)

REMEMBER!

Hold the pencil near the tip; use arm motion; draw lines with a single stroke; and do not move the paper.

PAINT CAN

SOCKET WRENCH

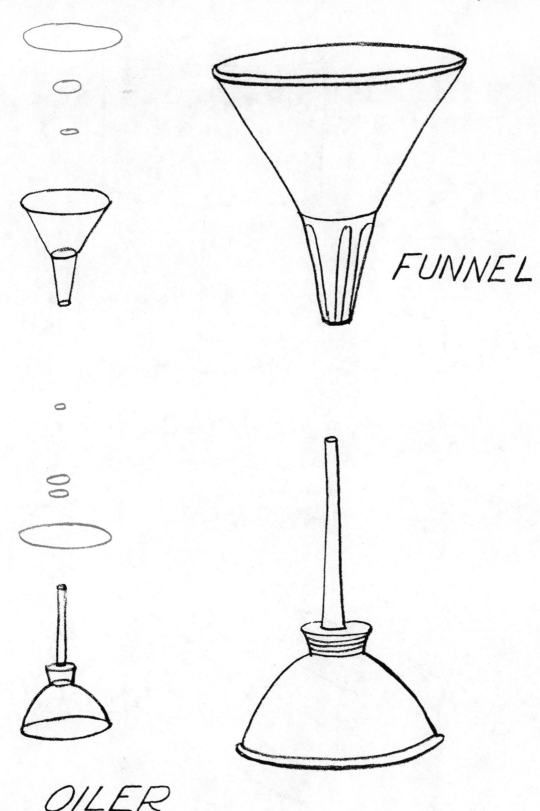

FUNNEL

OILER

TABLE LAMP

MALLET

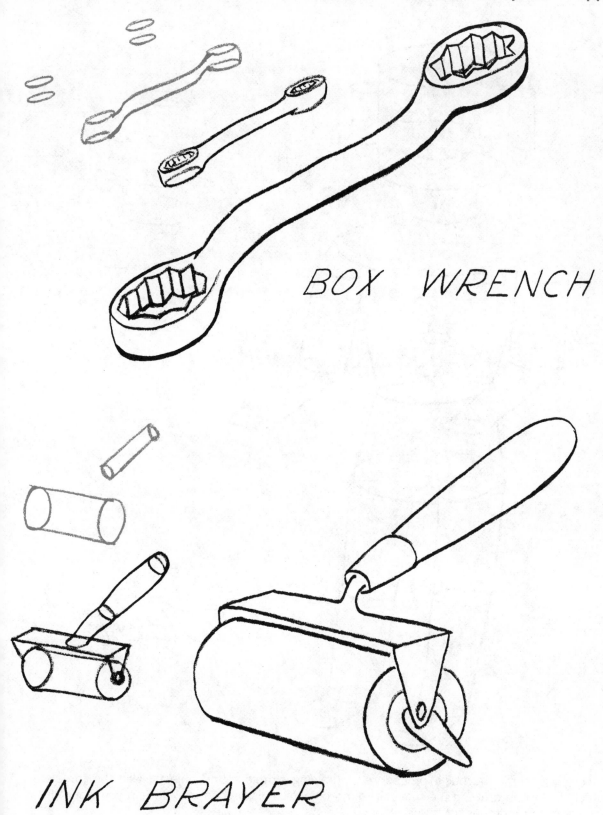

BOX WRENCH

INK BRAYER

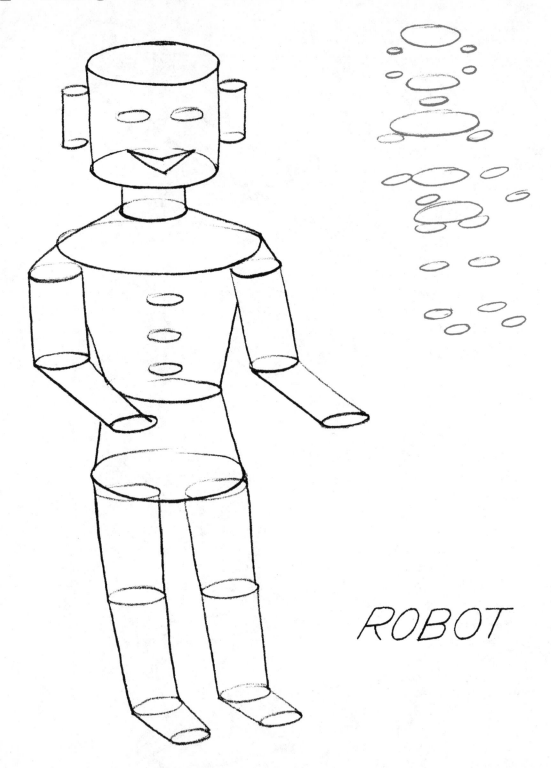

ROBOT

Now you know the basic procedure of drawing simple round objects. Use the three-step procedure when drawing the mass of round objects. This procedure will help you when drawing various proportions for round objects.

Drawing Pictorials of Square Objects Freehand

Pictorial views of square objects are drawn so that the front, top, and end are shown. When the mass of square objects is studied, the top view often stands out; therefore the freehand drawing should begin with this view first.

By drawing the top view first, your hand will not block your view as you continue to draw the remainder of the object. Your hand will block your view if you begin drawing from the bottom toward the top of the object.

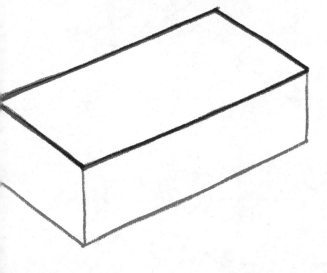

There are four steps in drawing the mass for square objects.

First, draw the two long lines of the top at a 30° angle.

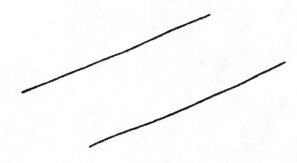

Second, draw the two short lines at a 30° angle to complete the top.

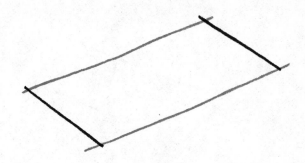

Third, draw vertical lines down from each of the three front corners of the top.

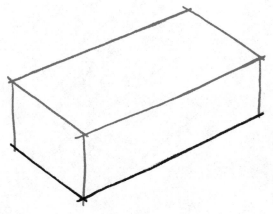

Last, draw the two bottom lines parallel to the lines in the top.

Using a full sheet of paper, draw six or eight pictorial views of the tops of square objects. This problem gives you drawing practice of the first two steps of drawing the mass of square objects.

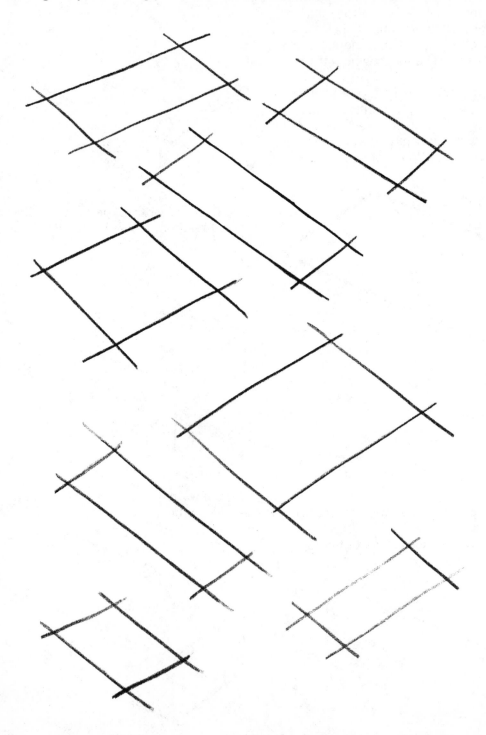

Problem 7
Drawing Square Masses

On a full sheet of paper, draw pictorial views of the mass of six or eight large, square objects. You will now practice procedure steps three and four for drawing the mass of square objects.

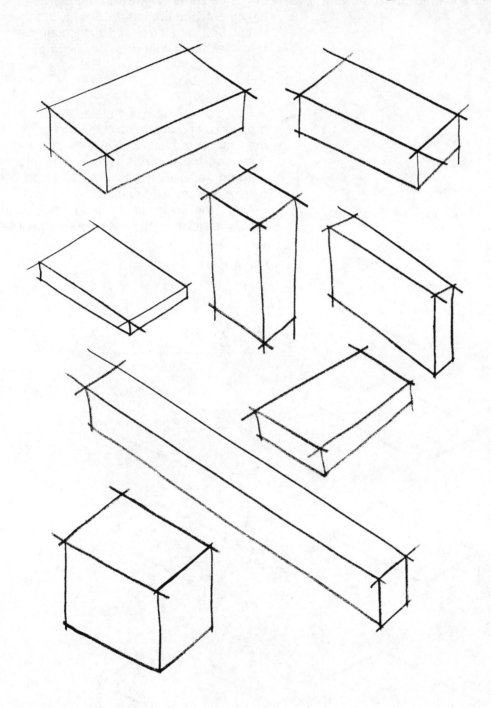

Parallel Line Sets

Notice there are three sets of parallel lines in the mass of a square pictorial drawing. Two of the sets are 30° from horizontal while one set is vertical.

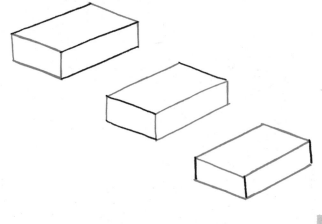

The detail should be added after the mass of the object is drawn with the correct angle, alignment, and proportion. Start with the large detail first and then add the small parts of the object until your drawing is complete.

Errors to Avoid

Now that you have completed the drawing of problems of square objects, compare your drawings to the following examples. If you are repeating these errors, you should practice drawing square masses until you can complete a drawing without errors.

Avoid the errors as shown in the colored area when forming the lines of a square object.

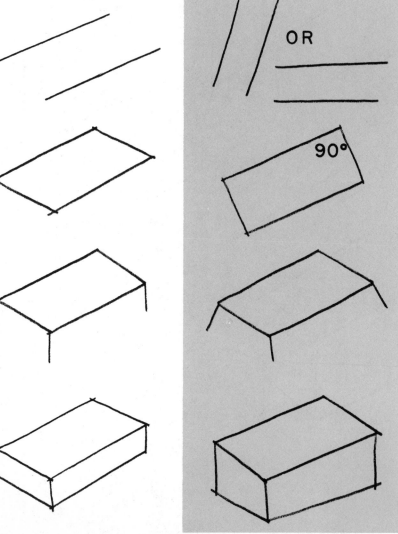

Problem 8
Practice Square Objects

Draw six or more of the square objects shown on the following pages. Four drawings should fill a full sheet of paper. Make large freehand drawings of these objects. By drawing large, you will more easily practice using relaxed arm motion, giving you the best results. (Note: it is not necessary to draw the small examples used to show the drawing procedure.)

┌─ REMEMBER! ───

Hold the pencil near the tip; use arm motion; draw lines with a single stroke; and do not move the paper.

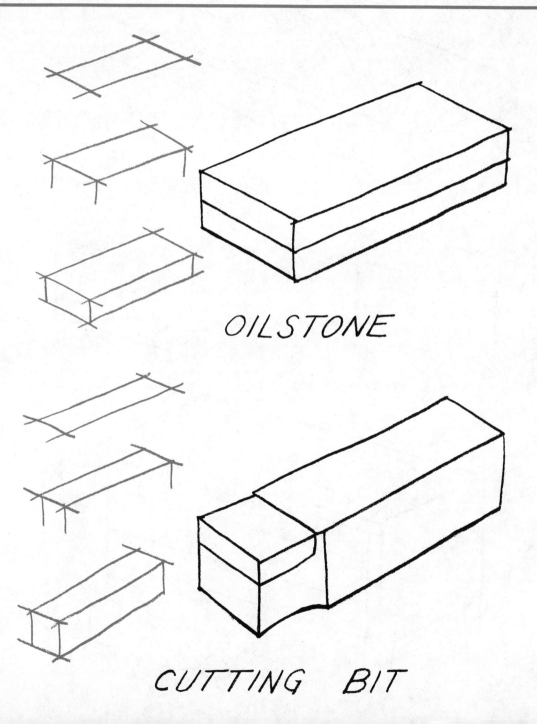

OILSTONE

CUTTING   BIT

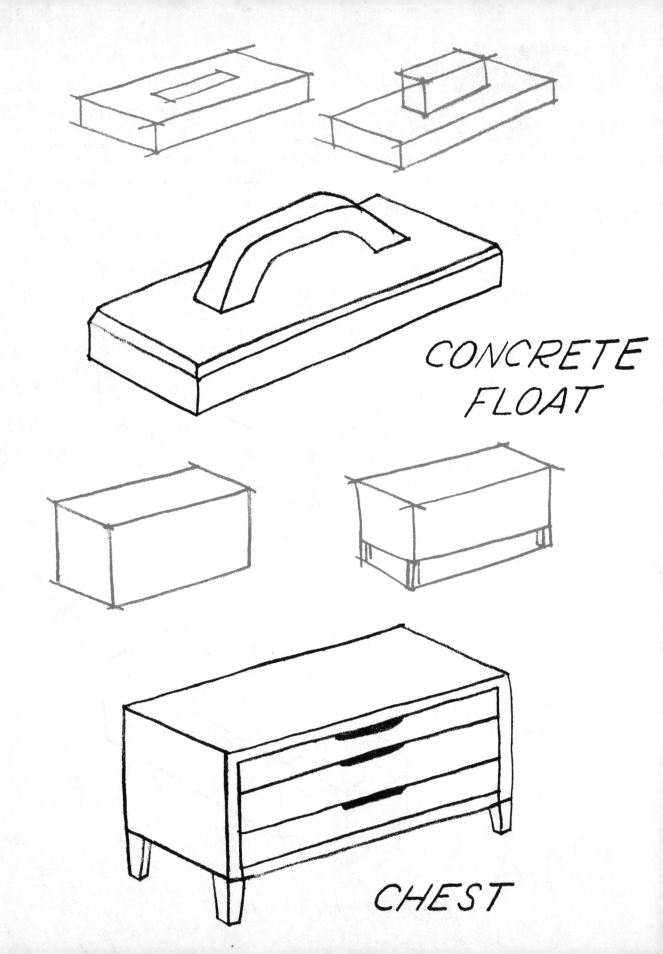

CONCRETE
FLOAT

CHEST

TAPE RULE

TELEVISION

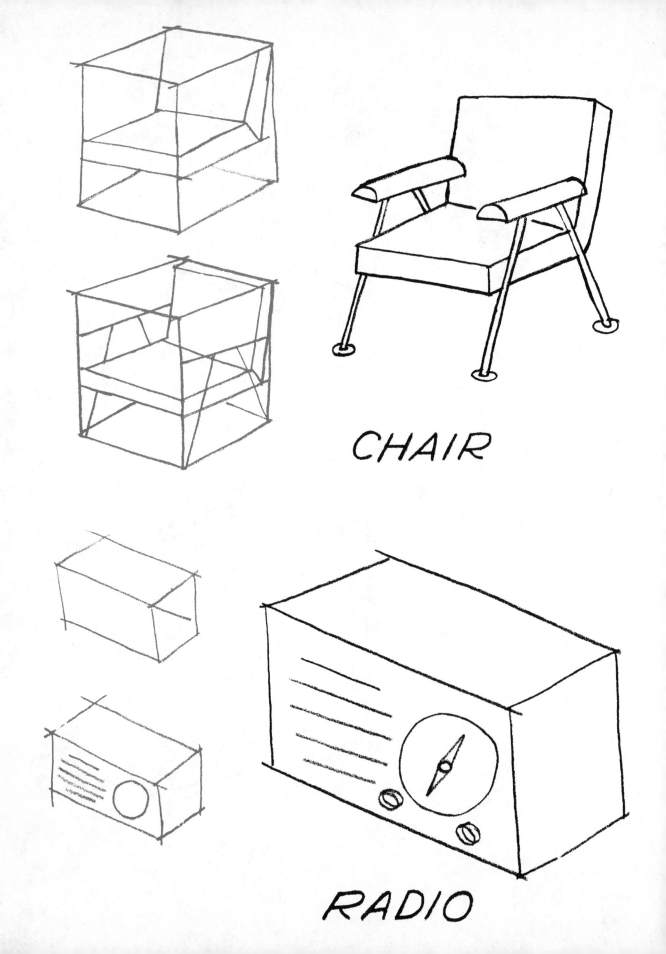

CHAIR

RADIO

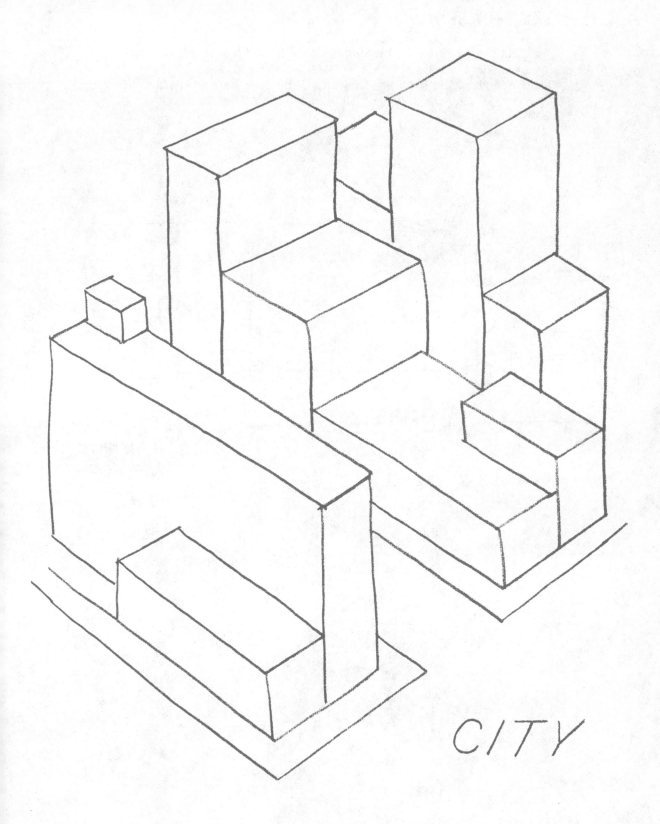

CITY

Drawing Flat Objects by Freehand

A flat object is primarily *two-dimensional*. Its width and length is more important than its thickness; therefore the thickness is not shown. If you try to show the thickness view, it will be a very small, narrow line. This narrow view has very little value in describing the object.

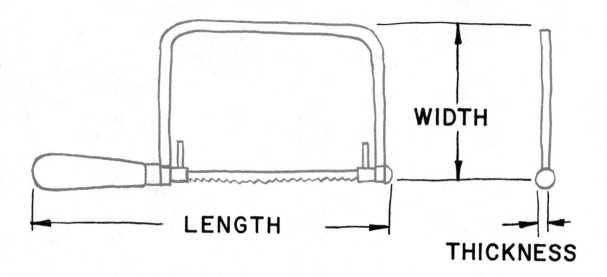

Problem 9
Flat Object Exercises

To draw flat objects, start with the largest or primary line and continue to block out (form) the shape of the object. Make six or more of the following objects large enough so that no more than four of them fill a sheet of paper.

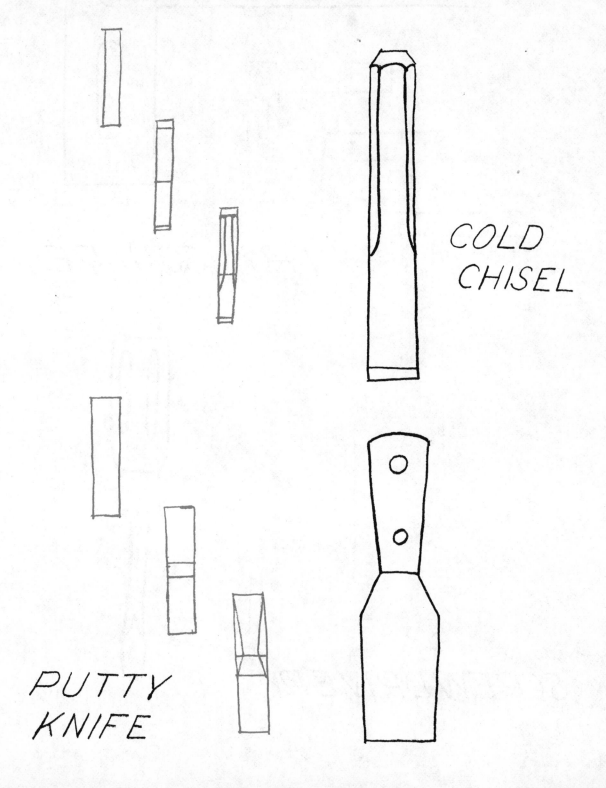

COLD CHISEL

PUTTY KNIFE

TRY SQUARE

SCREWDRIVER

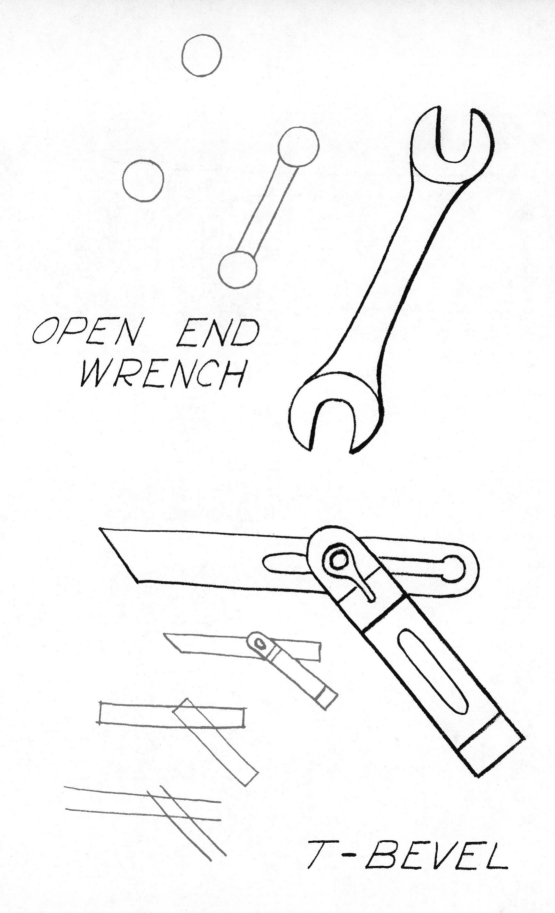

OPEN END
WRENCH

T-BEVEL

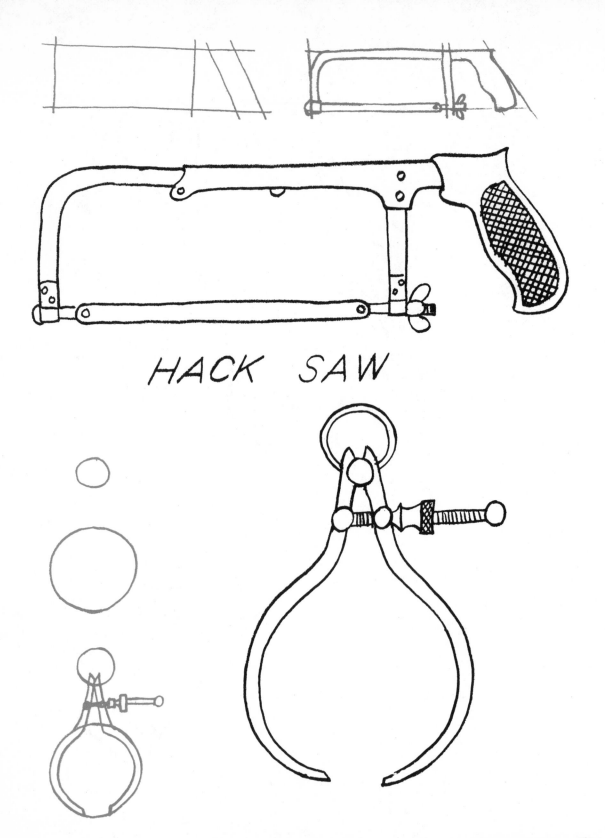

HACK SAW

OUTSIDE CALIPERS

Practice • Practice • Practice • Practice • Practice • Practice • Practice • Practice

The following examples should be used for developing your freehand drawing skill. Make large drawings and use arm motion. The mass of the object may be drawn with very light lines until the desired angle, alignment, and proportion are achieved. When the lines are satisfactory, they can be darkened.

You should practice drawing the following objects until you have developed your skill so that other people can understand what you are describing.

┌─ REMEMBER! ──────────────────┐
│ Make your lines with single strokes. │
└──────────────────────────────┘

BOWL

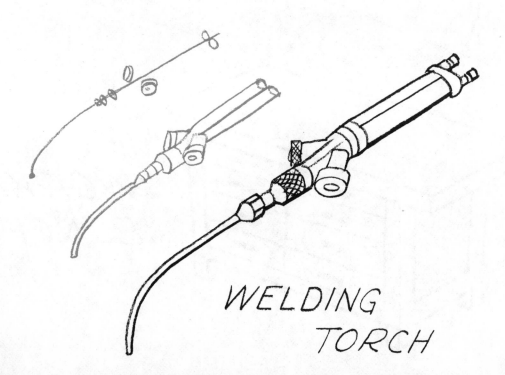

WELDING
TORCH

COFFEE TABLE

WORK
BENCH

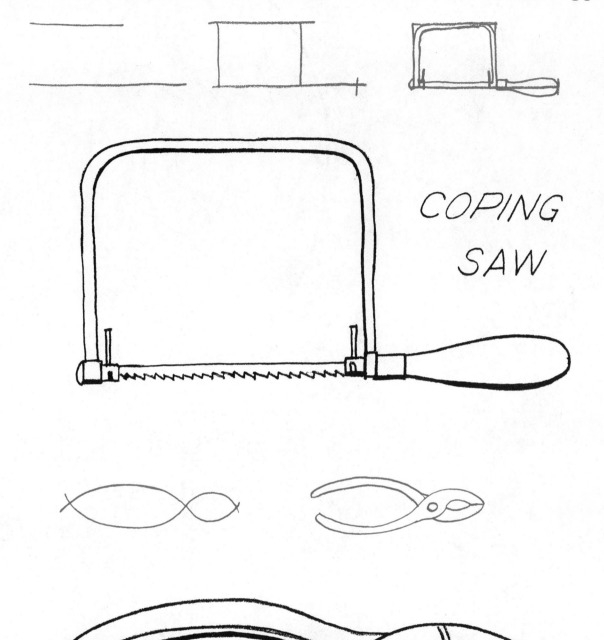

COPING
SAW

COMBINATION   PLIERS

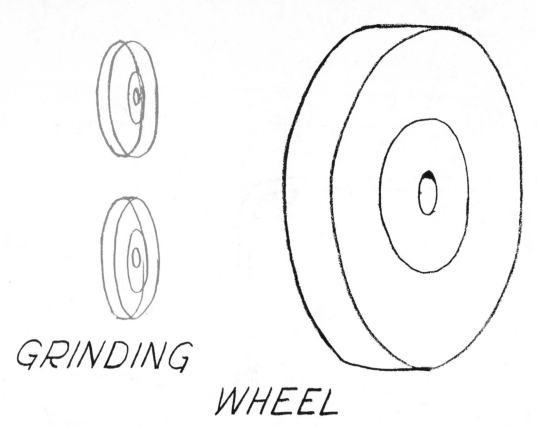

GRINDING

WHEEL

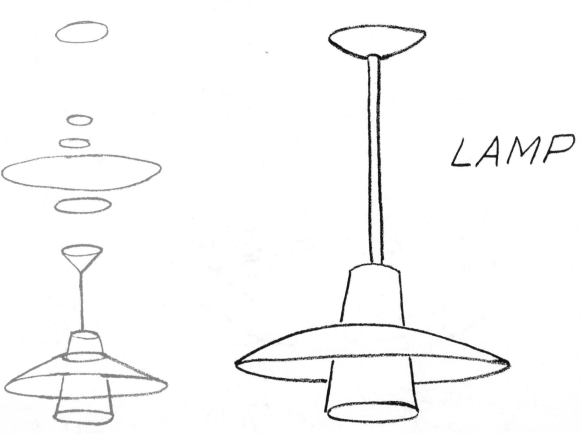

LAMP

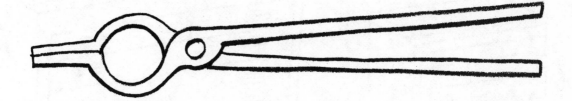

FORGING   TONGS

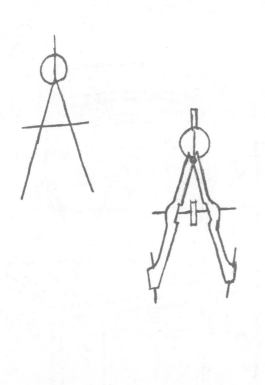

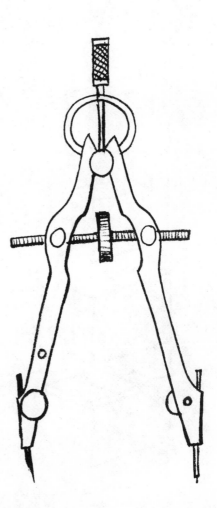

COMPASS

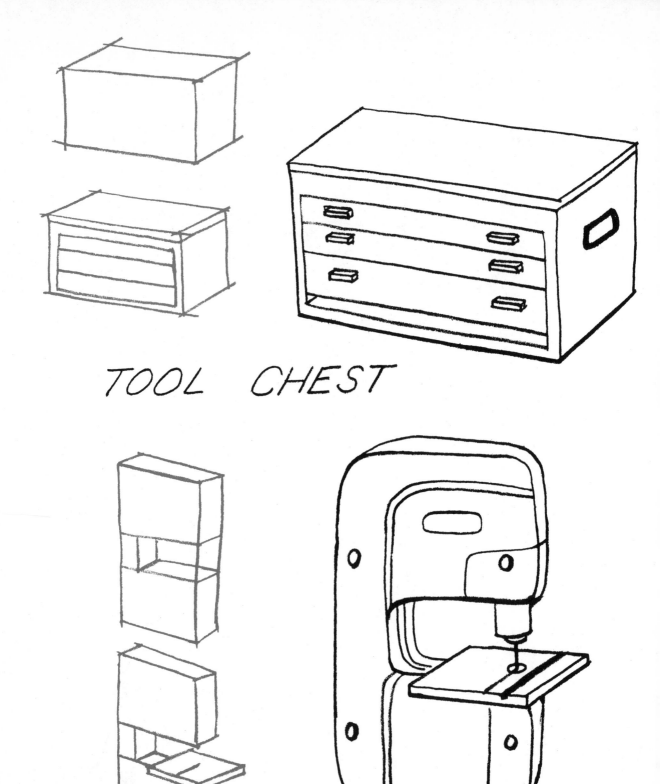

TOOL CHEST

BAND SAW

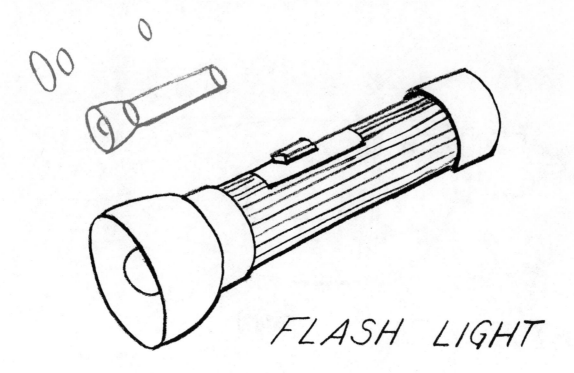

FLASH LIGHT

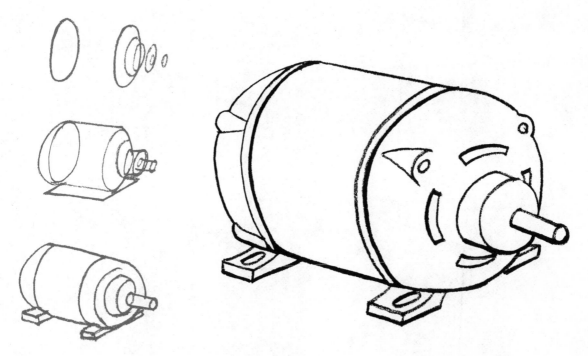

ELECTRIC MOTOR

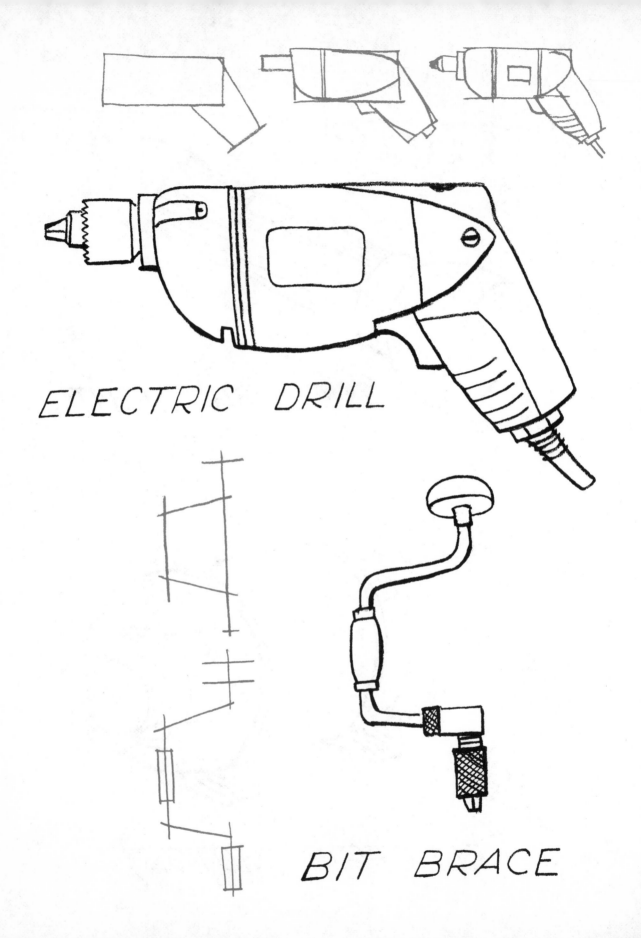

ELECTRIC DRILL

BIT BRACE

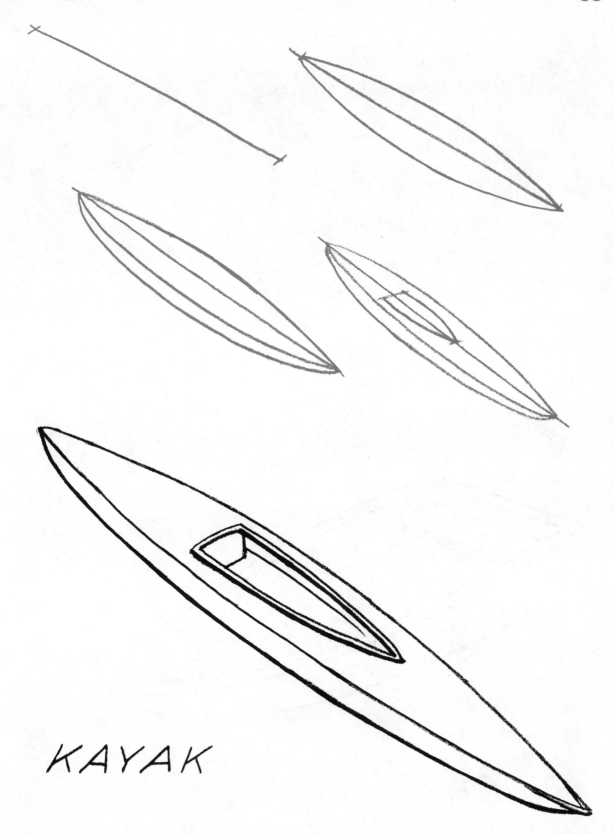

KAYAK

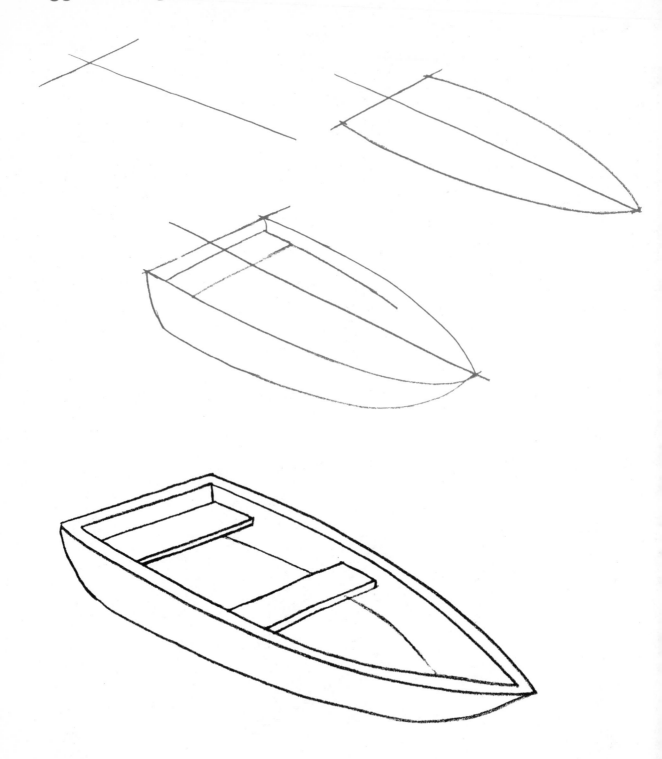

DINGHY

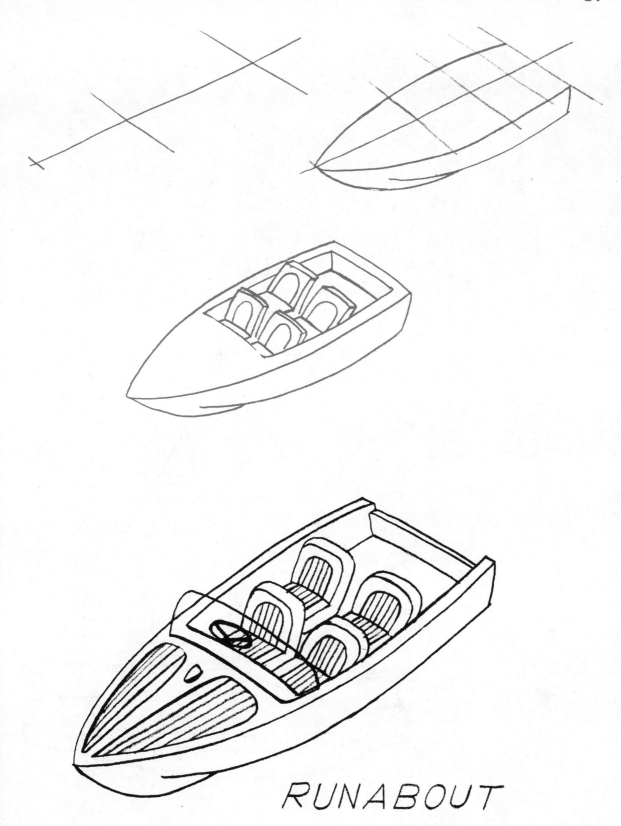

RUNABOUT

SAIL BOAT

SAIL PLANE

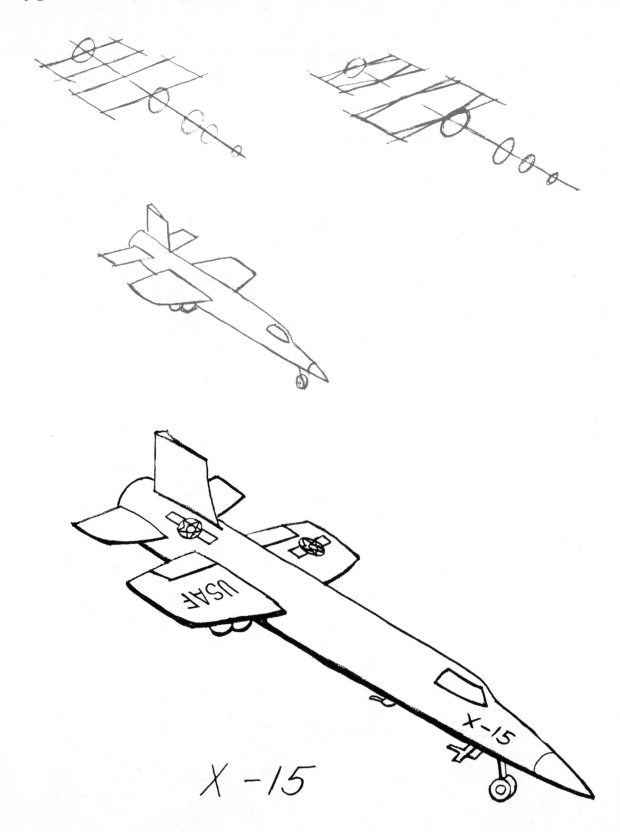

X - 15

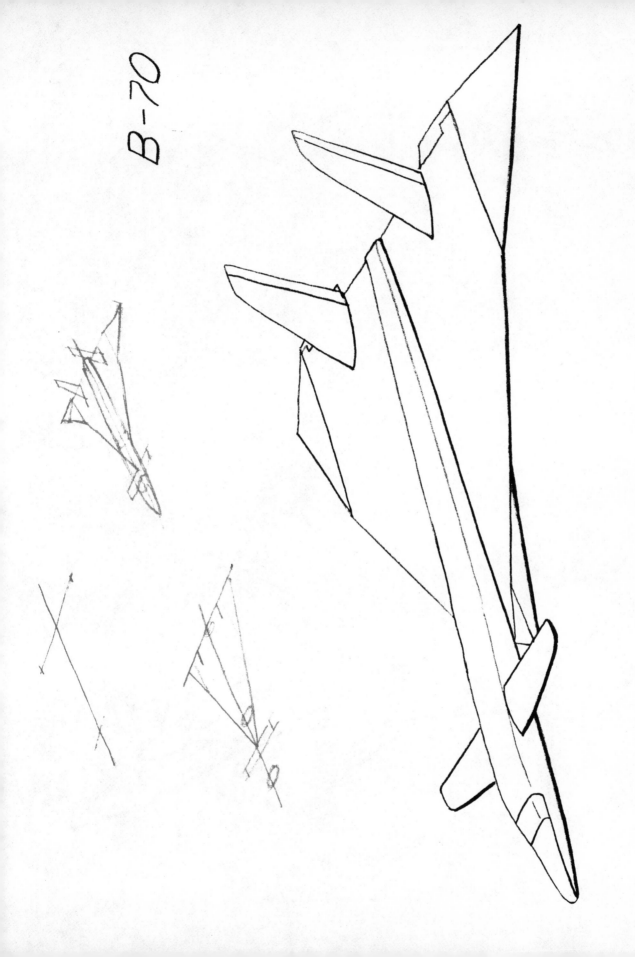

B-70

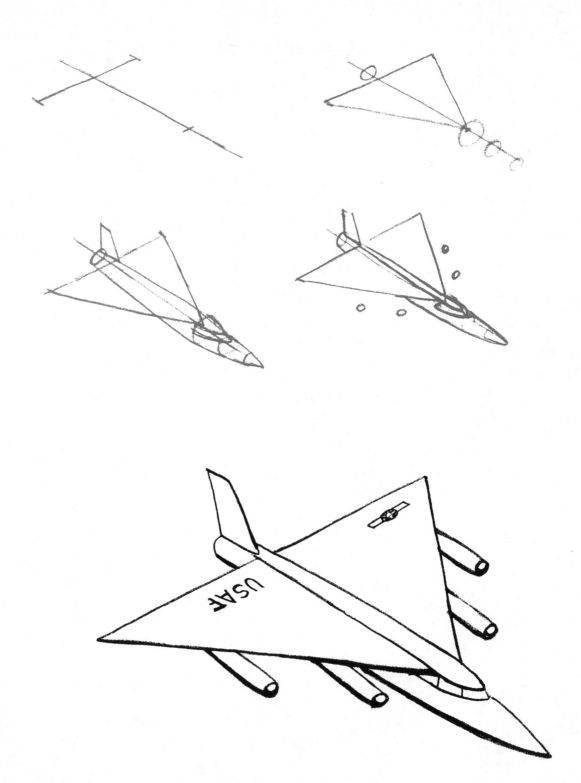

JEEP

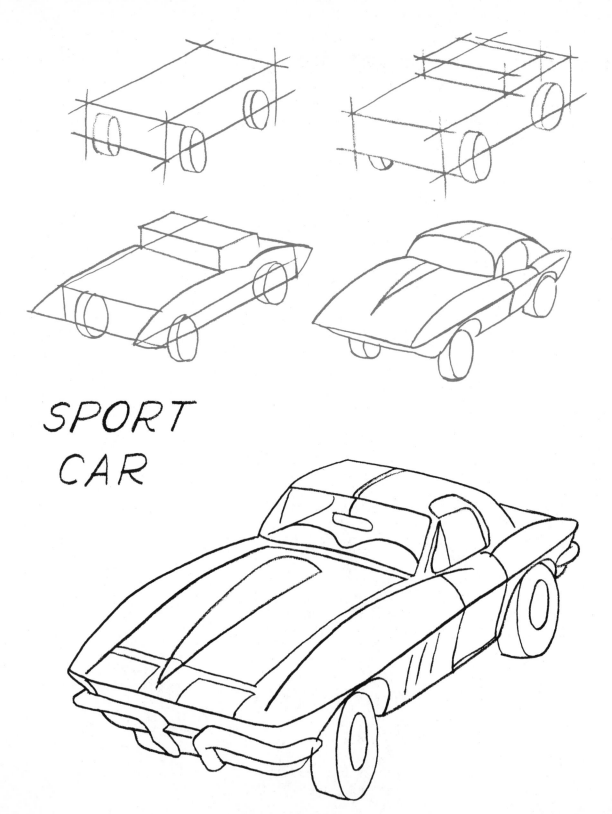

SPORT
CAR

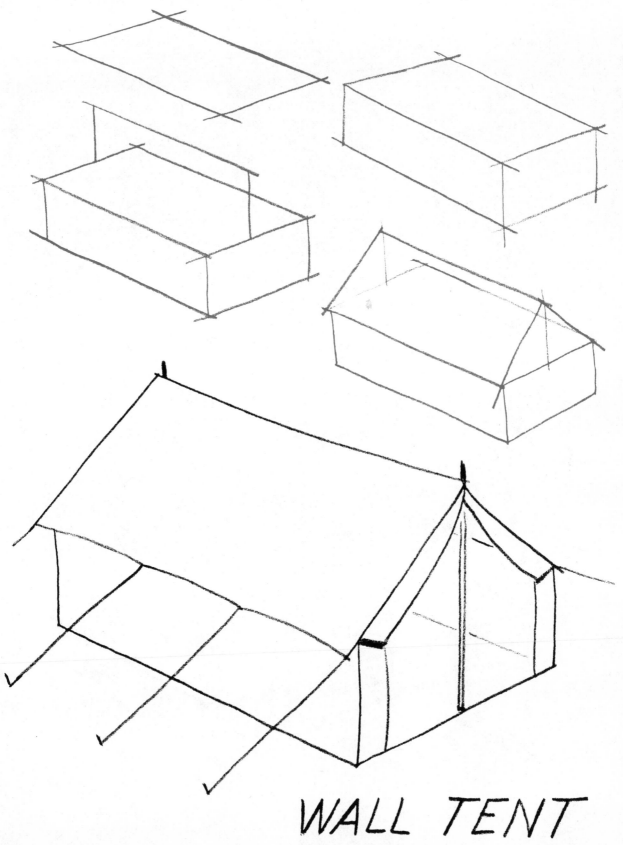

WALL TENT

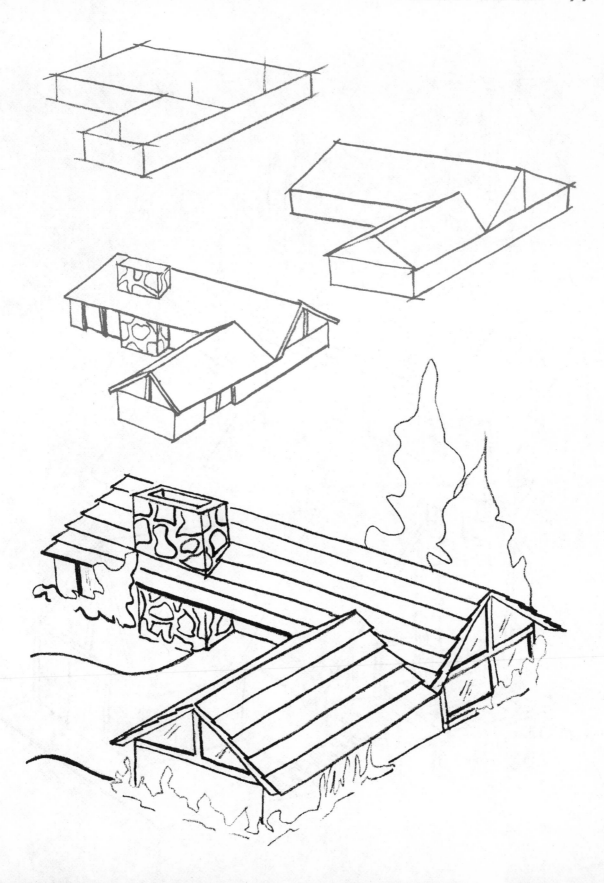

Pictorial Skill Development

The following illustrations are finished freehand drawings. The directions as to how they were developed are not included. You should be able to draw them freehand without difficulty, by using the procedures you have learned in previous drawings.

REMEMBER!
Start with the basic shape of the mass and work from large parts to small details. Relax!

Problem 10
Practice Pictorial Exercises

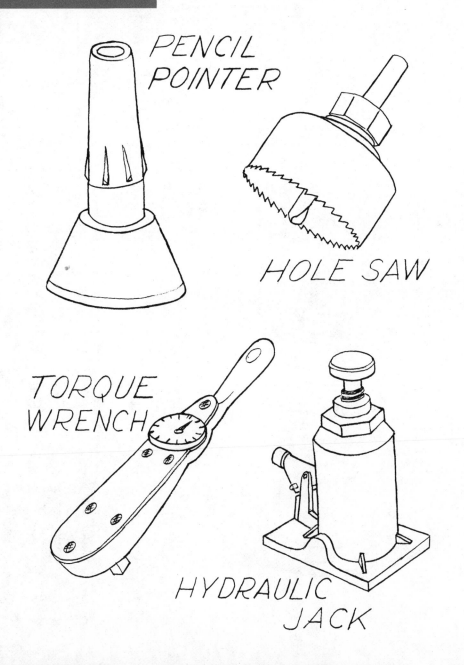

PENCIL POINTER

HOLE SAW

TORQUE WRENCH

HYDRAULIC JACK

APOLLO

RADIO
SPEAKER

ROUTER

ON OFF

UNITED STATES

USA USA

SABER SAW

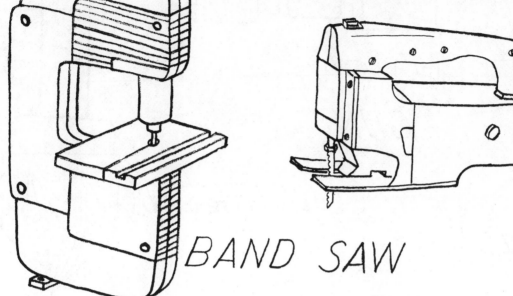

BAND SAW

CHAIR

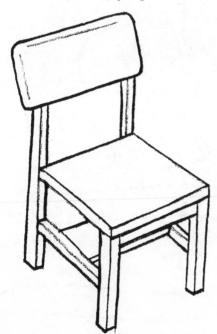

TOOL CHEST

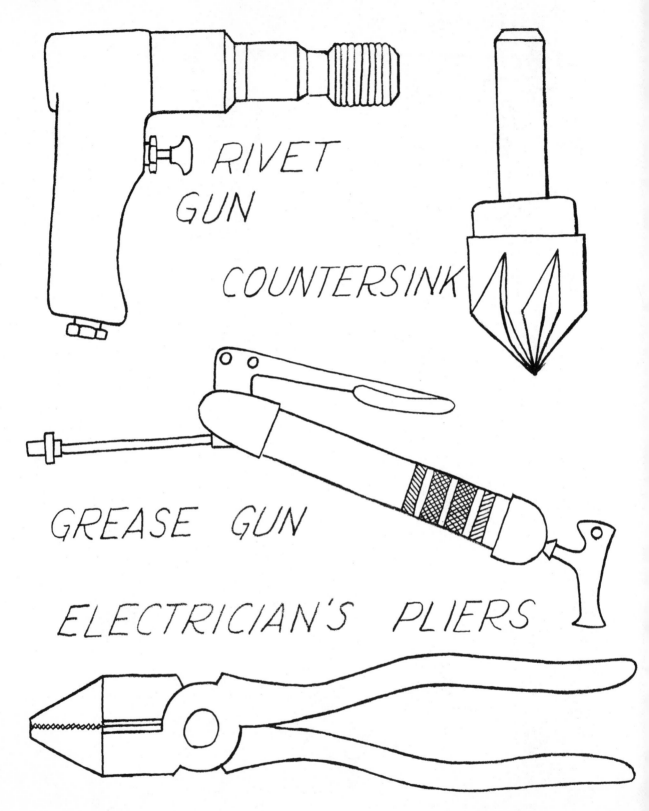

RIVET
GUN

COUNTERSINK

GREASE GUN

ELECTRICIAN'S PLIERS

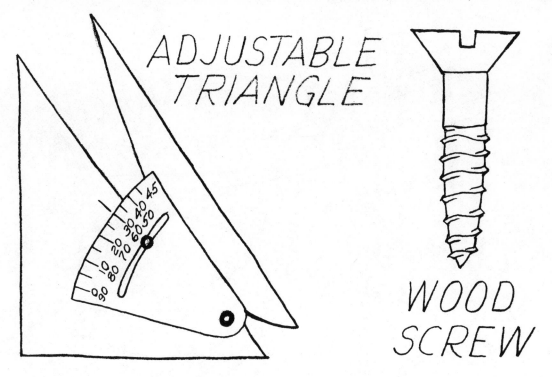

ADJUSTABLE
TRIANGLE

WOOD
SCREW

SNIPS

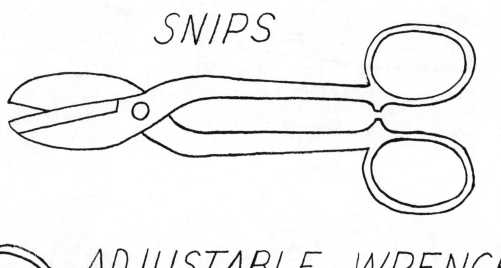

ADJUSTABLE WRENCH

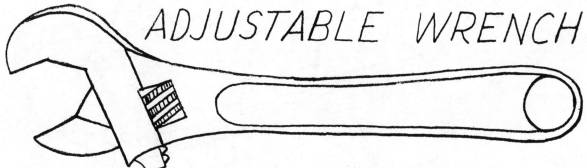

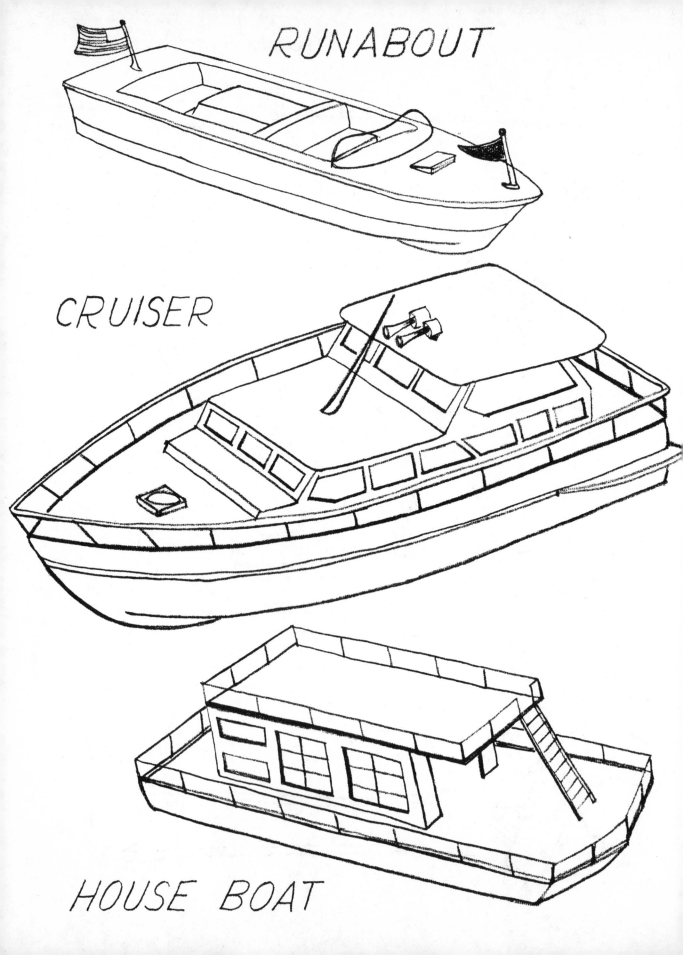

RUNABOUT

CRUISER

HOUSE BOAT

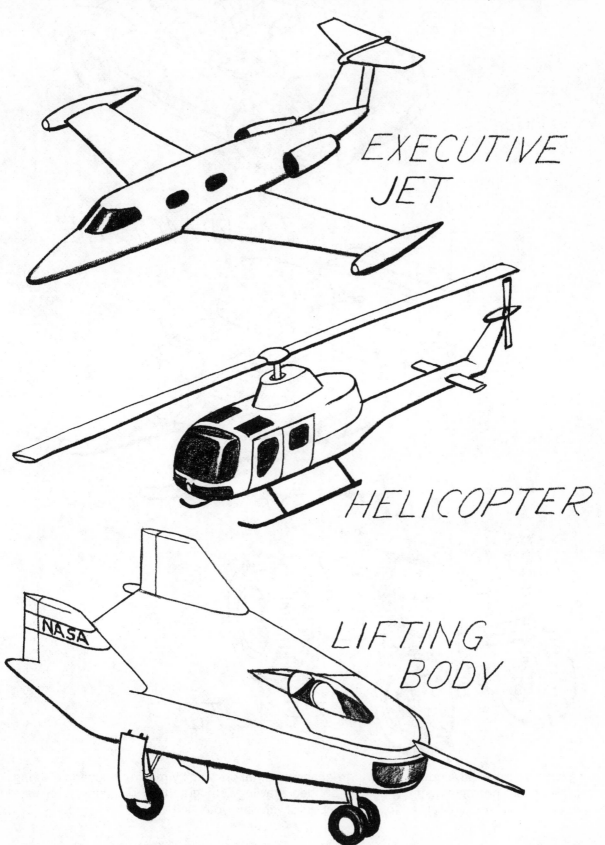

EXECUTIVE JET

HELICOPTER

LIFTING BODY

NASA

SPORTS CAR

SNOWMOBILE

TRACTOR

You can further develop your skill in freehand pictorial drawing by making freehand drawings of the project photographs in Chapter 6 entitled Drawing Orthographic Projections. After using pictures, draw from models as the next step in developing your skill.

Working Drawings

Working drawings are more technically described as *orthographic projection* drawings. Orthographic projection is a system of drawing in which the front, top, and side views are separated and the lines representing edges lie at right angles to the plane of projection. A right angle is 90° such as the corner of a square. The views are labelled on the following examples to help you understand this system.

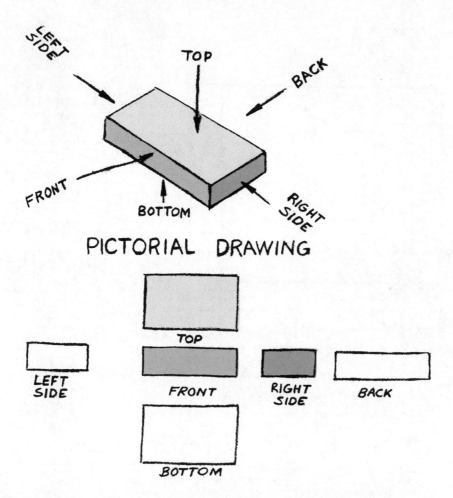

PICTORIAL DRAWING

ORTHOGRAPHIC PROJECTION DRAWING

In the example of an orthographic projection drawing, all views are shown. When drawings are made, only the views needed to show the shape of the object are used. Drawing the orthographic views by free-hand is a rapid method of recording the object. After the drawing has been recorded you can study the object and add corrections to improve the drawing. This freehand drawing can later be drawn mechanically. It can function as the working drawing to guide you or others when manufacturing the object.

The orthographic projection system of freehand drawing is used to express the detailed shape of an object clearly and only requires the minimum number of tools. Measurements and notes can be shown most accurately with this type of drawing. It is the most commonly used method of drawing things to be built. A freehand working drawing is shown in the following example.

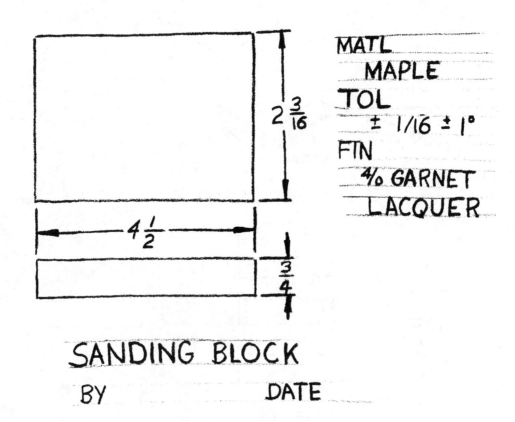

MATL
 MAPLE
TOL
 ± 1/16 ± 1°
FIN
 4/0 GARNET
 LACQUER

SANDING BLOCK

BY   DATE

Types of Lines

In orthographic projection drawing, it is customary to use several types or weights of lines to make the drawing as clear as possible. These customary lines are shown in the example.

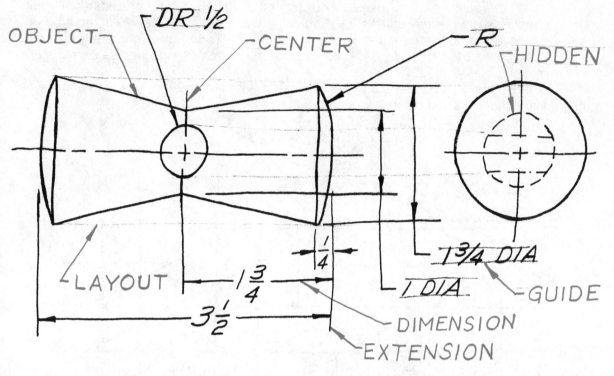

LINES   WIDTH   DENSITY

LINES	WIDTH	DENSITY
LAYOUT AND GUIDE	NARROW	LIGHT
OBJECT	WIDE	DARK
CENTER	NARROW	DARK
EXTENSION AND DIMENSION	NARROW	DARK
HIDDEN	NARROW	DARK

ARROWHEADS AND LETTERING SHOULD BE DRAWN WITH WIDE DARK LINES

In making orthographic projection drawings, there are several basic abilities necessary for good results. These abilities are developed by using and practicing correct procedures. The following examples show the procedures for developing these basic abilities. You should practice these procedures as exercises before making drawings. To improve your skill with these procedures, *practice them often for short periods of time. Several short practice sessions are better than a single long period.*

Practice the following exercises until you can skillfully combine the various elements of orthographic projections into complete, accurate drawings.

ANGLES

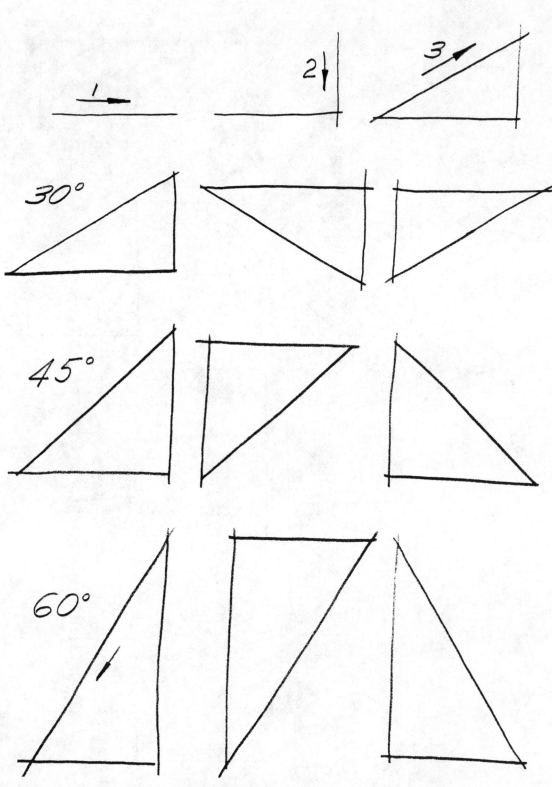

ARCS

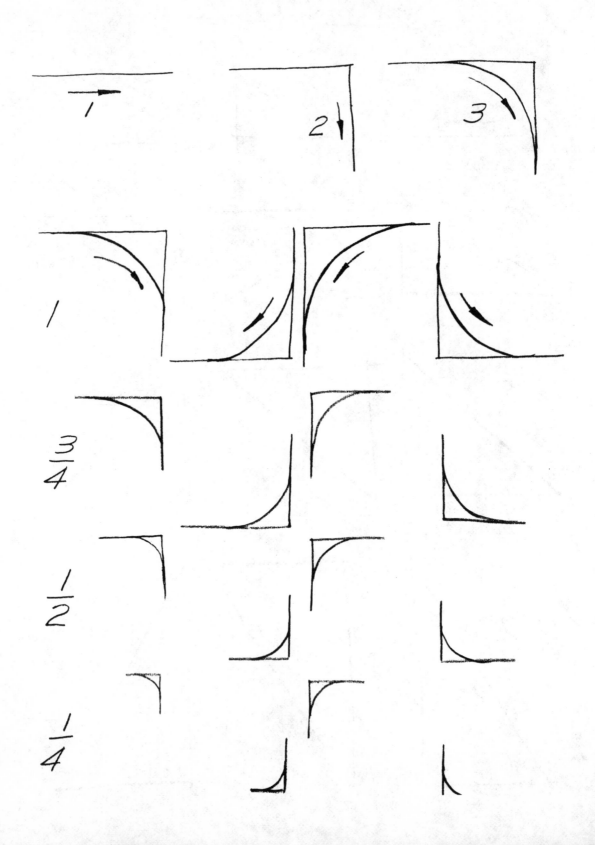

CIRCLES

ARROWHEADS

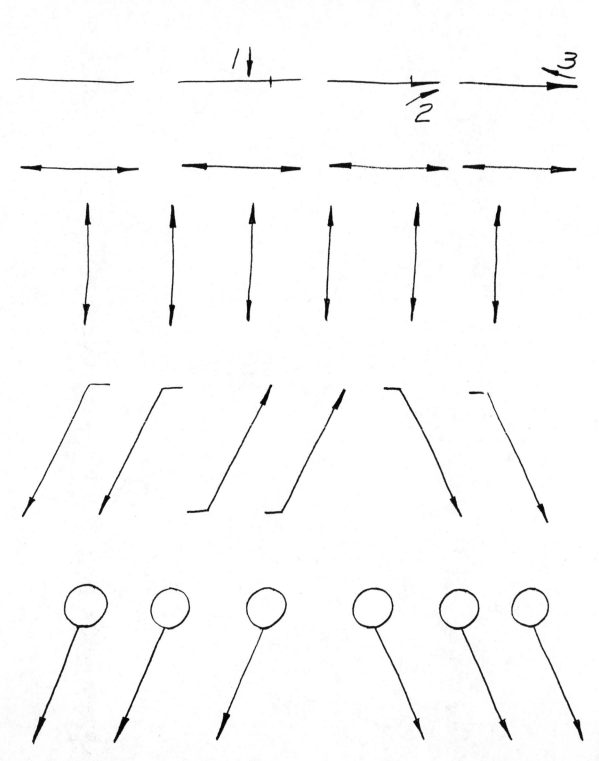

LETTERING

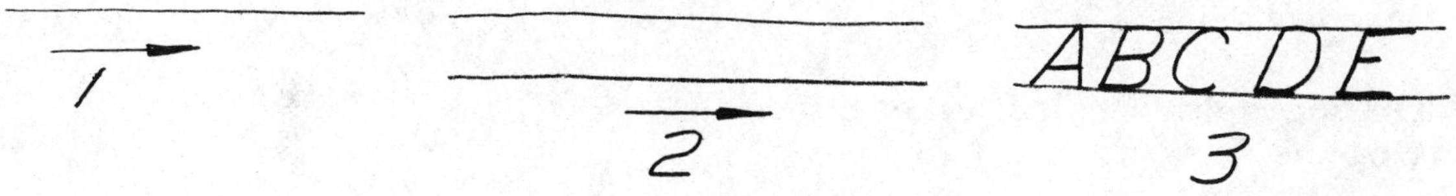

1 →

2 →

ABCDE

3

SET 1

ABCDEFGHIJKLMNOPQRSTUVWXYZ

1234567890 $\frac{1}{2}$ $\frac{3}{4}$ $\frac{7}{8}$ $\frac{3}{16}$ 1234567890

SET 2

ABCDEFGHIJKLMNOPQRSTUVWXYZ

1234567890 $\frac{1}{2}$ $\frac{3}{8}$ $\frac{1}{16}$ $\frac{5}{8}$ $\frac{1}{4}$ 1234567890

SET 3

STUDY THE SHAPE OF EACH LETTER,

USE GUIDELINES AND RELAX.

SET 4

45°X 1,/16 CHAM $\frac{9}{32}$ DR-32 HLS $\frac{1}{16}$ R

TOL ± 1/16   610 GARNET   SAW CUT

SET 5

11/16 DR-2 HLS   45° $2\frac{3}{16}$ $4\frac{1}{2}$ MAPLE

1/8 DR-3 HLS   LACQUER   RELAX

Before a freehand orthographic drawing is started, the object or structure should be studied to determine its basic shape. Usually the basic shape will be square (a rectangular solid) or round (a cylinder). In order to develop the ability to make good freehand orthographic projection drawings, the examples should be drawn according to the procedure shown.

Orthographic Projection of Square Objects

These examples show a step-by-step procedure for making freehand orthographic projection drawings of objects that are basically square. Follow the step-by-step procedure and study the systematic method of drawing

the SANDING BLOCK and the V-BLOCK. Notice that the main difference in these two examples is:

a. Horizontal lines are the dominant features of the sanding block.
b. Vertical lines are the dominant features of the V-block.

Sanding Block Drawing Procedure

Example is shown below.
Study the example and you will observe that most of the lines in the sanding block are horizontal.
Step One:
This drawing is started by estimating and locating the distance of each vertical line across the paper.

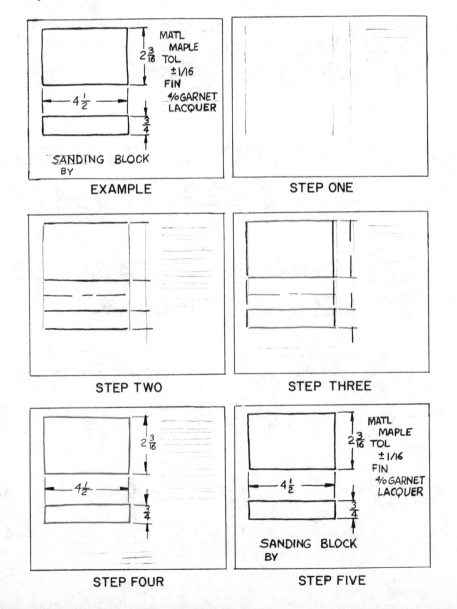

EXAMPLE

STEP ONE

STEP TWO

STEP THREE

STEP FOUR

STEP FIVE

Step Two:

Now draw narrow, light vertical lines.

Step Three:

Now the horizontal lines are drawn wider and darker.

Step Four:

Now the vertical lines are drawn wider and darker.

Step Five:

Now add the arrowheads to the dimension lines, add the dimensions, and add the lettering.

V-Block Drawing Procedure

Example is shown below.

Study the example and you will observe that most of the lines in the V-block are vertical.

Step One:

This drawing is started by estimating and locating the distance of each horizontal line across the paper.

Step Two:

Now draw narrow, light horizontal lines.

Step Three:

Now the vertical lines are drawn wider and darker.

Step Four:

Now the horizontal lines are drawn wider and darker.

Step Five:

Now add the arrowheads to the dimension lines, add the dimensions, and add the lettering.

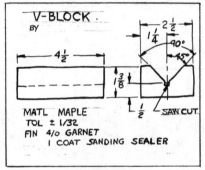

EXAMPLE

STEP ONE

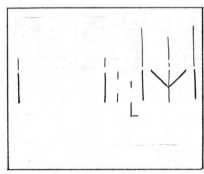

STEP TWO

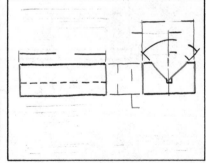

STEP THREE

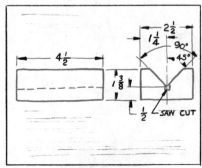

STEP FOUR

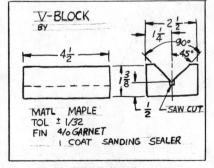

STEP FIVE

97

Problem 12
Practice the Drawing Procedure

Practice the step-by-step procedure shown with the SANDING BLOCK and V-BLOCK drawings as you make the freehand drawings of the following square objects. Use one full sheet of and draw each of the following examples.

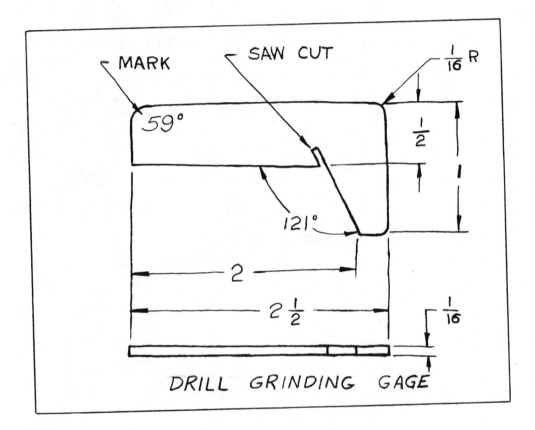

DRILL GRINDING GAGE

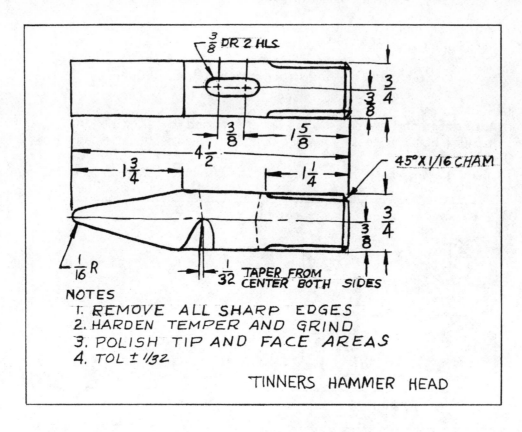

$\frac{3}{8}$ DR 2 HLS

45°X 1/16 CHAM

$\frac{3}{4}$

$\frac{3}{8}$

$\frac{3}{8}$ ← $1\frac{5}{8}$

$4\frac{1}{2}$

$1\frac{3}{4}$

$1\frac{1}{4}$

$\frac{3}{4}$

$\frac{3}{8}$

$\frac{1}{16}$ R

$\frac{1}{32}$ TAPER FROM CENTER BOTH SIDES

NOTES
1. REMOVE ALL SHARP EDGES
2. HARDEN TEMPER AND GRIND
3. POLISH TIP AND FACE AREAS
4. TOL ± 1/32

TINNERS HAMMER HEAD

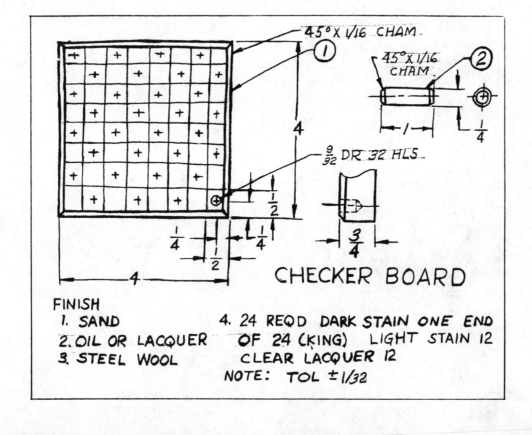

45°X 1/16 CHAM

45°X 1/16 CHAM

$\frac{9}{32}$ DR 32 HLS

4

1

2

$\frac{1}{4}$

$\frac{1}{2}$

$\frac{1}{4}$

$\frac{1}{4}$

$\frac{1}{2}$

$\frac{3}{4}$

4

CHECKER BOARD

FINISH
1. SAND
2. OIL OR LACQUER
3. STEEL WOOL

4. 24 REQD DARK STAIN ONE END OF 24 (KING) LIGHT STAIN 12
   CLEAR LACQUER 12
NOTE: TOL ± 1/32

Round Objects

Step-by-step procedures for making freehand orthographic drawings of round objects are shown in the following examples.

Freehand Drawing Procedure for Round Objects

Example:
Study the orthographic examples in the upper left hand corner of the MALLET HEAD and FUNNEL drawings. Basically, these are round objects that consist of circles and arcs.

Step One:
This type of drawing is started by measuring the distance of each vertical line. Then draw

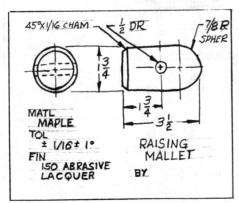

EXAMPLE

STEP ONE

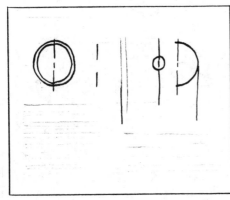

STEP TWO

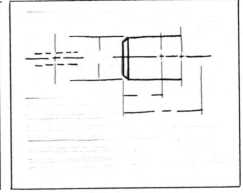

STEP THREE

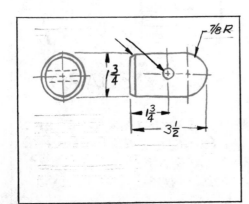

STEP FOUR

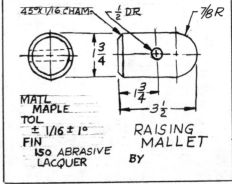

STEP FIVE

the vertical lines with narrow, light lines.

Step Two:
   Now estimate and locate the position of the horizontal lines. Then draw them with narrow, light lines.

Step Three:
   Now draw the circles and arcs. Also draw in the wide, dark vertical lines.

Step Four:
   Now darken the horizontal lines.

Step Five:
   Now add the arrowheads to the dimension lines, add the dimensions, and add the lettering.

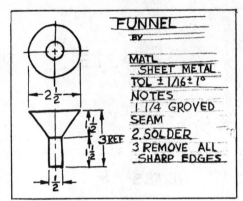

EXAMPLE

STEP ONE

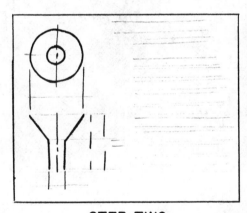

STEP TWO

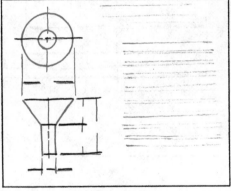

STEP THREE

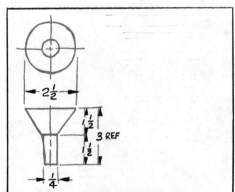

STEP FOUR

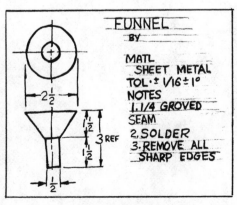

STEP FIVE

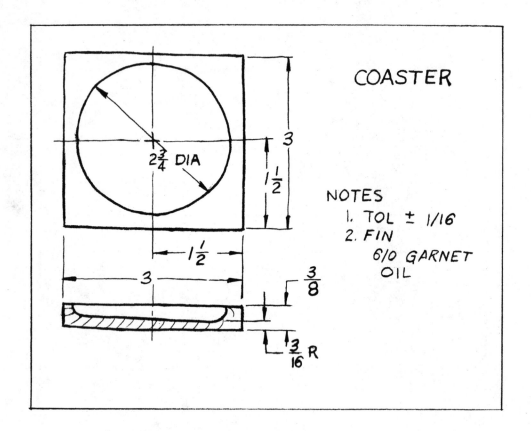

Practice the procedures shown with the MALLET HEAD and FUNNEL drawings as you make freehand drawings of the following objects, pages 102 and 103.

COASTER

$2\frac{3}{4}$ DIA

3

$1\frac{1}{2}$

$1\frac{1}{2}$

3

$\frac{3}{8}$

$\frac{3}{16}$ R

NOTES
  1. TOL ± 1/16
  2. FIN
     6/0 GARNET
     OIL

GAVEL HEAD

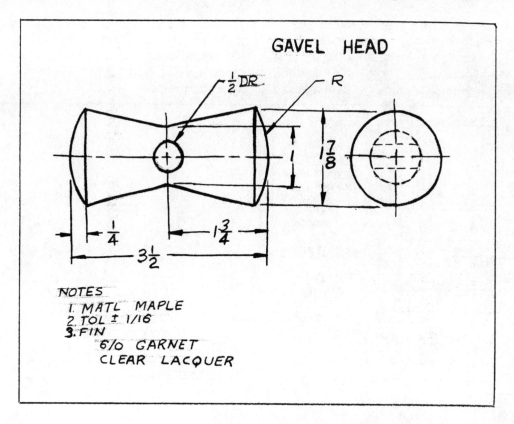

NOTES
1. MATL MAPLE
2. TOL ± 1/16
3. FIN
    6/0 GARNET
    CLEAR LACQUER

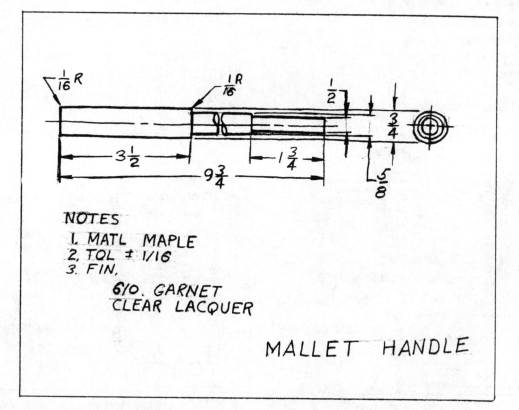

NOTES
1. MATL MAPLE
2. TOL ± 1/16
3. FIN,
    6/0. GARNET
    CLEAR LACQUER

MALLET HANDLE

Assembly Drawings

Assembly drawings show objects made of several parts. When the drawing gives all the necessary information for making the parts of the assembly, as well as how it fits together, it is called a *detail assembly*. A suggested procedure is shown for making freehand assembly drawings.

Study the examples in the KICKING TEE and the PICTURE FRAME drawings. Now analyze Steps One through Five to understand how to complete this type of drawing, pages 104 and 105.

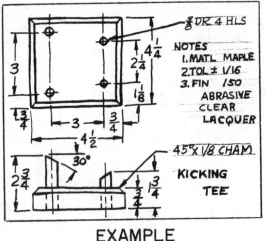

EXAMPLE

STEP ONE

STEP TWO

STEP THREE

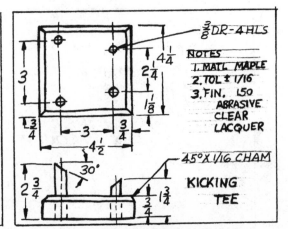

STEP FOUR

STEP FIVE

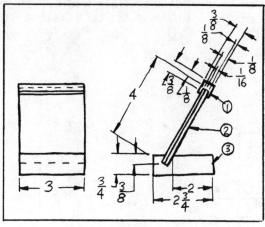

EXAMPLE

STEP ONE

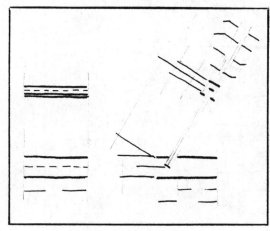

STEP TWO

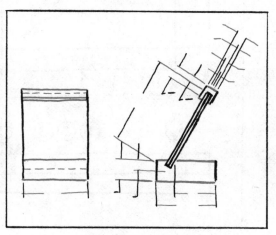

STEP THREE

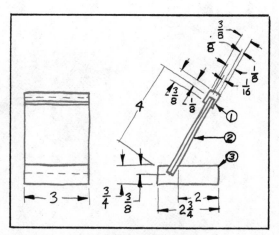

STEP FOUR

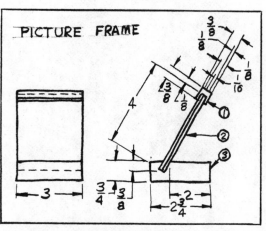

PICTURE FRAME

STEP FIVE

Examples of freehand working drawings are shown for your practice in developing the ability to make good drawings, pages 106 and 107.

When you are capable of drawing objects that are accurate and easy to understand, you have achieved a satisfactory freehand drawing ability. Remember that it is less costly to correct drawings than it is to correct a product that was manufactured wrong because of a drawing error.

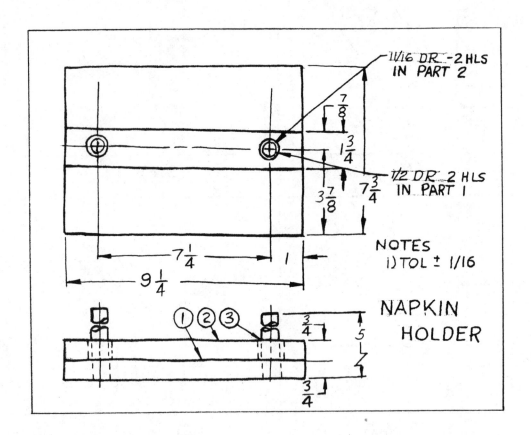

NOTES
i) TOL ± 1/16

NAPKIN HOLDER

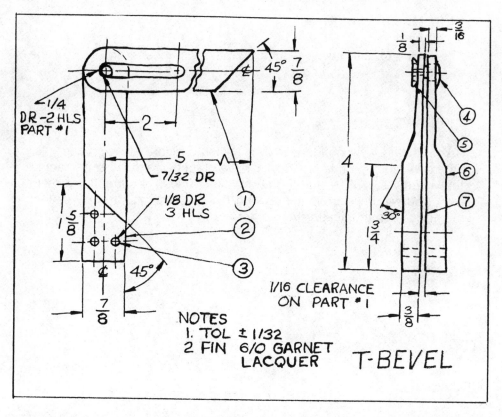

1/4
DR-2 HLS
PART #1

2

5

7/32 DR

1/8 DR
3 HLS

45° 7/8

5/8

7/8

45°

① ② ③

3/16

1/8

4

30°

4
3/4

3/8

④ ⑤ ⑥ ⑦

1/16 CLEARANCE
ON PART #1

NOTES
1. TOL ± 1/32
2 FIN 6/0 GARNET
LACQUER

T-BEVEL

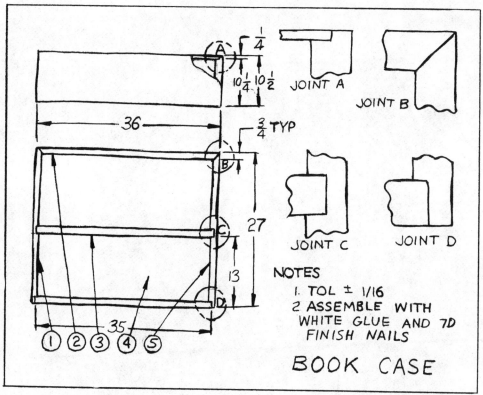

A

1/4

10 1/4 10 1/2

JOINT A

JOINT B

36

3/4 TYP

B

27

C

13

D

35

① ② ③ ④ ⑤

JOINT C   JOINT D

NOTES
1. TOL ± 1/16
2 ASSEMBLE WITH
WHITE GLUE AND 7D
FINISH NAILS

BOOK CASE

Skill Development

Further skill can be developed by making freehand drawings of the projects shown in Chapters 6, 7, 8, 9, 11, and 12.

Summary

You should feel confident in your ability to record ideas on paper for others to see and understand. You have practiced a drawing procedure that improves your freehand drawing skill. If you keep practicing regularly, you will develop your freehand drawing ability into an excellent method of communicating with other people.

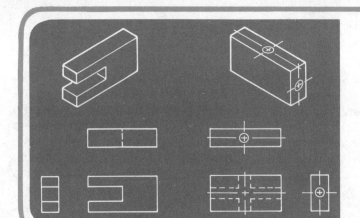

Drafting Conventional Practices

Why Study This Chapter?

The study of CONVENTIONAL PRACTICES will show you how to:

1. Use different sizes of drawings.
2. Lay out the border, title block, and list of material.
3. Select views, draw lines, and dimension and label orthographic projections.
4. Show special views on orthographic projections.
5. Check finished drawings carefully.

You will want to refer to this chapter again later when you need to recall the correct procedure for making your drawings. The drafting practices in this chapter are a good review when you need a better understanding of the drawing methods introduced to you in Chapters 5, 6, 7, 8, 9, 10, and 11.

Conventional practices are accepted or "standard" methods of performing or communicating the work to be done. They have been developed over years of use by draftsmen and engineers. Standards for drawings, or conventional practices, are agreed upon by people representing many industries and printed in books called *United States of America Standards Institute (USAS) Drafting Manuals*. This association was originally called the *American Standards Association (ASA)*. Individual companies also develop *Drafting Room Manuals* as guides to their draftsmen. It is important that conventional practices are used so that drawings can be correctly understood. Basic conventional practices used in drafting are described in this chapter. You should gain an understanding of them and use this chapter for reference when making drawings.

Sheet Sizes

Drawings are made on standard-size sheets of paper measuring in multiples of 8½″ × 11″, 11″ × 17″, and 17″ × 22″. A letter symbol is used to identify each sheet size. Selection of an appropriate sheet size for a drawing depends upon the size of the object to be drawn. Draftsmen usually refer to the sheet sizes as A (8½″ × 11″), B (11″ × 17″), or C (17″ × 22″). There are also sizes D and E. Large sheets are used for very large objects like engines, transmissions, etc. As a student, you will not use the larger sheets since you will study a variety of small, simple objects.

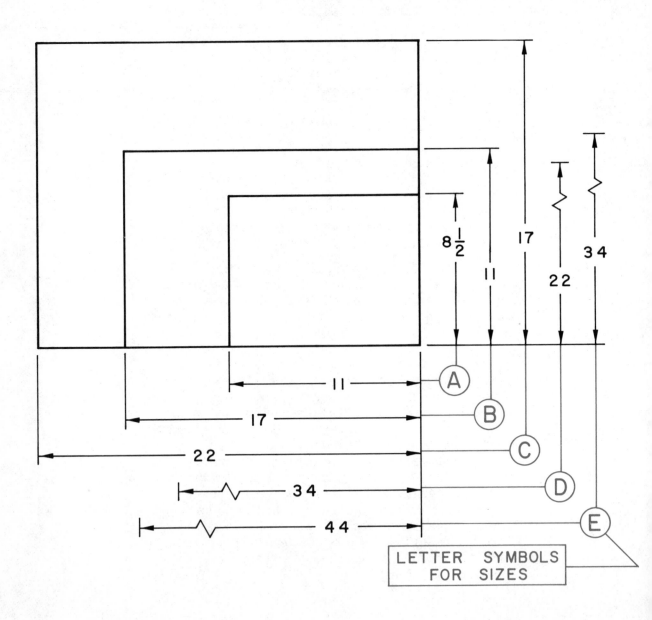

LETTER SYMBOLS FOR SIZES

Generally, mechanical objects are drawn full-size or half-size to fit on the paper. Buildings are usually drawn so that ¼″ or ⅛″ equals 1′-0″. The sheet size selected should allow adequate space for notes and dimensions. A or B size sheets are used when drawing small, simple objects because the objects do not require a lot of notes and dimensions. Complex objects require many notes and dimensions. Therefore, size C, D, or E sheets must be used.

Sheet Layout

A sheet layout consists of the border line, title block, and list of material. The sheet layout provides an organized method of showing needed information on the drawing. With the exception of the narrow, light layout lines and guide lines for lettering, all lines for the sheet layout are drawn dark and wide.

Lines for the border, title block and list of material are drawn into position on your paper with narrow, light layout lines. The lines are then drawn wider and darker after the layout has been completed.

Border Size

Borders for A, B, and C sheet sizes may be drawn as illustrated. This layout allows room for notebook binding of the drawings you have done as you learn.

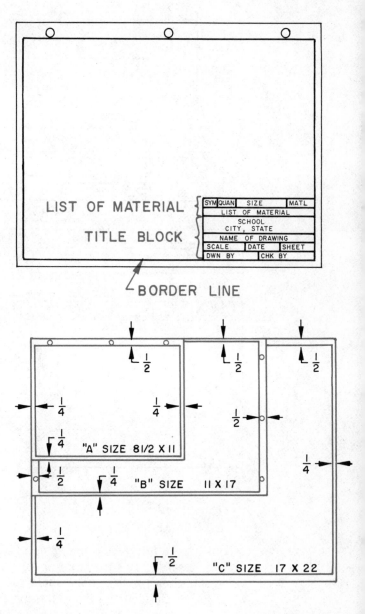

Title Block and List of Material

The title block and list of material should appear in the lower right-hand corner of the sheet. Each company may have a different style for drawing the block. The size of the title block and list of material used in this book is shown in the illustration. This size was selected to record the important information about the objects you will be drawing.

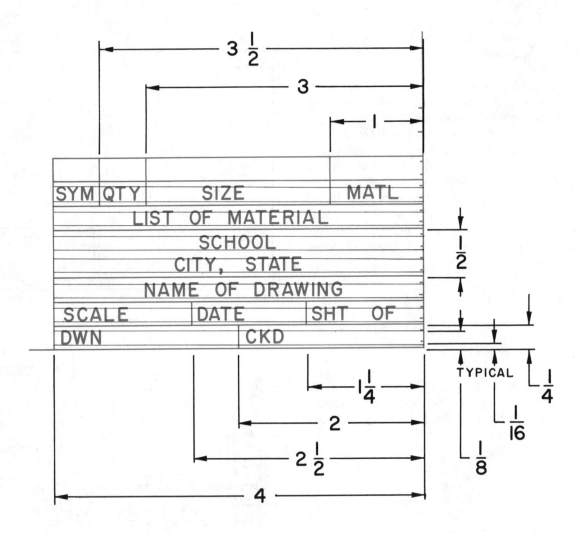

In the *title block*, the *scale* is always the ratio of the drawing size to one full unit of measurement, such as $1 = 1$ for full size. For a half-size drawing, the scale would read $\frac{1}{2} = 1$. A double scale is shown as $2 = 1$. One-fourth inch to the foot is expressed as $\frac{1}{4}'' = 1'\text{-}0''$.

Dimensions showing the size of a part in the *list of material* are shown in the following order:
1. Square or rectangular parts—
   Thickness × Width × Length
   Example: ¾ × 2⁹⁄₁₆ × 4½
2. Round or cylindrical parts—
   Diameter × Length
   Example: 1¾ Dia × 3½
3. Hexagon—
   Hexagon (across flats) × Length
   Example: ⅝ Hex × 5
4. Octagon—
   Octagon (across flats) × Length
   Example: ½ Oct × 3

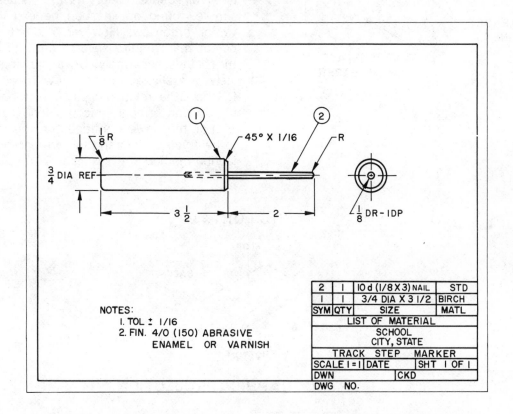

NOTES:
1. TOL ± 1/16
2. FIN. 4/0 (150) ABRASIVE
   ENAMEL OR VARNISH

SYM	QTY	SIZE	MATL
2	1	10 d (1/8 X 3) NAIL	STD
1	1	3/4 DIA X 3 1/2	BIRCH

LIST OF MATERIAL

SCHOOL
CITY, STATE

TRACK STEP MARKER

SCALE 1=1	DATE		SHT 1 OF 1
DWN		CKD	
DWG NO.			

Study the *List of Material* for the TRACK STEP MARKER. Above the column marked SYM (symbol), the parts are numbered 1 and 2. Notice that these numbers begin at the bottom and build upward. This is a correct conventional practice. This allows the draftsman to add symbols as the drawing is developed. The symbol numbers (1 and 2) are used to explain the list of material. The number 1 and 2 are placed in circles called *balloons*. The symbol numbers are recorded in the list of material and they are identified in the balloons to indicate the part being described.

Orthographic Projection Drawing

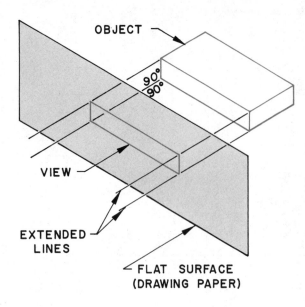

Orthographic projection drawings show the exact shape and size of parts or structures. It is the most widely used drawing method practiced in drafting. The term *orthographic projection* means the view is formed on a flat surface by drawing parallel lines from the faces of an object at 90° to the flat surface. It can be easily understood by looking at the example on the left.

In orthographic projection, there are six main views that can be shown. They are the (1) front, (2) back, (3) top, (4) bottom, (5) right-side, and (6) left-side views. Side views are sometimes called end views. All rectangular or square objects have six sides. Most simple, round objects can be explained in two or three views. However, a complex round object may require several views to explain the details accurately. On a drawing, these views are aligned in position with each other to show the relationships. A pictorial drawing and an orthographic projection drawing, with all the views identified, are shown below to help you understand the orthographic projection method of drawing.

PICTORIAL

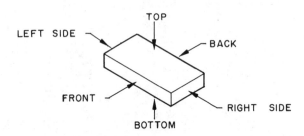

ORTHOGRAPHIC PROJECTION

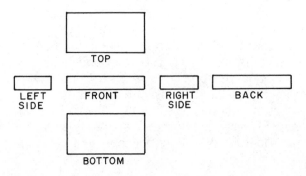

Selection of Views

In an orthographic projection drawing, the draftsman uses only the views needed to show the shape of the object clearly. Notice that the views are aligned exactly with each other. They are either on the right or left side or on the top or bottom. Side views may be projected to the side of the top view when space is needed on the drawing sheet. Enough space should be left between the views to allow proper placing of the dimensions.

The problems in this book have been provided to give you experience in using tools and to acquaint you with a variety of drawing techniques. It is important that you learn how to select the views which express the shape of each object. The following rules will help you understand how to select the proper view. The problems in this book will show you various types of objects and specify the best view selection so you will learn this technique quickly and accurately.

The following rules should be used as guides in selecting the correct views for an orthographic projection drawing. Study the rules and learn why a particular view should be selected to express the size and shape of an object.

1. Use as few views as needed to show the shape of the object clearly.
2. *Always* use the front view.
3. The back view is only used when other views will not clearly show the shape. Since it is seldom used, the back view should be labeled (back view) whenever it is used.
4. Use the top view instead of the bottom view if both views show the same detail.
5. The right side view is used in place of the left side view when both views show the same detail.
6. Use the view which reduces the use of hidden lines.

These rules have been used in the following examples.

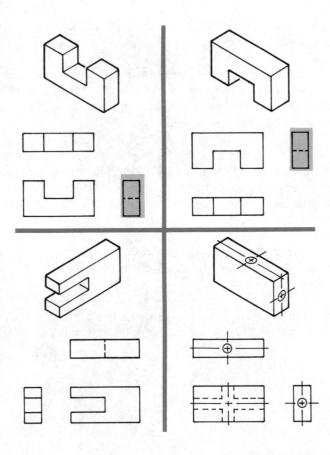

Conventional Lines

Conventional lines are of a prescribed width and/or pattern, according to their use on a drawing. By using conventional lines, it is much easier to express clearly and understand the drawing. All lines needed on a drawing should be drawn dense, dark black. It is the width that varies; not the blackness. The diagram on page 117 shows the names, use, pattern, and width of the basic lines used in drafting.

Study the diagram and observe the different types of drawing lines. These lines are used when planning and drawing any type of object. The lines are labelled as layout, object, center, extension, dimension, hidden, guide, and border lines.

Layout lines are drawn with a narrow, light density. They are used when planning the position and line lengths on a drawing.

Object lines are drawn with a wide, dark line and are used to represent the shape of the object.

Center lines are drawn with alternating long and short lines which are narrow and dark in density.

Extension and dimension lines are drawn narrow and dark. Extension lines are used to extend the size of the object so that dimension lines can be drawn near the views. Dimension lines and dimensions are used to explain the size and shape of the object.

Hidden lines are drawn dark with a medium width. They are formed with short dashes (approximately ⅛" long) to show the shape and position of internal or posterior (rear view) surfaces. Drawing views should be selected so that the hidden lines are held to a minimum when describing an object.

Guide lines are drawn narrow and very light in density. They are similar to layout lines. They are used to control the size and location of notes, lettering, or numbers.

Border lines are used to form the frame for the drawing, the title block, and the list of material. They are drawn wide and dark.

CONVENTIONAL LINES

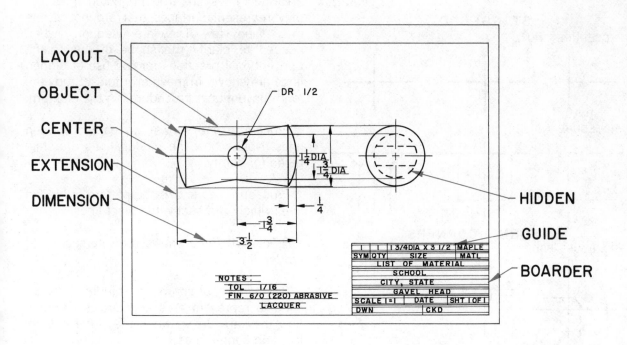

LINES

LINES		WIDTH	DENSITY
LAYOUT	————————————	NARROW	LIGHT
OBJECT	————————————	WIDE	DARK
CENTER	— · — — — · — —	NARROW	DARK
EXTENSION DIMENSION	——— ———	NARROW	DARK
HIDDEN	– – – – – – –	MEDIUM	DARK
GUIDE	————————————	NARROW	LIGHT
BOARDER	————————————	WIDE	DARK

ARROWHEADS AND LETTERING SHOULD BE
DRAWN WITH WIDE DARK LINES

PROCEDURE ONE

STAGGERED

PROCEDURE TWO

PROCEDURE THREE

FORM   CORNERS

PROCEDURE FOUR

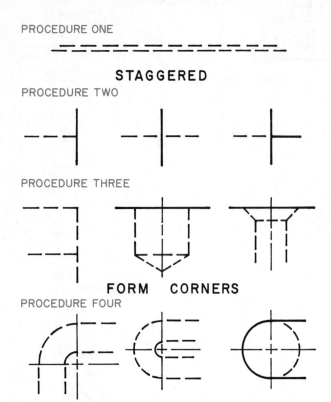

Hidden Lines

Hidden lines are true projected lines but they represent surfaces that are not visible in a given view. They are used only when needed to clarify the shape of the object. Conventional practices for the use of hidden lines are shown in these examples. Study the four conventional procedures in the diagram.

Procedure one shows two parallel hidden lines. Notice how the hidden lines are staggered for clarity.

Procedure two shows the pattern of hidden lines which intersect with object lines.

Procedure three shows the intersection of hidden lines.

Procedure four shows how hidden lines are used to represent arcs and circles. Observe how they are drawn when they intersect object and center lines.

MEASURED $\frac{1}{8}$ $\frac{1}{4}$ APPROXIMATE

TOUCHES

$\frac{1}{2}$

SPACE   APPROXIMATE

$\frac{1}{16}$ $\frac{3}{16}$

DIMENSION LINE

ARROWHEAD

EXTENSION LINE

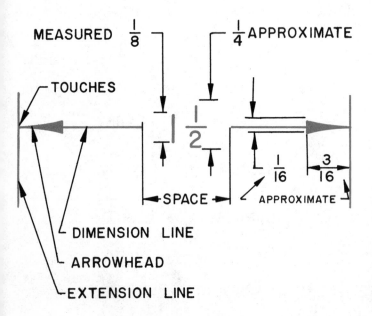

Dimensions

Dimensions are the measurements of the object. They are recorded on the drawing to describe size of parts or structures accurately. A complete dimension requires dimension lines, extension lines, arrowheads, and numbers.

This diagram shows the conventional practices used to describe the size of the object. Lines, arrowheads, and numbers explain the size and relationship of parts. Observe that the arrowhead touches the extension line. Also, notice the space left in the dimension line so the number can be added (1½). The arrowhead is approximately 3/16″ long and 1/16″ wide. Notice the position of the 1½. The whole number (1) is approximately ⅛″ high and the fraction (½) is approximately ¼″ high.

The two types of dimensions are *size* and *location* dimensions. Together, they describe the shape and size of an object.

Sizes shown in dimensions often require the use of fractions or decimal numbers. At beginning or basic levels of drafting, the fractions are used because they are more easily understood.

Study the example, TYPES OF DIMENSIONS. The *size* dimensions explain the size of the block and hole. The *location* dimensions show the exact center position of the hole from the edges of the block.

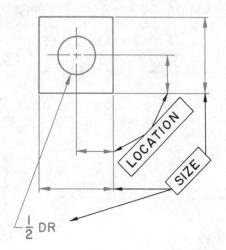

TYPES OF DIMENSIONS

Dimensioning Methods

You have studied that drawing lines and the placement of views are important to show the relationship of one surface to another. Now you will learn that dimensions are used to control the size and shape of objects. It is important that you learn and understand the following dimensioning methods and conventional practices.

Unidirectional and *aligned* are the two methods of placing the numbers with the dimension lines. With the unidirectional method, all figures read from the bottom of the page. In the aligned method, the numbers are lined up with the dimension lines so they read from the *bottom* or the *right-hand* edge of the drawing. The unidirectional method of dimensioning is generally used in all fields of drafting except civil and architectural drafting where the aligned method is used.

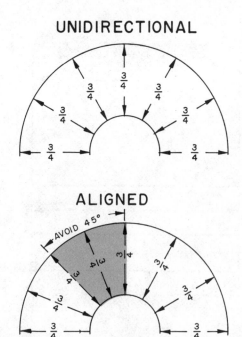

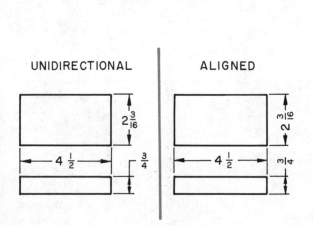

Placement of Dimensions

The term *placement of dimensions* means the arrangement or positioning of the measurements on a drawing. By following these conventional practices in the placement of dimensions, a drawing can be read with ease and accuracy. (In the following examples color screens have been placed over the incorrect drawing practices.)

1. Place dimensions *off the views*. Color screen area is wrong.

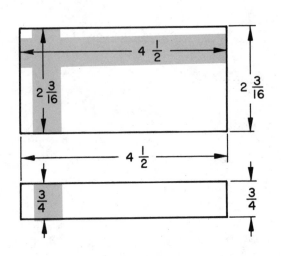

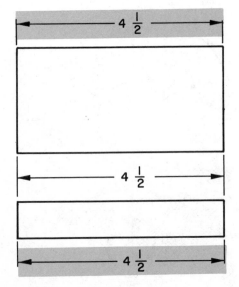

2. Dimension lines *should be spaced ½" from object lines* and other dimension lines. This space may be reduced to ⅜" when necessary. Extension lines should start ¹/₁₆" from object lines and pass the arrowhead ⅛" (estimate these measurements). Also observe the leader (slanted line showing ⅜" drill note) is drawn with the horizontal part of the leader spaced ½" from the object line.

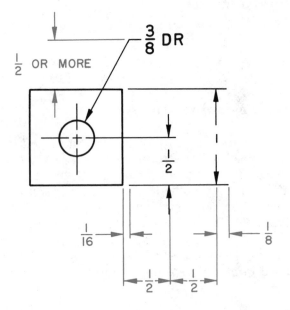

3. Place dimensions *between the views*.

┌─ REMEMBER! ──────────────┐
The color screen shows the wrong method.
└──────────────────────────┘

When the dimension is between the view, it is easier to read with minimum eye movement.

4. Dimensions *should be placed to the right* of views. When the dimensions and the title block are located to the right of the views, it is easier to read with minimum eye movement.

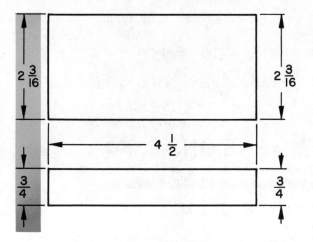

5. Place dimensions *below the views*. In this position, it is easy to read and compare to the title block.

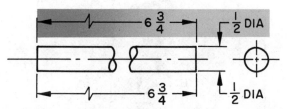

6. Dimensions should be *placed near detail*. In this example it required drawing extension lines across the entire view to follow previous rules. Detail placed in a position where it is difficult to read is shown in the colored area.

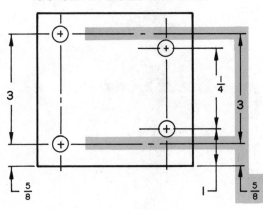

7. Avoid dimensioning hidden lines. *Do not dimension hidden lines* when the dimension can be shown in another view. Dimensioning a hidden line is difficult to understand as shown in the colored area. The ½″ dimension of the object line is easily understood in the right-hand view.

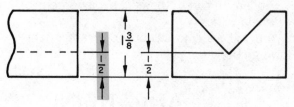

8. When several dimensions are placed near each other, they should be separated or *staggered so they are easily understood.*

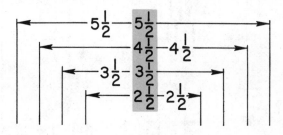

9. When possible, avoid crossing dimension lines with extension leaders or other dimension lines.

10. *Do not break extension lines* as they cross other extension lines. The left view of the illustration shows the incorrect practice in the colored area.

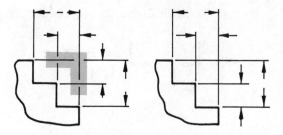

Arranging Dimensions

The following examples show various ways of arranging dimensions in both horizontal and vertical measurements. Study the three conventional practices that are used.

Procedure one shows the placement of the arrowheads and the dimensions outside the narrow space of the extension lines.

Procedure two shows the placement of the dimension between the extension lines; however, there is not enough space to include the arrowheads.

Procedure three shows the placement of the arrowheads and the dimension between the extension lines.

You will learn to select the arrangement of dimensions as you do the problems in the following chapter.

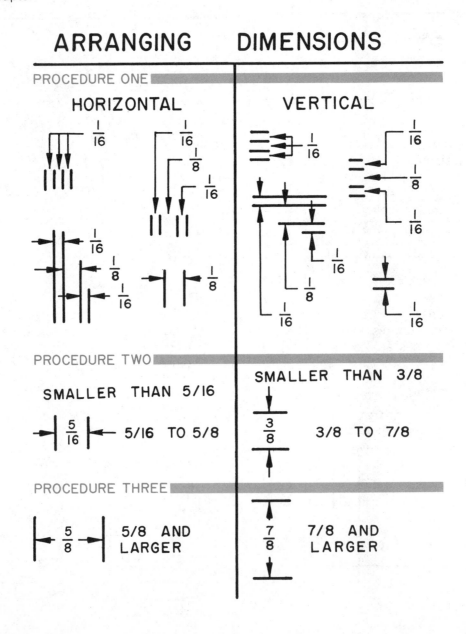

Dimensioning Practices

Round parts such as rods and shafts should be dimensioned across the center line and never on the round view. The dimensions in the colored area show a practice that should be avoided.

ROUND PARTS

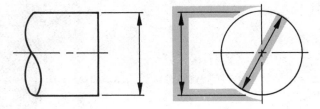

The location and size dimensions for holes are placed on the view showing the shape of the hole. The dimensions in the colored area are difficult to understand. Also remember dimensioning hidden lines is considered to be a poor practice.

HOLES

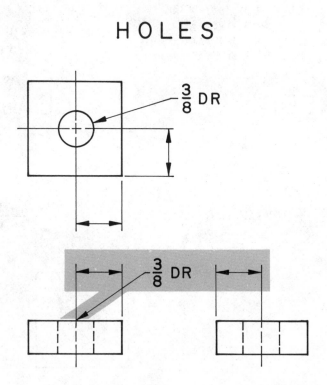

Leaders

Leaders are connected to a narrow *slanted* line that ends with an arrowhead. The narrow horizontal line portion is approximately ⅛″ to ¼″ long. They are used to connect notes or dimensions with the area or part which is being described.

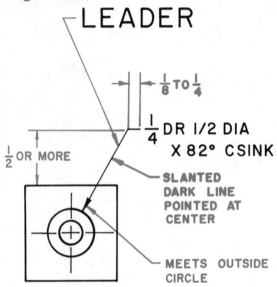

2. The leader line must slant considerably from the horizontal position and the vertical position. Angles of 15°, 30°, 45°, 60°, or 75° are commonly used.

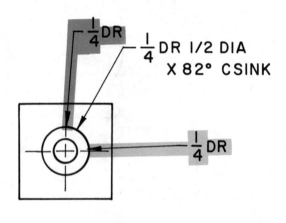

1. Generally the short, narrow horizontal line of a leader should be at the beginning of the note or dimension. It should be placed at one-half the height of the lettering.

3. If extended, the slanted line of a leader would point to the center of the operation. The colored area shows the wrong practice.

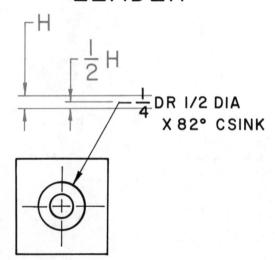

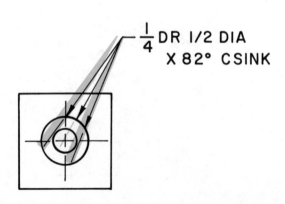

4. The leader ends at the outside edge of the line that shows a series of operations, such as the diameter of the countersink hole in the illustration. The colored area shows the wrong practice.

LEADER

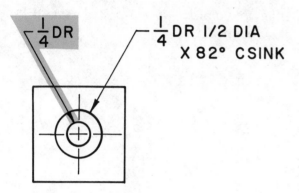

5. A leader should never cross another leader. The colored area is the wrong practice.

LEADERS

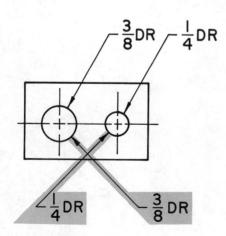

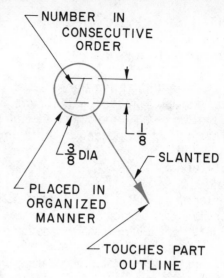

Balloons

Balloons are used to designate different parts in an assembly drawing. The numbers should be in consecutive order.

These numbers correspond with the SYM (symbol) column of the *List of Material* of each title block. Balloons should be placed in an organized manner with the circles following horizontal or vertical lines. The arrows extending from the circles should be slanted and should not cross other balloon arrows. These arrows should not be horizontal or vertical. The arrows should touch the object line of the part.

Arrowheads

Arrowheads are used to show where a line stops. They also connect dimensions and notes for detail references on the drawing. Many arrowheads are used in drafting; therefore it is important to be able to form them properly.

There is a special way to make arrowheads. In Chapter 5, DRAWING MECHANICALLY, you will practice making the arrowhead with three pencil strokes.

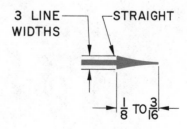

Labelling Drawings

You have studied how the selection of views, types of lines, and dimensioning methods are used to graphically represent objects. Now you will learn that various labelling techniques are used to add detail to the object. Labelling is added with lettering, notes, and abbreviations. These are basic practices needed to communicate the description of the object's parts and assembly.

Lettering

Lettering is placed on drawings to describe sizes, materials, conditions, and machining operations of the object. *The first requirement of lettering is legibility.* After you can make legible letters, it is necessary to develop speed. The lettering must be placed neatly on a drawing. The single-stroke Gothic letters shown meet all requirements. Lettering should be ⅛″ to ³⁄₁₆″ high and may be vertical or slanted. *All the lettering on a drawing should be the same height and style.*

VERTICAL GOTHIC

A   B   C   D   E   F   G

H   I   J   K   L   M   N

O   P   Q   R   S   T   U

V   W   X   Y   Z   &

1   2   3   4   5   6   7

8   9   0

SLANTED GOTHIC

A   B   C   D   E   F   G

H   I   J   K   L   M   N

O   P   Q   R   S   T   U

V   W   X   Y   Z   &

1   2   3   4   5   6   7

8   9   0

There are two styles of fractions, and each requires special attention in lettering. One style of fraction uses a short horizontal line to separate the numerator (top number) from the denominator (bottom number). The other style uses a slanted or diagonal line which extends slightly below and above the numbers. In either style the numbers should not touch the fraction line.

Horizontal fraction lines are used in dimensions and when notes with leaders begin with a fraction. Slanted fraction lines are used in notes, the title blocks, and the list of material.

FRACTIONS

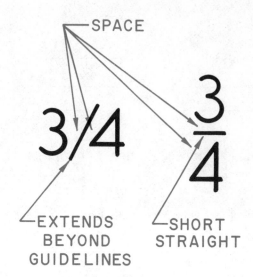

SPACE

EXTENDS BEYOND GUIDELINES

SHORT STRAIGHT

GENERAL NOTE AREAS

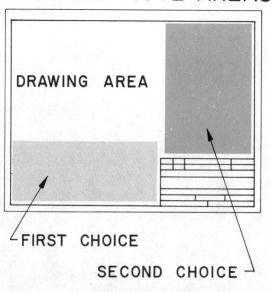

DRAWING AREA

FIRST CHOICE

SECOND CHOICE

Notes

Notes are short explanations used on drawings to tell how certain operations are to be performed. Notes describe the size, condition, and shape of the object. All notes should read in the order of the work to be done or in order of their need. The two types of notes used in drafting are (1) *general notes* and (2) *operation notes*.

General notes refer to the entire part or the entire drawing. Tolerances, radii, heat treatment, removal of sharp edges, and finishes are commonly included in general notes. These notes are placed either to the left or above the title block on a drawing.

OPERATION NOTES

Operation notes give instructions for work to be done. These notes are placed on the drawing and located near the part or assembly being explained. They should be positioned near the view and near the location specifying where the work is to be done. Operation notes are connected with leaders to the place where the work is to be done. Some operation notes commonly used with leaders are shown in the examples.

The note in the example explains that a hole is to be drilled with a ¼″ diameter. It will also have an 82° × ½″ countersink. A production worker can select the tools and perform the operation to make this hole by reading the note.

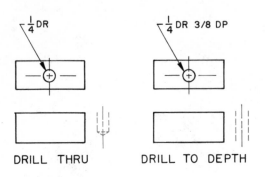

DRILL THRU   DRILL TO DEPTH

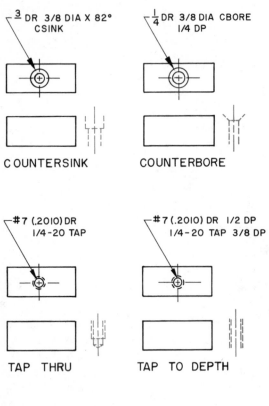

COUNTERSINK   COUNTERBORE

TAP THRU   TAP TO DEPTH

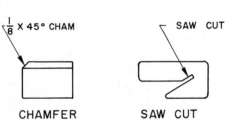

CHAMFER   SAW CUT

LEADER

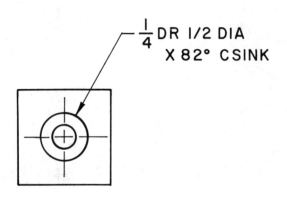

Abbreviations

Abbreviations are shortened forms of words. Their use in drafting saves time in lettering and space on the drawing. There are many words used in drafting that have accepted abbreviations. Generally, abbreviations used on drawings require no periods, except those abbreviations that spell words such as: Finish—Fin.; Inch—" or IN.; Number—No. Abbreviations should not be used if there is a possibility of being misunderstood. Some of the basic, conventional abbreviations are shown. Complete lists are available from the United States of America Standard Institute Drafting Manuals (USAS; formerly ASA, the American Standards Association).

Aluminum	AL	Machine Steel	MS
And	&	Material	MATL
Assembly	ASSY	Nominal	NOM
Bearing	BRG	Number	NO. #
Bushing	BUSH.	Octagon	OCT
Center Line	₵	Outside Diameter	OD
Chamfer	CHAM	Press Fit	PF
Check (ed) (er)	CHK	Plus or Minus	±
Cold Rolled Steel	CRS	Quantity	QTY
Counterbore	CBORE	Radius	RAD, R
Countersink	CSINK	Ream	RM
Deep	DP	Reference	REF
Degree (s)	(°) DEG	Required	REQD
Detail (ed) (er)	DET	Screw	SCR
Dowel	DWL	Screw Threads	
Drawing	DWG	American National	
Drawn	DWN	Course	NC
Drill	DR	American National	
Finish	FIN.	Fine	NF
Fixture	FIXT	Slip Fit	SF
Grind, Ground	G, GRD	Standard	STD
Harden	HDN	Steel	STL
Head	HD	Symbol	SYM
Hexagon	HEX	Thread	THD
Holes	HLS	Through	THRU
Hot Rolled Steel	HRS	Times or By	X
Inch (es)	" IN.	Tolerance	TOL
Inside Diameter	ID	Typical	TYP

Special Views

Basic orthographic projection drawings may not express an object accurately. Therefore, additional practices have been developed to express the parts or assemblies of unusual shapes. These special practices involve the use of breaks, section views, auxiliary views and enlarged views.

Breaks

The use of conventional breaks is a common drafting practice. Long rods, shafts, pipes, tubes, bars, beams, and boards would require very long pieces of paper if drawn in their full lengths. The ends of such shapes can be brought closer together by removing the middle portion or the long section which is all alike. Conventional practices for showing breaks are shown in these examples.

Example one shows the type of break used for solid bars.

Example two shows a conventional break used for hollow tubing or pipe.

Example three shows a short-section break for solid, rectangular material.

Example four shows a long-section break for large rectangular material.

The lines in conventional breaks are usually drawn freehand *except* for the section lines and for very large rectangular parts which are drawn with a straightedge.

Section Views

Section views show a portion of the object or assembly. They are used to show detail shapes inside the objects. With some section views, a *cutting-plane line* is used to show the path of the cutting plane.

Several types of section views are used in drafting. Some of the common conventional practices used in sectioning are described as follows:

1. *Full-section views* are used to show complex inside detail when outside detail is simple.

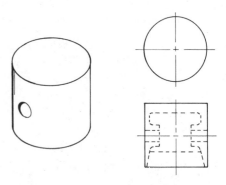

WITHOUT   SECTION

FULL   SECTION

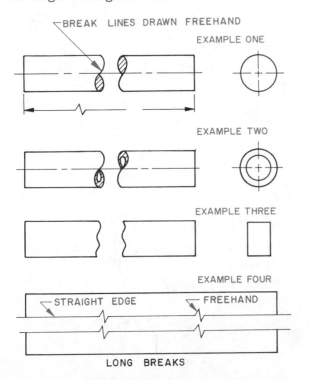

BREAK LINES DRAWN FREEHAND

EXAMPLE ONE

EXAMPLE TWO

EXAMPLE THREE

EXAMPLE FOUR

STRAIGHT EDGE   FREEHAND

LONG   BREAKS

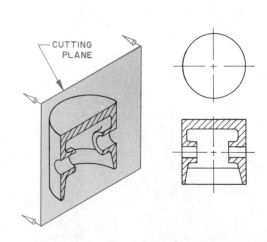

CUTTING PLANE

2. *Half-section views* show inside and outside detail.

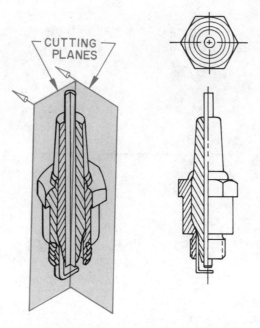

3. *Broken-section views* are used in showing only a portion of interior detail. A broken section view may be used when internal parts of the object must be dimensioned. This sectioning method eliminates the need to dimension hidden lines.

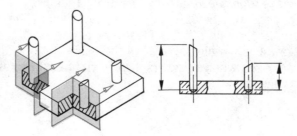

4. *Revolved-section views* are obtained when a cutting plane is passed through the part at a 90° angle to the center axis, and the resulting section is revolved 90° into the plane surface of the paper. Object lines may or may not be removed by using break lines on each side of the section.

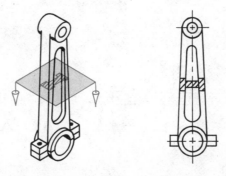

5. *Cutting-plane line* and *section letters*. Cutting-plane lines show the edge of the cutting plane as it passes through an object. They show the path a cutting plane follows through a view. Section letters are used to label cutting-plane lines with their section views. The letters are drawn ⅜" or ½" high.

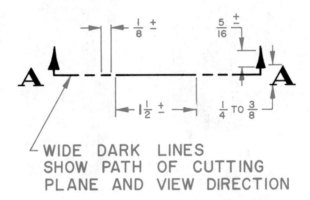

WIDE DARK LINES
SHOW PATH OF CUTTING
PLANE AND VIEW DIRECTION

Cutting-plane lines and section letters are drawn and used as shown in the examples of removed and offset section views. They are used only when the path of the cutting plane is not clear.

6. *Removed-section views* are moved from their regular position to another location. They should be placed behind the arrowheads and cutting-plane line. If the removed-section view is not a direct projection, it is usually labelled with section letters. Also, section letters are used when removing two or more sections as illustrated in this drawing.

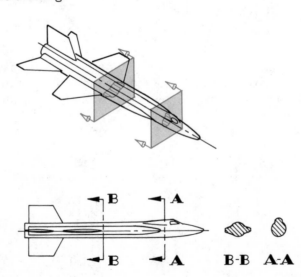

7. *Offset-section views* are drawn when the object is not cut by one continuous plane. They should be placed behind the arrowheads and cutting-plane line. If the offset section is not a direct projection, it is labelled with section letters. The example shown is a direct projection, therefore letters are not required.

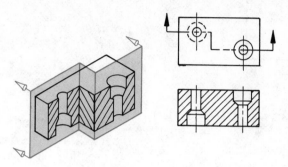

8. *Section lines* are symbols or representations made up of various line patterns. The symbol for cast iron may be used to represent any material. Section lines are spaced by eye and *should be drawn after all dimensions and notes have been put on the drawing.* Some basic section-line symbols are shown. Additional section-line symbols are shown in the USAS (or ASA) drafting manuals.

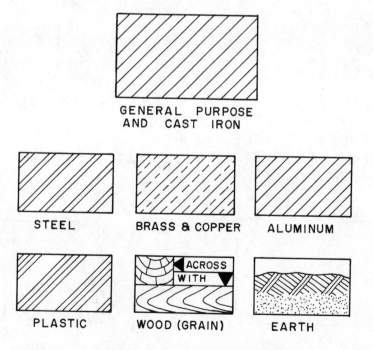

GENERAL PURPOSE AND CAST IRON

STEEL   BRASS & COPPER   ALUMINUM

PLASTIC   WOOD (GRAIN)   EARTH

① SECTION LINES DO NOT CROSS LEADER, EXTENSION, OR DIMENSION LINES

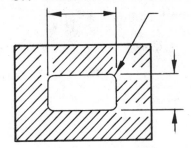

② ADJACENT PARTS HAVE SECTION LINES AT DIFFERENT ANGLES

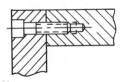

③ NO SECTION LINES WHEN THERE IS NO INSIDE DETAIL.

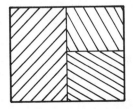

④ LARGE AREAS DO NOT NEED COMPLETE SECTION LINES.

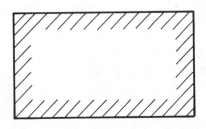

The use of section lines is shown in the following examples. Study the six different practices and refer to them when you draw sections.

Example one shows that section lines do not cross leader, extension, or dimension lines.

Example two shows that adjacent parts have section lines at different angles.

Example three shows that section lines are not drawn on a view of an internal detail.

Example four shows that sections of large objects do not need complete section lines. This practice will save you drawing time.

Example five shows that section lines should be drawn at an angle to the object lines. Avoid drawing them parallel to object lines.

Example six shows that thin portions of an object have no section lines.

⑤ SECTION LINES SHOULD NOT BE PARALLEL TO OBJECT LINES.

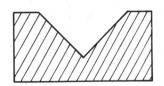

⑥ THIN PORTIONS HAVE NO SECTION LINES.

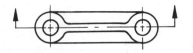

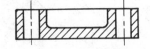

Auxiliary Views

Auxiliary views show the true shape of slanted or angular surfaces. They are used to locate and give the size of details on the slanted surface. Auxiliary views are drawn by projecting lines 90° from the slanted surface and developing the view by drawing the true lengths with a scale.

Study the front view of the orthographic projection. You can see that the slanted surface does not show the true shape of the object. The auxiliary view has been projected from the top view so that the true size and shape can be seen.

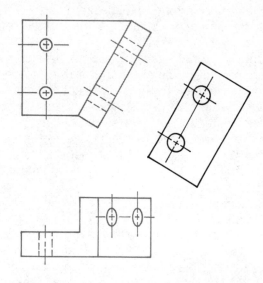

Enlarged Views

Enlarged views are used to better express small details. The enlargement is easily understood and dimensioned.

In this example, the small view adequately represents the overall description of the object. However, the angle of the point are difficult to understand. A *phantom line* (long line and two dashes) is used to identify the portion to be enlarged and the location of the enlarged view.

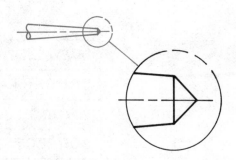

Checking Drawings

In industry, the checking system is used to increase the draftsman's speed. While the draftsman is concerned with neatness and accuracy, he must also learn to work rapidly. When a draftsman works at a rapid pace to lower the cost of the drawing, he sometimes makes minor errors. The checker is an aid to the draftsman by controlling the amount of errors on the drawing.

Checking drawings is the process of closely examining every detail on the drawing to determine whether or not it is correct and complete. Design concepts, lines, dimensions, notes, materials, etc. are studied in the process of checking drawings. Any errors on a drawing could result in extra expenses if such a drawing were to be used as a guide in manufacturing the object.

Checking a drawing involves the following basic steps:

1. A print or copy of the drawing is made and given to a checker or a person who is responsible for examining the drawings.
2. In an organized manner, the design, views, lines, dimensions, notes, materials, spelling and other aspects of the drawing are studied for correctness.
3. Everything on the print or copy that is found to be correctly done is marked with a green or yellow pencil. (Shown in the example with gray.)
4. Each item on the print that is wrong is marked with a red pencil. The correct information is added to the print with the red pencil. (Shown in the example with color.)
5. The print that has been checked is known as a *checker print*. The checker print is returned to the draftsman who changes the original drawing as directed by the checker print.
6. The corrected drawing and the checker print are returned to the checker who examines them to see that all corrections have been made. The red marks on the checker print are marked with blue pencil if the corrections have been made on the drawing. If the corrections have not been made, the indicated error on the checker print is circled in red.
7. The checker print and drawing are exchanged between the draftsman and the checker until all corrections have been made on the drawing and the checker approves it.

Checking and correcting drawings is a well-organized and complete process to help prevent costly errors in making the product. Notice the chart showing the uses of checking colors. An example of a checker print is shown.

CHECKING COLORS

MEANING	NORMAL COLOR	CODE COLOR
CORRECT	YELLOW OR GREEN	GRAY
WRONG	RED	BLUE
CORRECTED	BLUE	

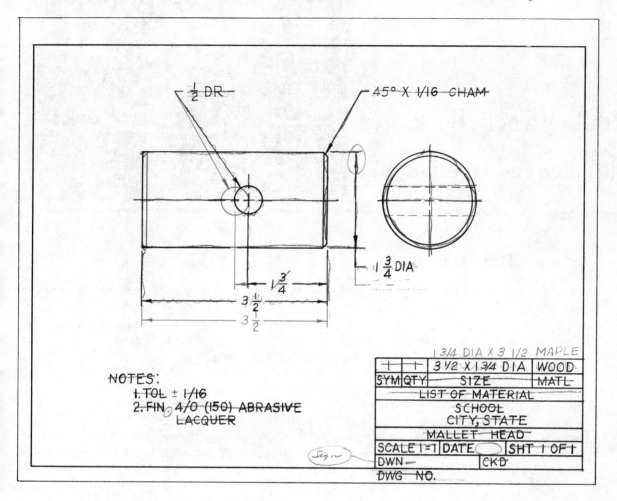

NOTES:
1. TOL ± 1/16
2. FIN 4/0 (150) ABRASIVE LACQUER

		1 3/4 DIA X 3 1/2 MAPLE	
+	+	3 1/2 X 1 3/4 DIA	WOOD
SYM	QTY	SIZE	MATL
LIST OF MATERIAL			
SCHOOL CITY, STATE			
MALLET HEAD			
SCALE 1=1	DATE		SHT 1 OF 1
DWN		CKD	
DWG NO.			

Pictorial Drawings

Conventional practices are also used when drawing pictorially. Many of the conventional practices discussed in this chapter are basically the same for pictorial drawing. You will learn more practices in Chapter 7, DRAWING PICTORIALS.

Summary

The conventional practices that you have studied in this chapter will be used in the remaining chapters. You will apply what you have been studying by doing the problems in the following chapters.

Always refer to this chapter as you are drawing so that you apply the proper *conventional practices*. When you begin to draw, you will have to:
1. Select the proper paper size and do the layout.
2. Use the orthographic projection conventional practices to express the views of the object.
3. Use the dimensioning method to control the size of the object.
4. Add labelling to the drawing when describing the details.
5. Use *special views* to express the drawing accurately.
6. Before your drawing is complete, it must checked and corrected.

4

Drafting Tools, Books, Supplies and Equipment

Why Study This Chapter?

The study of DRAFTING TOOLS, BOOKS, SUPPLIES, AND EQUIPMENT will help you learn the correct names of these items and tell you about:

1. Tools as they are classified according to their use for making lines; pointing or sharpening pencils; measuring distances; drawing straight, circular, or irregularly curved lines; drawing symbols or standard object outlines; and cutting supplies.
2. Books that are used as sources of information by draftsmen.
3. Supplies that are used for drawing surfaces; marking lines; erasing; coating and protecting drawing surfaces; holding and cleaning drawings; and duplicating drawings.
4. Equipment that gives the draftsman a comfortable and functional place to work.

Learning how to use these tools and supplies will help you improve your drawing ability. You will want to refer back to this chapter when the drawing problem requires the use of a tool that you have forgotten. Use this chapter to help you solve the drawing problems in other chapters.

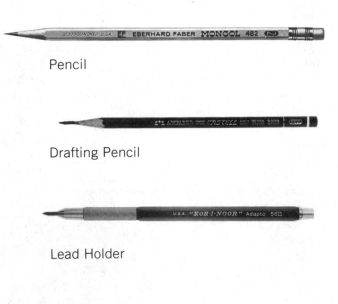

Pencil

Drafting Pencil

Lead Holder

Ruling Pen

Fountain Pen

Many useful tools, books, supplies, and items of equipment are used in making drawings. Drafting tools are commonly called *instruments*. Through the proper use of instruments and materials, good drawings can be made in a minimum amount of time. The draftsman spends most of his time working with tools and materials and must become very skilled in their use.

Tools

Lines

Most lines in drafting are made with a pencil, although many drawings are inked. There are many types of pencils and pens available for use in drawing. The basic ones are shown on page 138.

Pointing

Drafting pencils and leads need special care in preparing them for use. Any of several pieces of equipment can be used in sharpening pencils and pointing their leads. The sharpener removes only the wood from the pencil. The pointer sharpens the lead for making lines.

Drafting Pencil Sharpener

Lead Pointer

Desk Top Lead Pointer

Pocket lead Pointer

Erasing

It is necessary to use erasing tools in properly preparing and correcting drawings. The eraser or the erasing machine is used to remove lines. An erasing shield is used when it is necessary to remove a line that is close to other lines on the drawing that are not being removed. The shield protects the good lines. The duster is used to remove eraser and lead dust from the drawing.

Measuring

The two basic types of measurements made in drafting are (1) *distances* and (2) *angles*. There is a variety of tools for making each of these types of measurements. Scales and proportional dividers and pantographs are used to measure distances. Scales are available in many designs. Angles are measured with protractors and adjustable triangles.

Eraser

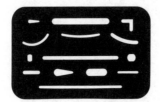

Erasing Shield

Duster

Erasing Machine

Triangular Architect's Scale

Flat Engineering Scale

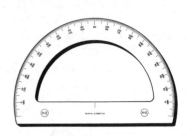

Protractor

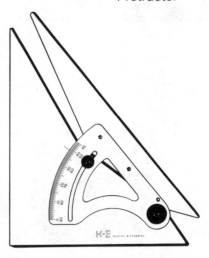

Adjustable Triangle

Proportional
Dividers

Pantograph

Straight Line

Most lines drawn in drafting require the use of straightedge tools. The T-square has been used for many years, but has been generally replaced by the parallel straightedge and drafting machines, which are faster and easier tools to use. Triangles are used to make straight lines at angles. Drafting machines do the combined operations of the parallel straightedges, triangles, protractors, and scales.

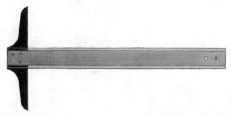

T-Square

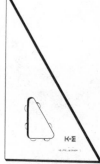

30°–60° Triangle

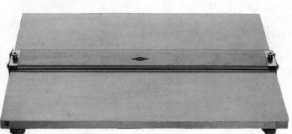

Parallel Straightedge and Drawing Board

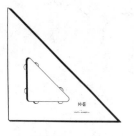

45° Triangle

Drafting Machine

Drawing Board

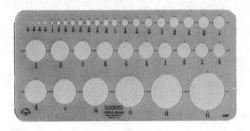

Circle Template

Circles

Circles and arcs are made with two basic types of tools. These are the circle template and the various types of compasses. The inexpensive circle template or guide is the fastest tool to use in making small circles and arcs. A compass should be used when several arcs or circles are to be made from a common center point. Bow compasses are used for medium-sized circles. The drop-bow compass is used for making small circles. Large circles are drawn with a beam compass.

Bow Compass

Drop Bow Compass

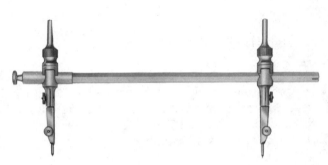

Beam Compass

Irregular Curve (26)

Irregular Curves

Irregular curves, commonly called "french curves", are available in many shapes. They are used as a guide in completing irregularly curved lines.

Irregular Curve (13)

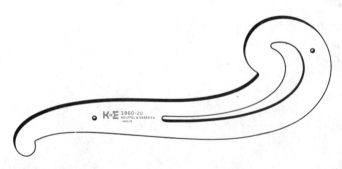

Irregular Curve (20)

Templates

Templates are used to draw accurately and quickly the various details, symbols, and lettering on drawings. There are dozens of templates available in many shapes and sizes. A few of the most commonly used templates are shown.

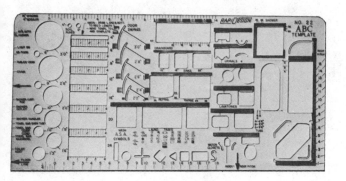

Architectural Template

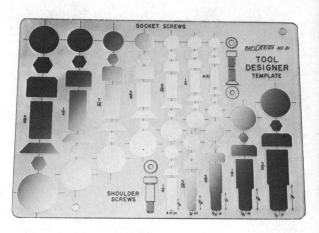

Tooling Template

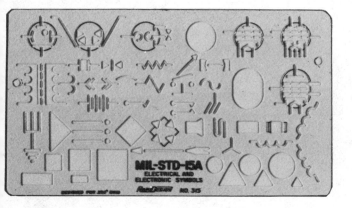

Electronic Template

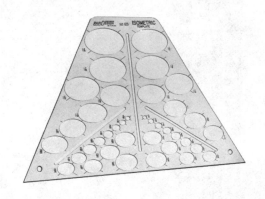

Ellipse Template

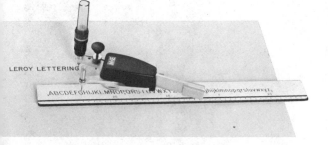

Leroy Lettering Template

Wrico Lettering Template

Cutting

Knives and shears are used to cut materials such as tape and printed symbols being applied to drawings. They are also used to cut sheets of paper and plastic drawing film.

X-Acto Knife

Shears

Books

Draftsmen use many technical books, catalogs, and other literature in their work. Two commonly used reference books are shown.

Machinery's Handbook

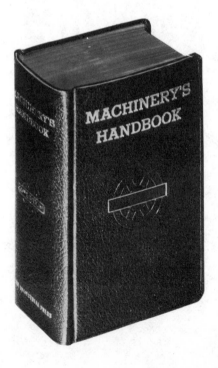

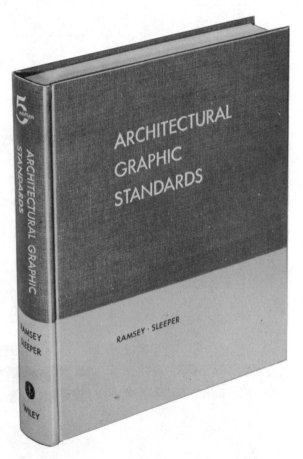

Architectural Graphic Standards

Supplies

Supplies used in basic drafting can be classified as: (1) surface, (2) marking, (3) holding, (4) cleaning and protecting, and (5) duplicating. It is advisable to use good quality supplies in drafting because their cost is small compared to the time involved in making a drawing.

Surfaces

Paper used in drafting comes in many types, qualities, sizes, and packages. Generally, it is used in sizes which are multiples of 8½ × 11", such as: 11" × 17", 17" × 22", etc. Drafting papers are available in packages of sheets, padded sheets, and rolls. Most drafting paper can be obtained with printed line patterns on them to assist in drawing certain types of work. The line patterns are generally printed in a very light blue color that will not reproduce in copy machines. When the line pattern is wanted on the copies or prints, a black or dark brown (sepia) printed-line drafting paper should be used.

1. *Duplicator paper* is a low-cost paper used for freehand drawings. Plain white notebook paper can be used for the same purpose.
2. *Tracing paper or vellum* costs about ten times as much as duplicator paper. Tracing paper is used in nearly all drafting work because it can be easily used in making low cost copies of a drawing.

It should have five important qualities.
   a. *Tooth*, or roughness which holds lines.
   b. *Strength*, which prevents tearing.
   c. *Translucency*, which permits light to pass through it easily.
   d. *Erasability*, which allows erasing to be done completely.
   e. *Stability*, which means the paper does not change size with changes in the weather.
3. *Drawing paper* costs about the same as tracing paper and should have the same characteristics and qualities, except for translucency. It is used primarily in technical illustration drafting. Drawing paper is available in several colors, but white is used almost entirely.
4. *Plastic drawing film* is available in thin sheets with a rough or toothed surface. It is used for very accurate or expensive drawings. Like paper, it is available in sheet and roll form. Plastic drawing film costs about five times as much as tracing paper.
5. *Drawing board cover paper* is a plastic-coated, heavy, high-quality paper used to cover drawing boards. This paper provides an excellent drawing surface and protects the drawing board.

Marking

Pencil lead comes in a variety of colors, qualities, and degrees of hardness.

Drafting Pencil

Drafting Lead

Drawing ink is available in many colors, but black is the most often used.

Drafting Ink

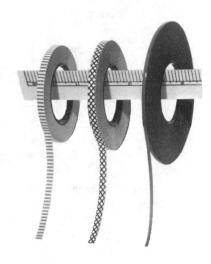

Drawing Tape

Drawing tape is used for making accurate lines on drawings. It is available in many widths, patterns, and colors. It is very useful because it can be easily removed if errors are made.

Preprinted sheets of lettering, symbols, pictures, and patterns are available with adhesive back surface for easy application to drawings.

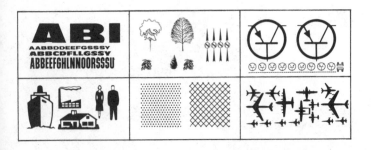

Preprinted Sheets

Erasing

Erasers are available in many forms and several different compositions. The "pink pearl" is most commonly used.

Eraser

Coating

A protective coating or "fixative" is often sprayed over drawings and illustrations so pencil and chalk lines will not smear.

Protective Coating

Holding

Drafting tape (often called masking tape) comes in several widths and is used for mounting the drawing paper to the board.

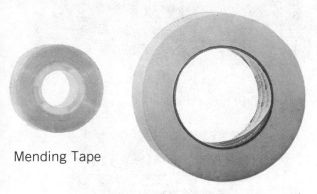

Mending Tape

Drafting Tape

Mending tape is a translucent material used to repair torn drawing paper or splice sheets of drawing materials together.

Cleaning

Wiping with a cloth moistened with denatured or rubbing alcohol is the best way to clean drafting tools and equipment. Alcohol dissolves dirt easily and dries quickly.

Soap and water can be used to clean drafting tools, but water is slow in drying and may cause metal parts to rust.

Reproducing

Diazo paper is coated with a material that is sensitive to bright light and it fades when exposed. It is used in making copies of drawings made on tracing paper. Diazo paper comes in many printing colors. The commonly used colors are white paper with blue or black lines. It costs about half as much as tracing paper.

Liquid developing solutions are used to change the unexposed lines on diazo paper to a color such as blue, black, or brown. Ammonia is the solution most commonly used.

Equipment

Furniture of special design helps make drawing work easier for the draftsman. There are special seats, tables, lamps, and storage equipment for his use.

Student Drawing Table

Student Drawing Stool

Professional Drawing Table

Whiteprinter machines are used to make copies or prints of drawings.

Professional Drawing Chair

School Whiteprinter Machine

Professional Whiteprinter Machine

Drafting Lamp

Microfilming equipment is used to photograph drawings for easy storage and reproduction.

Drawing File Cabinet

Microfilm Camera

Paper trimmers are used to cut paper to size, leaving a straight edge and square corners.

Drawing Trimmer

Microfilm Reader-Printer

Summary

Now that you have learned the names and purposes of tools, books, supplies, and equipment, the procedures and skill required to do mechanical drawing will be explained in the next chapter so you may practice what you have learned.

5

Drawing Mechanically

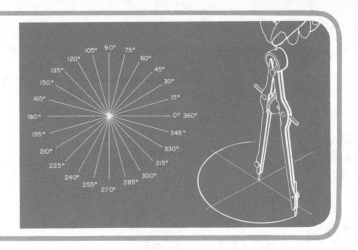

Why Study This Chapter?

DRAWING MECHANICALLY will explain how to:

1. Use the drafting tools you studied in Chapter 4.
2. Apply the conventional practices you studied in Chapter 3.
3. Make mechanical drawings by showing you how to:
   a. Measure distance and locate specific points.
   b. Make scale drawings.
   c. Prepare and use a pencil.
   d. Draw different types of horizontal, vertical, and angular straight lines.
   e. Draw circles and arcs with templates and compasses.
   f. Draw irregularly curved lines with irregularly curved tools.
   g. Erase lines and keep drawings clean.
   h. Letter, draw arrowheads, and place dimensions on drawings.
   i. Make simple geometric drawings.

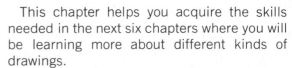

This chapter helps you acquire the skills needed in the next six chapters where you will be learning more about different kinds of drawings.

Draftsmen spend most of their time drawing mechanically and must acquire accuracy and speed in performing operations with drafting tools. The tools or instruments are used to measure, locate and guide the making of accurate lines on a surface. Draftsmen become very skilled with drafting tools. You can learn to draw with accuracy and speed by performing the basic mechanical drawing operations according to the following instructions.

Measuring Length

Length is measured to find the distance from one point to another point. It is called *linear* measurement. The system used in the United States for measuring length involves such units as yards, feet, and inches with fractions.

1 yard = 3 feet
1 foot = 12 inches

Draftsmen and many craftsmen use the 12″ scale with 1/16″ divisions as the basic tool for measuring length. The flat scale and the triangular scale are the two shapes of scales used by draftsmen.

Inches are commonly divided into 16 equal parts on scales. You must understand this system of measurement before accurate drawing is possible. The following diagrams show how an inch is divided into 16 equal parts.

FRACTIONS OF AN INCH

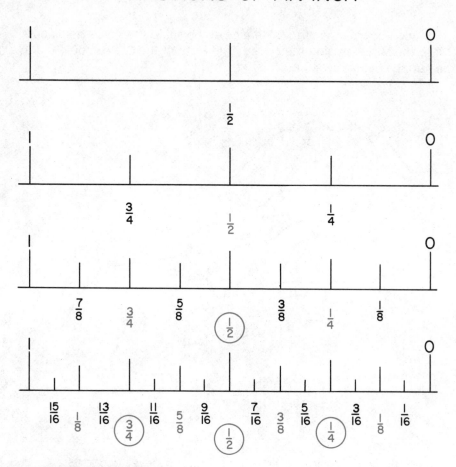

Problem 15
Reading Fractions of an Inch

All fractional units of an inch should be memorized as shown in the illustration. Drill and practice will help you learn these units if you start at the top of the illustration. The circled fractions act as a guide or reference point in reading the smaller lines on either side. Notice that the ½ mark is the longest and each set of fractions (¼'s, ⅛'s, and ¹⁄₁₆'s) is shown with marks of equal length.

After you have studied the FRACTIONS OF AN INCH illustration, start at the top by covering the fractions below each scale and learn the meaning of each division mark. As you understand each set of divisional marks, lower the sheet of paper to the next set. When reading a measuring scale, read the full units first and then read the fractions of the unit.

For accuracy in measuring, the face of the scale should be held about 90° to the surface being measured. The edge of the scale should touch the surface being measured.

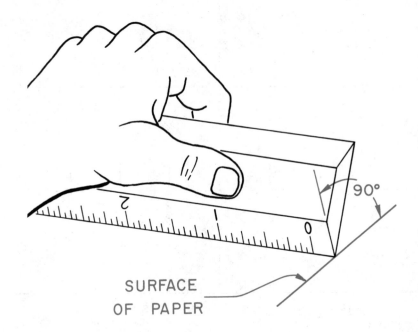

SURFACE
OF PAPER

Keep the scale clean, never mark on it, and never use it as a guide in drawing lines. Measuring is the only function of a scale. Other tools are used as guides in drawing lines.

Problem 16
Measuring Length

Practice using the scale correctly by measuring the distances between the marks shown below. Record your answers on the edge of a piece of writing paper.

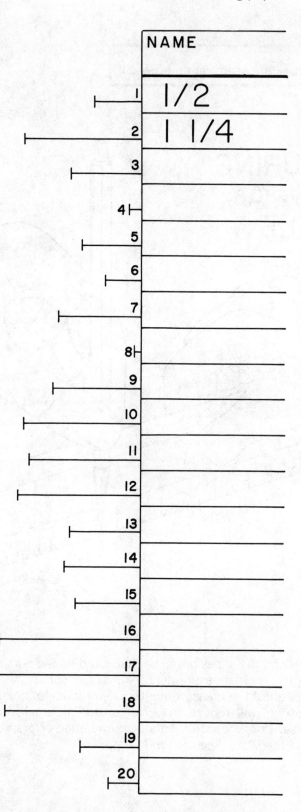

NAME

1	1/2
2	1 1/4
3	
4	
5	
6	
7	
8	
9	
10	
11	
12	
13	
14	
15	
16	
17	
18	
19	
20	

153

When measuring distances on a drawing, mark them with a sharply pointed pencil. Place small marks on the drawing surface to record each distance.

> **CAUTION!**
> Never mark the scale with the pencil!

MEASURING WITH A SCALE

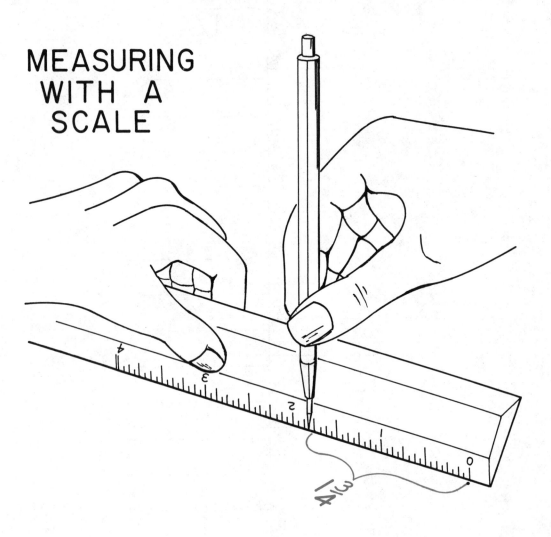

When several distances are to be measured end to end, avoid moving the scale for each measurement. The scale should be held in one position for all of the measurements. The practice of holding the scale in one position will reduce the error of adding small mistakes when making a series of measurements. Accumulation errors are avoided by not moving the scale. See the top of page 155.

AVOID ADDED ERRORS

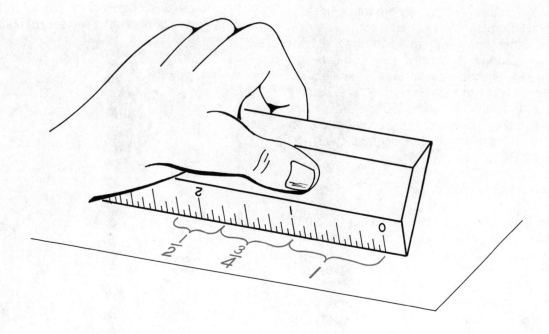

Dividers

Dividers are used to transfer dimensions or sizes from one location to another. With two plain-tapered steel points installed in a compass, it becomes a divider.

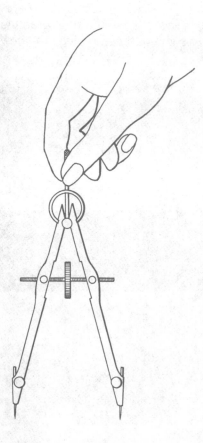

Scale Drawings

When practical, drawings are made full size (1 = 1). Sometimes it is better to make drawings either larger or smaller than the item being planned. Normally, large objects are drawn in reduced sizes of ¼ or ½ scale. Very large items such as buildings are usually drawn to a scale of: ¼" = 1'-0" or ⅛" = 1'-0". Items being increased in size (enlarged) on a drawing are drawn 2 or 4 times their normal size.

Measuring to Scale

Measurements for scale drawings should be made with an appropriate tool. It is not necessary or advisable to mathematically compute enlargements or reductions to make such measurements. For quarter or half size the scale is marked with the same pattern of line lengths for the fractions as full size, but the space between the lines has been reduced to the ¼ or ½ size. Scales (tools) are available for all conventional drafting practices. Portions of some of these scales are shown.

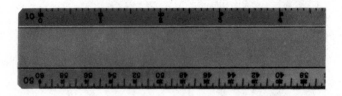

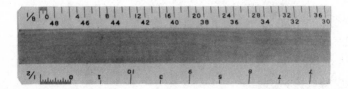

For unusual scale measurements or ratios, *proportional dividers* are used. The proportion on the dividers is changed by adjusting the pivoting device between the two sets of points.

Mounting the Paper

After the paper has been selected, the sheet is held on the drawing board with small pieces of masking tape. The bottom edge of the sheet should be 4" to 8" from the bottom edge of the drawing board if space permits. To mount the paper, place the lower edge on the top edge of the parallel-straightedge, drafting machine horizontal scale, or a T-square. With small pieces of drafting tape, fasten the two top corners of the paper to the drawing board.

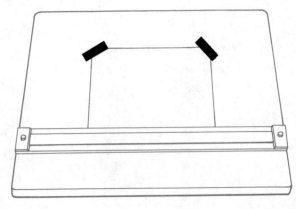

To secure the bottom corners of the sheet, lower the parallel edge, drafting machine horizontal scale, or T-square and place pieces of tape across each bottom corner.

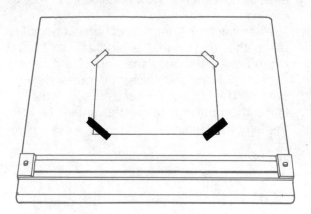

The paper should then be checked to see that it is aligned properly.

Pencils and Leads

Most industrial drawings are drawn with pencil on tracing paper. Pencils used in drafting include the common *wood type* and the *lead holder*. The wood pencil is less expensive but requires more time to maintain. The wood must be cut back or sharpened repeatedly as the lead is used. Lead holders or mechanical pencils are very convenient to use since they do not require sharpening. The lead is fed through and held by a mechanical chuck in the lead holder.

Both types of pencils use the same quality lead. The pieces of lead used in the lead holder are called *refill leads*. Drafting pencils and refill leads cost two or three times as much as common pencils due to the quality

and grading. The hardness of drafting pencils and leads is shown by a number and the letter H or the letter B. The *B series of lead is softer than the H series* and is used for freehand drawing. For most drafting work, the H series is used.

PENCIL LEAD HARDNESS

6B	5B	4B	3B	2B	B	H	2H	3H	4H	5H	6H
VERY SOFT			SOFT			HARD			VERY HARD		
ART WORK						DRAWINGS			LAYOUT		

The identification mark which shows the type of lead is printed on the side of the pencil or refill lead near the top end. Be careful not to remove or sharpen the grading identification from the pencil or lead.

LEAD MARKING

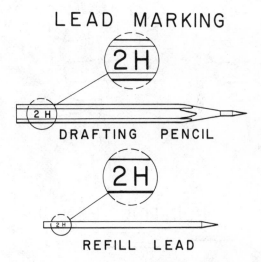

Light lines are generally drawn with a 4H or harder lead. Other lines and lettering are done with an H or 2H lead.

There are four steps in preparing a pencil or lead for use in drafting.

1. Sharpening or extending the lead.
2. Pointing the lead.
3. Cleaning the lead.
4. Conditioning the point.

DRAFTING PENCIL

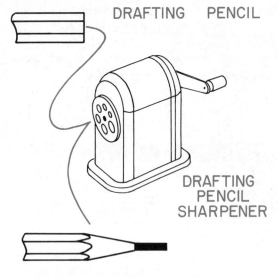

DRAFTING PENCIL SHARPENER

Sharpening or Extending The Lead

A special sharpener is used to sharpen wood drafting pencils. The drafting pencil sharpener removes the wood to expose about ½" of the lead.

When a lead holder or mechanical pencil is used, the lead should extend about ½". To extend the lead, hold the end of the pencil about ½" from a surface and press the top button. This allows the lead to slide out. Release the button to allow the chuck to hold the lead in position.

EXTENDING LEAD

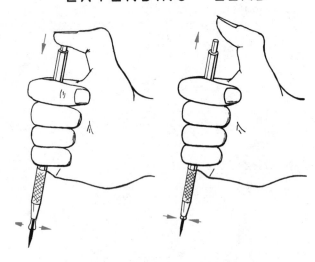

Pointing the Lead

After the drafting pencil has been sharpened or the lead extended, it can be pointed with a sandpaper pad or a mechanical pointer. The pencil is held in one hand and the pointer in the other.

POINTING PENCIL

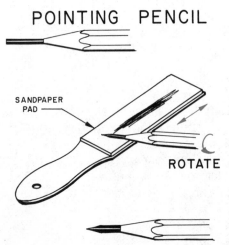

SANDPAPER PAD

ROTATE

POINTING LEAD

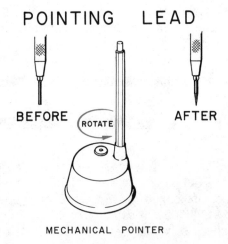

BEFORE   ROTATE   AFTER

MECHANICAL POINTER

Cleaning the Lead

The lead can be cleaned with a cloth or by sticking it into a piece of soft foam plastic.

Conditioning the Pencil

Pointed lead should be conditioned in order to obtain the best results in drawing. Lead is conditioned by lightly moving the sharp point in a circular motion on a piece of paper to remove the very sharp, weak point on the tip.

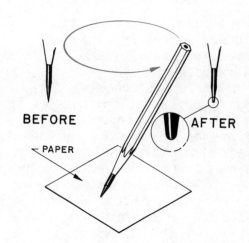

BEFORE **AFTER** PAPER

How to Draw Lines

After the pencil point has been properly prepared, lines can be drawn. Since drawings are almost always used to make prints and lines of poor quality will not reproduce on a print, good lines are essential in making useful drawings. When lines do not reproduce from the drawing to the print, the workman making the part cannot interpret the print accurately.

Drafting tools such as straightedges, triangles, templates, and irregular curves are used as guides in making lines with a pencil. The point of the pencil should contact the paper at the place where the edge of the guiding tool meets the paper.

The pencil should slant slightly in the direction in which the line is being drawn. By applying a firm downward pressure and slowly rotating the pencil, a dense, even line can be drawn. The pencil is rotated slowly as the lead is put on the paper so the line will be an even width. It is often necessary to draw over lines several times to produce the desired quality of blackness.

PENCIL MOTION

PRESS DOWN

ROTATE SLOWLY AS POINT WEARS

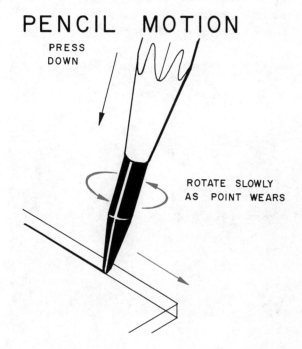

PENCIL POSITION

DRAFTING TOOL

PAPER

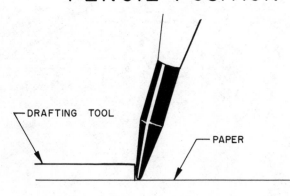

By selecting the correct, flat, worn area on the tip of the lead, a line of any desired width can be drawn. A small area on the point will produce narrow lines while a large area on the point makes wide lines.

As the pencil tip contacts the paper, a good sense of touch and finger control is necessary to select the correct flat area to be used When the line is drawn, proper rotation of the pencil will produce an even width line. Skill in preparing and using the pencil will produce the desired density and width of line. Line density of drawings made on tracing paper can be checked by holding the paper in front of a bright light. If any light comes through the line, more lead is needed on the line in order to make a good print. All lines on a drawing should be made a dense black in widths which vary according to their function.

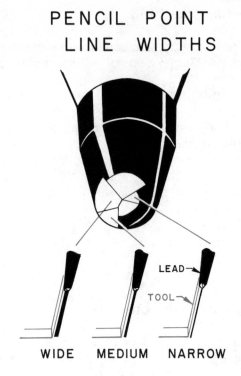

PENCIL POINT LINE WIDTHS

WIDE   MEDIUM   NARROW

Horizontal Lines

Horizontal lines are made with a parallel edge, T-square, or drafting machine as a guide. The following instruction shows how horizontal lines should be drawn with a T-square and a parallel edge.

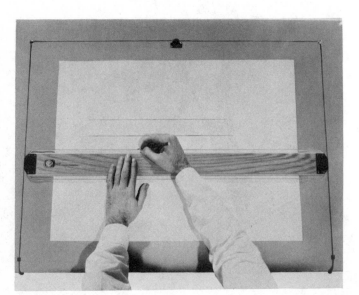

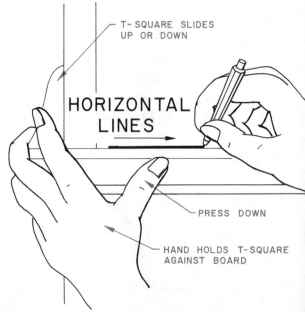

HORIZONTAL LINES

T-SQUARE SLIDES UP OR DOWN

PRESS DOWN

HAND HOLDS T-SQUARE AGAINST BOARD

Vertical Lines

Vertical lines are drawn along the vertical edge of a triangle which has been placed against a T-square or parallel edge. With a drafting machine vertical lines can be made with the vertical scale or triangles, whichever is faster.

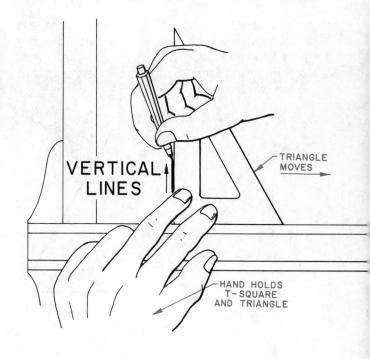

Angular Lines

Lines that are not vertical or horizontal may be called slanted, angular or inclined lines. An *angle* is the open area of figure formed between two lines or surfaces that meet at a point.

Angles are measured by the number of degrees included between the lines. An arc would be drawn with its center at the intersection of lines or surfaces of the angle. An *arc* is part of a circle. There are 360 degrees in a complete circle. The following diagram shows some of the common angles in a circle.

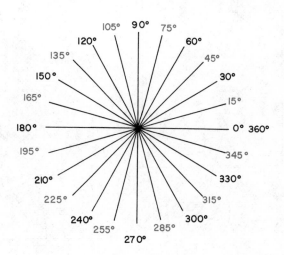

In drafting, the 45°-90° triangle and the 30° -60° -90° triangle are used for drawing common angles.

Angles at each 15° space can be drawn with the two triangles.

DRAWING COMMON ANGLES

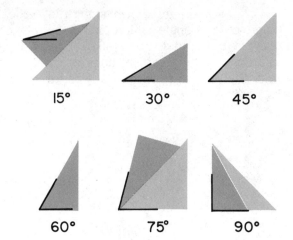

15° 30° 45°

60° 75° 90°

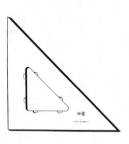

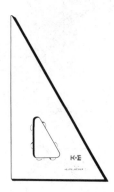

Other angles are measured and drawn with an adjustable triangle or a protractor. Drafting machines can also be used to measure and draw any angle.

ADJUSTABLE TRIANGLE

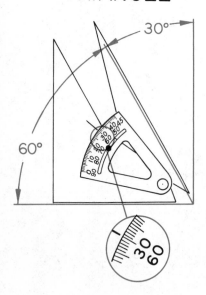

PROTRACTOR

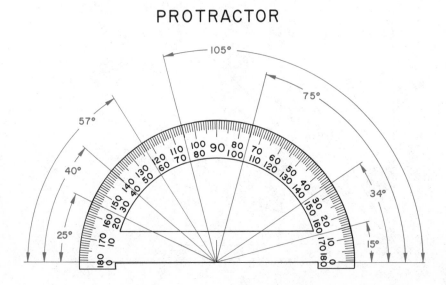

Drawing Circles and Arcs

A circle is a single curved line, every point of which is equally distant from the point at the center. The parts of a circle are the center, diameter, radius, and circumference.

In drafting, the center of a circle is usually shown by the point where two center lines cross. Circles are specified by their diameter. The *diameter* is the length of a straight line passing through the center from one side of the circle to the other. The *radius* is one half the diameter or the distance from the center to the edge of the circle. The *circumference* is the distance around the circle.

An *arc* is a portion of a circle. It is measured by the size of the radius and the angle included.

A line is *tangent* when it touches a curved line or surface but does not cross it.

Circles and arcs are used very often in making drawings. A circle template, drop-bow compass, bow compass, or beam compass is used to draw circles and arcs mechanically.

Circle Template

The circle template is a thin piece of plastic with a series of various-sized circles cut in it. The size of each circle is printed on the template along with lines showing the center lines. The circles in the template make an allowance for the pencil point in order to produce a drawing of the correct size.

CIRCLE

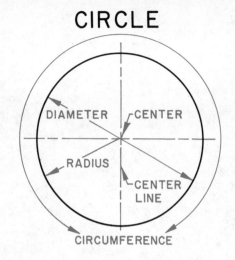

ARC

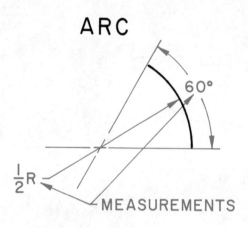

TANGENT

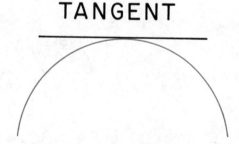

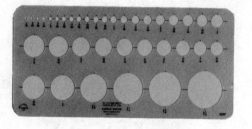

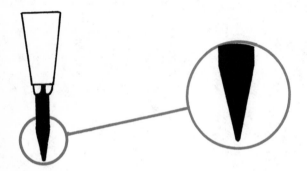

The circle template is the fastest and easiest tool to use in drawing circles and arcs. In using the circle template, these steps should be followed:

1. Locate the center of the desired circle on the drawing with *light* vertical and horizontal lines.

2. Correctly point the pencil.

3. Select the proper size circle on the template.

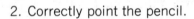

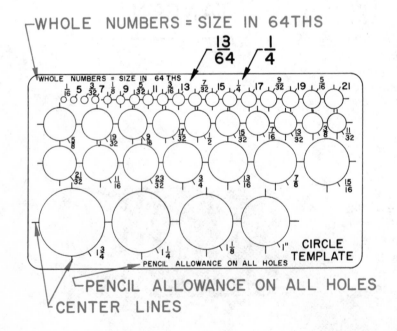

WHOLE NUMBERS = SIZE IN 64THS

$\frac{13}{64}$ $\frac{1}{4}$

PENCIL ALLOWANCE ON ALL HOLES

CENTER LINES

4. Center the circle in the template on the location as indicated by the light horizontal and vertical lines.

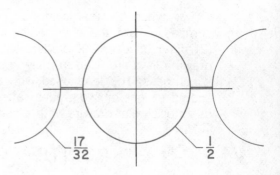

5. Keep the pencil point against the edge of the template where it meets the paper.

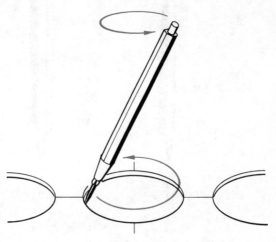

Compasses

Three compasses commonly used in drafting are the (1) drop-bow compass, (2) bow compass, and (3) beam compass. Compasses are used primarily for drawing circles that are not included on a circle template. You should practice using a compass to draw several circles having a common center.

Two types of steel points furnished with compasses are the (1) *shouldered* and the (2) *plain divider*. A shouldered point and a drawing lead are used in making circles with a compass. The lead used with a compass should be one or two grades softer than that used for similar drawing with a pencil.

POINTS

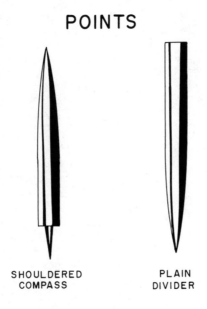

SHOULDERED
COMPASS

PLAIN
DIVIDER

The steps in using a compass are as follows:
1. *Extend the lead* from ⅜″ to ½″ beyond the metal portion of the compass.

COMPASS LEAD

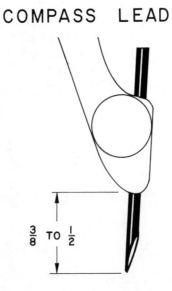

$\frac{3}{8}$ TO $\frac{1}{2}$

CAUTION!

Be sure the remaining lead is long enough to extend through the clamping portion to prevent damage to the compass.

2. *Point the lead* with a sandpaper pad as shown. The strokes should run with the length of the lead. Notice the compass is rotated from side-to-side around the lead as it is pointed.

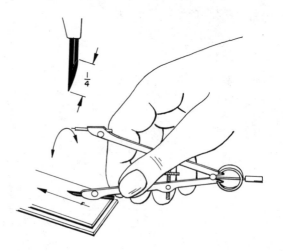

$\frac{1}{4}$

3. *Condition the lead* on the paper by removing the very sharp tip as shown.

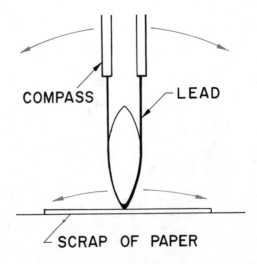

COMPASS   LEAD

SCRAP OF PAPER

4. With the compass in a closed position, *adjust the metal point* until the shoulder is extended the same length as the lead.

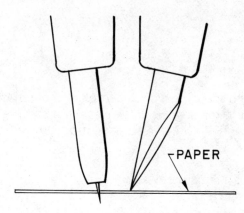

5. With the center adjustment screw, *set the distance between the lead and metal points* to the desired radius (½ the diameter) by using a scale.

```
┌─CAUTION!──────────────────────────┐
│                                   │
│  Do not mark the scale with compass points. │
│                                   │
└───────────────────────────────────┘
```

SETTING COMPASS

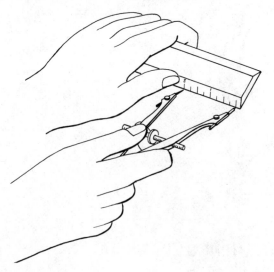

6. *Draw a circle on a scrap of paper* and check it for size with a scale. Adjust compass until desired circle size is produced.

7. Place the shouldered metal point on the center lines of the circle or arc to be drawn. The metal point should be gently forced into the paper.

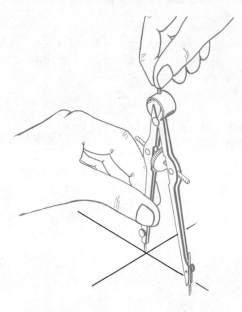

8. *Slant the top of the compass slightly* in the direction the lead point is to move and turn the compass around the metal point until the desired line is achieved.

Practice • Practice • Practice • Practice • Practice • Practice • Practice • Practice

On a piece of paper draw various sizes of circles to learn the proper use of the compasses and circle templates. Draw 4 to 6 circles with each tool. This will prepare you to use the compass and template when a drawing requires a circle.

Problem 17
Drawing a Round Corner

Draw arcs that are connected with straight lines as shown, using a circle template or compass. A considerable amount of practice is usually required to make good drawings with a compass. Study the example showing how to draw a round corner. Follow these steps of procedure when making a round corner.

Step One:
   You see a square layout representing the corner of a square object.
Step Two:
   You see that an arc has been drawn in the corner by using a circle template or a compass.
Step Three:
   You see that the connecting lines and the center lines have been darkened.

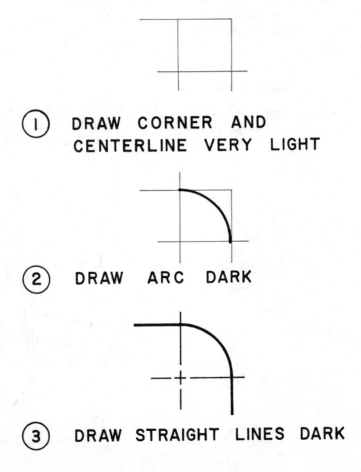

(1) DRAW CORNER AND
CENTERLINE VERY LIGHT

(2) DRAW ARC DARK

(3) DRAW STRAIGHT LINES DARK

Curved Lines

Curved lines that are not circles or arcs are called *irregular curves*. They form many parts of airplanes, boats, and automobiles. Irregular curves are often started by drawing freehand and are then finished with thin plastic tools called *irregular curves* or *"french curves"*.

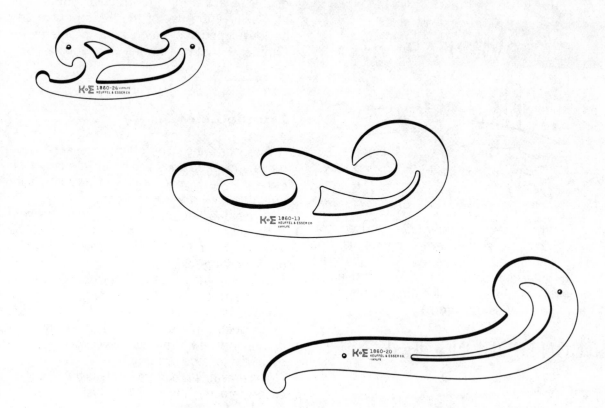

How To Draw Curved Lines

Use an irregular curve as a guide to form irregular lines, using these helpful suggestions:

1. Select the tool having the curve that follows the greatest portion of the desired line.

2. As the line becomes straighter, the irregular curve should be used in a position to form the longest, possible part of the line.

CURVE SIZE

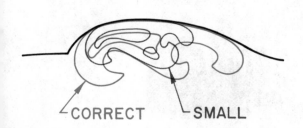

CORRECT POSITION

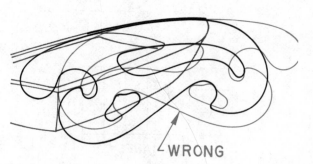

3. Usually, curved lines will have to be drawn in several sections with the irregular curve. Each setting of the irregular curve should overlap part of the line that has been drawn.

OVERLAP

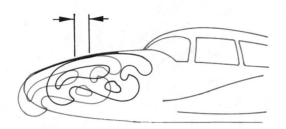

4. When the irregular curve is used correctly, a single, even, continous line will result.

Irregular curved lines can be controlled by a series of dimensions locating points along the line or by using a grid.

CONTROLLING IRREGULAR LINES

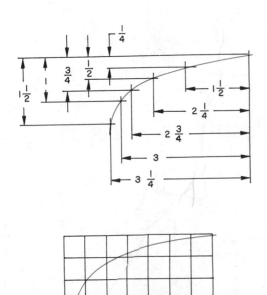

I/2 **SQUARES**

For practice in the use of an irregular curve, place a piece of tracing paper over a picture of an object with irregular curved lines such as a boat, airplane, or car and trace the outline of the object using the irregular curve. Further skill in the use of the french curve can be developed by completing problems in Chapter 9 entitled Drawing with Grids.

Erasing Lines

When drawing, it is often necessary to remove undesired lines and other marks with an eraser. A very good eraser to use is a soft, pink one known as "Pink Pearl."

A mistake left on a drawing can be very expensive in manufacturing. It can also be very expensive to make new drawings instead of correcting existing drawings by erasing errors. For these reasons, errors should be erased and corrected on the original drawing when it is practical. Erasing prevents errors in producing parts and often saves the cost of making new drawings. *Skill in erasing is essential to good drafting.*

The erasing procedure involves the use of an eraser, erasing shield, and a dusting brush.

Special care must be taken in using the eraser and erasing shield. By following these practices, good results can be achieved:

1. Clean the eraser on a scrap of paper or cloth before applying it to the drawing.
2. Cover the good portion of the drawing around the mistake with an erasing shield. Leave the drawing mistake exposed through an opening in the shield.
3. Lightly and slowly rub the lines to be removed with the eraser. Gentle erasing will prevent staining the drawing surface.

ERASING LINES

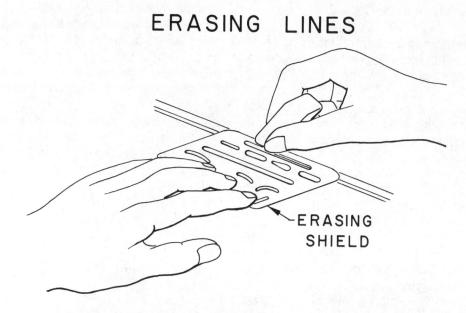

ERASING
SHIELD

Erasing can also be done with erasing machines.

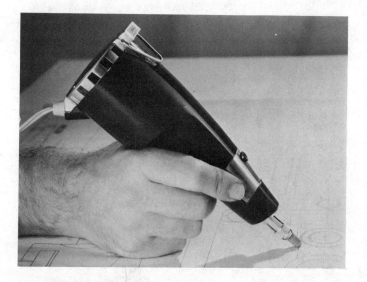

4. Make sure that the undesired lines or marks are completely removed.
5. With the dusting brush, remove all the eraser dust from the drawing.

Draw a series of lines spaced about $\frac{1}{16}$" apart. Then with an erasing shield and eraser remove alternate lines. Use these tools in correcting misspelled words and changing numbers in dimensions or notes.

Keeping Drawings Clean

Drawings should be kept clean in order to produce good prints as well as for general appearance. The following practices will help keep drawings clean.

1. *Keep your hands clean* by washing them before beginning work on a drawing. Whenever your hands become dirty while drawing, wash them.
2. *Keep drafting tools clean* by wiping them with a soft cloth daily, or more often if needed. Clean the drafting tools as needed with alcohol, or soap and water.
3. *Avoid touching the drawing paper* with the hands. Place a piece of paper under the hand while making arrowheads and doing lettering.
4. *Use the duster* to remove all dust after each series of lines is made or erased.
5. *Avoid sliding drafting tools* over large areas of the drawing. Lift the tools off the paper before moving them to another position on the drawing.

Lettering

Lettering is used to make dimensions and notes on drawings. The dimensions and notes give the size and other information necessary for project construction.

The accuracy of the completed project is dependent upon the quality of the numbers and letters on the drawing. Lettering is also important in applying for a job. The first contact with an employer will likely be through an employment form which the applicant completes by lettering, or as it is often called "printing." Sometimes the appearance of the application blank may determine whether or not an interview is granted. Lettering that is done incorrectly can result in your loss of employment opportunities or result in costly manufacturing errors due to your poor work on the job. With varying amounts of practice, nearly everyone can learn to letter well by following a few fundamental procedures.

Lettering is a kind of freehand drawing. Shape, angle, alignment, and proportion are fundamental to good freehand drawings whether it is a picture or lettering. The procedure for accomplishing good lettering is as follows:

1. Sit in a comfortable, naturally erect and relaxed position.

2. Use a well-sharpened soft (H) lead pencil with a slightly rounded point.

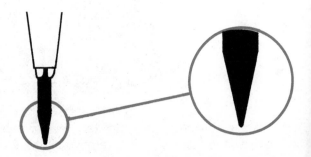

3. Hold the pencil the same as in writing with a relaxed hand. Finger and hand motions are used in making small sized lettering. For large letters, arm motion should be used as it is in freehand drawing.

HOLDING   PENCIL

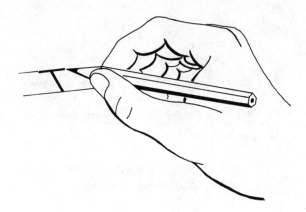

4. Measure and draw very light guidelines. All letters should touch both guidelines. Normally, guidelines are spaced 3/16″ or 1/8″ apart.

MEASURE
GUIDE
LINES

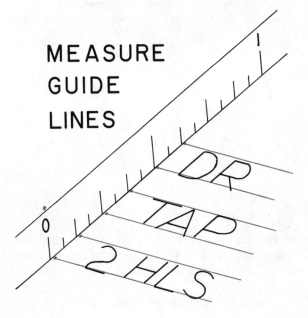

5. Use either vertical or slanted, single-stroke, uppercase, Gothic-style lettering. (See page 126.) The slope of slanted lettering should be to the right only. Try both the vertical and the slanted lettering to find out which is easiest for you. Develop your ability with the style you like best.

6. Study the basic shape of each letter and number carefully. Notice that the following lines are used in forming letters.

LETTERING   STROKES

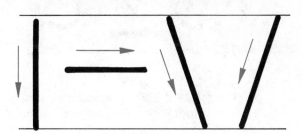

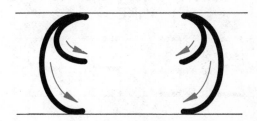

a. Straight lines of letters and numbers should be drawn straight.

STRAIGHT   LINES

b. Notice the position of the middle lines of lines of letters and numbers. The middle lines may be *below* center or *above* center.

MIDDLE AREA BELOW CENTER   **MIDDLE AREA ABOVE CENTER**

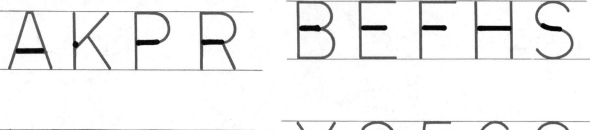

c. The top and bottom lines are straight or horizontal on these letters.

d. The figures are round on the top or bottom as shown.

STRAIGHT TOP AND BOTTOM LINES   **CURVED TOP AND BOTTOM LINES**

Problem 19
Learn Drafting Lettering

Draw the letters and numbers using the order of strokes as shown in the following examples. Be sure to keep all letters at the same angle. To learn the shape of the letters, practice lettering between guidelines spaced ⅜″ apart. As skill is developed, the space between guidelines should be reduced to ³⁄₁₆″ or ⅛″.

Practice lettering until you can form neat, legible letters. See examples on pages 175 and 176.

LETTERING STROKES

A B C D E F G

H I J K L M N

O P Q R S T U

V W X Y Z &

1 2 3 4 5

6 7 8 9 0

LETTERING   STROKES

A   B   C   D   E   F   G

H   I   J   K   L   M   N

O   P   Q   R   S   T   U

V   W   X   Y   Z   &

1   2   3   4   5

6   7   8   9   0

After learning the basic shape and strokes for lettering, practice lettering for many short periods of 5 to 15 minutes rather than a few longer periods.

Problem 21
Practice Spacing the Letters and Words

Once the correct shape of lettering is learned, practice making various notes to develop the correct spacing. In spacing the letters of words, the area rather than the clearance between letters should be nearly the same. Words should be spaced so they are clearly separated.

SPACING   LETTERING

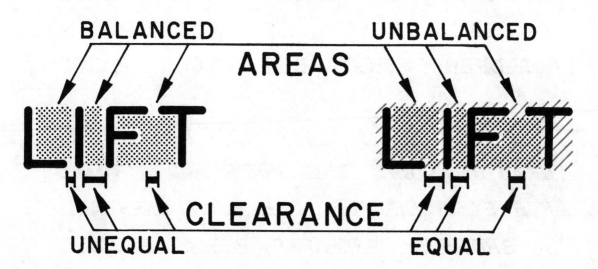

177

ABCDEFGHIJKLMNOPQRSTUVWXYZ

1 2 3 4 5 6 7 8 9 0   1/16 $\frac{1}{8}$ 3/16 $\frac{1}{4}$ 5/16 $\frac{3}{8}$ 7/16

ABCDEFGHIJKLMNOPQRSTUVWXYZ

1 2 3 4 5 6 7 8 9 0   1/2 $\frac{9}{16}$ 5/8 $\frac{11}{16}$ 3/4 $\frac{13}{16}$ 7/8 $\frac{15}{16}$

A B C D E F G H I J K L M N O P Q R S T U V W X Y Z

1 2 3 4 5 6 7 8 9 0   1/16 $\frac{1}{8}$ 3/16 $\frac{1}{4}$ 5/16 $\frac{3}{8}$ 7/16

A B C D E F G H I J K L M N O P Q R S T U V W X Y Z

1 2 3 4 5 6 7 8 9 0   1/2 $\frac{9}{16}$ 5/8 $\frac{11}{16}$ 3/4 $\frac{13}{16}$ 7/8 $\frac{15}{16}$

LETTERING IS A TYPE OF FREEHAND
DRAWING. STUDY THE SHAPE AND STROKES
FOR EACH LETTER. USE GUIDE LINES AND
A PROPERLY PREPARED PENCIL. RELAX

LETTERING IS A TYPE OF FREEHAND
DRAWING. STUDY THE SHAPE AND STROKES
FOR EACH LETTER. USE GUIDE LINES AND
A PROPERLY PREPARED PENCIL. RELAX

R = RADIUS , DIA = DIAMETER , DR= DRILL ,

CHAM = CHAMFER, TOL = TOLERANCE ,

± = PLUS OR MINUS , FIN. = FINISH, SYM = SYMBOL ,

MAT = MATERIAL, NO. = NUMBER

R = RADIUS , DIA = DIAMETER , DR = DRILL,

CHAM = CHAMFER, TOL = TOLERANCE ,

± = PLUS OR MINUS, FIN. = FINISH, SYM = SYMBOL,

MAT = MATERIAL , NO. = NUMBER

1 2 3 4 5 6 7 8 9 0   1 2 3 4 5 6 7 8 9 0

$\frac{3}{4}$ $2\frac{3}{16}$ $4\frac{1}{2}$ 90° $1\frac{3}{8}$ $2\frac{1}{2}$ $\frac{1}{32}$ 45°   30°

1/16   1/8   1/4   5/16   3/8   7/16   1/2   9/16

$\frac{5}{8}$ $\frac{11}{16}$ $\frac{3}{4}$ $\frac{13}{16}$ $\frac{7}{8}$ $\frac{15}{16}$ $5\frac{1}{2}$ $7\frac{3}{4}$ $8\frac{5}{16}$ $3\frac{3}{8}$

1 2 3 4 5 6 7 8 9 0   1 2 3 4 5 6 7 8 9 0

$\frac{3}{4}$ $2\frac{3}{16}$ $4\frac{1}{2}$ 90° $1\frac{3}{8}$ $2\frac{1}{2}$ $\frac{1}{32}$ 45°   90°

1/16   1/8   1/4   5/16   3/8   7/16   1/2   9/16

$\frac{5}{8}$ $\frac{11}{16}$ $\frac{3}{4}$ $\frac{13}{16}$ $\frac{7}{8}$ $\frac{15}{16}$ $5\frac{1}{2}$ $7\frac{3}{4}$ $8\frac{5}{16}$ $3\frac{3}{8}$

Arrowheads are drawn freehand with three strokes as shown. When made correctly, they should be solid black after the three strokes are completed and should not require "filling in."

Practice making arrowheads on a sheet of paper. When you are skilled enough to make five to ten arrowheads exactly alike, as described in the illustration, you have accomplished the skill.

ARROWHEAD

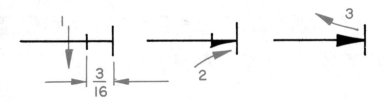

Geometric Drawing

Geometric drawing or construction deals with the properties, measurement, and relationships of points, lines, and shapes. Such drafting tools as scales, triangles, protractors, and templates were designed through the use of geometric drawing. Many other useful things can be made through its use. A few of the most commonly used processes are shown.

Bisecting a line is a method of finding the center of a line when a scale is not available. In drawing circles, it is sometimes necessary to find the center of a given diameter.

Bisecting a Line

How to find the center of a given line (A-B).

SOLUTION:
1. From point *A*, draw an arc with a compass.
2. Using the same radius, draw an arc from point *B*, intersecting arc *A* and making points *C* and *D*.
3. With a straightedge, draw a line through points *C* and *D*. The line *C–D* crosses the center of line *A–B* making point *E*. Line *C–D* is also square (90°) or perpendicular to line *A–B*.

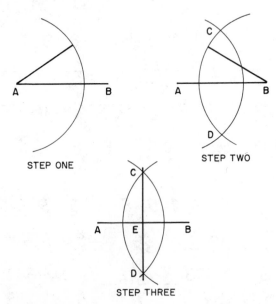

STEP ONE

STEP TWO

STEP THREE

BISECTING LINE

Equal Parts of a Line

How to divide any given line (*A–B*) into any given number (5) of equal parts.

SOLUTION:
There are two methods of solving this problem.

Method A

Method A requires the use of a scale:
1. At point *B*, draw a line *B–C* that is square (at 90°) with line *A–B*.
2. Place a scale so that the zero (0) mark is at point *A* of line *A–B*. Move the scale so that the fifth mark of any equal division is on line *B–C*. Mark five equal spaces which may each be ½", 1" or 2" etc. apart.
3. Draw lines square (at 90°) to line *A–B* from the measured points 1, 2, 3, and 4. Line *A–B* is divided into 5 equal parts.

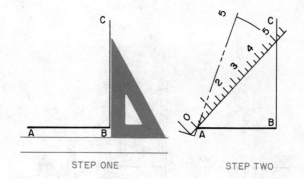

STEP ONE   STEP TWO

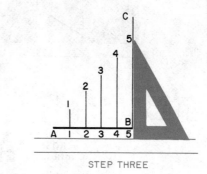

STEP THREE

DIVIDING   LINE

Method B

Method B requires the use of a compass.
1. At point *A*, draw line *A–C*.
2. With a compass or scale, mark 5 equal spaces on line *A–C*.
3. With a triangle and a straightedge, draw a line from 5 to *B*. Through points 1, 2, 3, and 4, draw lines parallel to 5–*B* and through line *A–B*. This divides given line *A–B* into 5 equal parts.

This procedure is useful when the division of a given distance results in measurements not included on a common scale. It is also used in developing complete measuring systems or scales different than those already available.

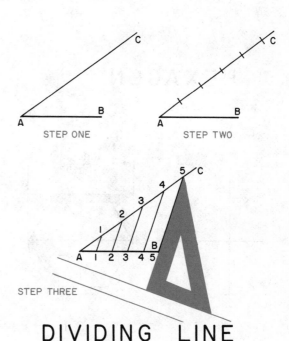

STEP ONE   STEP TWO

STEP THREE

DIVIDING   LINE

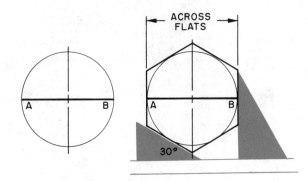

HEXAGON

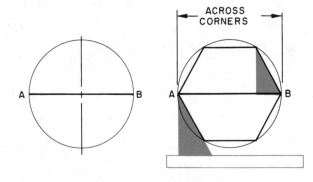

HEXAGON

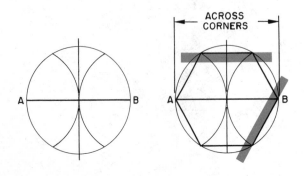

Drawing a Hexagon

A regular hexagon is a plane figure with *six equal sides* and *six equal angles*. Hexagon shapes are used very often for metal screws, nuts, bolts, and bars. Normally, the draftsman draws hexagons with a template, but templates are not always available. Hexagons are usually specified and the diameter measured across two of the flat surfaces.

Constructing a Hexagon Across the Flats

Given the size *A–B* across the flats, draw a hexagon.

SOLUTION:

1. With *A–B* as the diameter, draw a circle.
2. Using a 30°–60° triangle, draw lines tangent to the circle as shown.

Construct a Hexagon Across Corners

Given the size *A–B* across the flats, draw a hexagon.

SOLUTION:

1. With *A–B* as the diameter, draw a circle.
2. There are two ways of solving the problem.

Method A

Method A is the best and requires a 30°–60° triangle as shown.

Method B

Method B requires a compass and a straightedge as shown.

Drawing an Octagon

A regular octagon is a plane figure with *eight equal sides and eight equal angles.* Octagon shapes are used in making metal bars and in making some projects. Octagons are generally specified and the size measured across two of the flat surfaces.

Construct an Octagon Across the Flats

Given the size *A–B* across the flats, draw an octagon.

SOLUTION:

1. With *A–B* as the diameter, draw a circle.
2. Using a 45° triangle, draw lines tangent to the circle as shown.

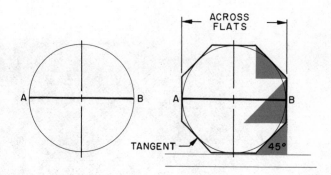

OCTAGON

Summary

By studying and practicing in this chapter, you have learned how to use the tools and the drawing procedures for making drawings. The procedures for drawing were introduced to you in the approximate order required for making orthographic and pictorial drawings. Now you are ready to learn How to Draw Orthographic Projections.

This object can be drawn in orthographic views to explain to workmen the details of making the finished design.

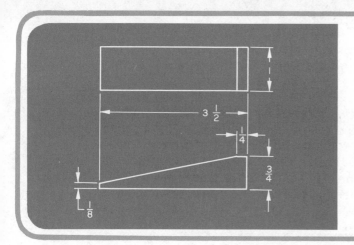

6

Drawing Orthographic Projections

Why Study This Chapter?

DRAWING ORTHOGRAPHIC PROJECTIONS will explain:
1. The six-step drawing procedure which helps you draw orthographic views quickly and accurately.
2. The different types of products which draftsmen draw, such as jigs, fixtures, gages, cutting or forming dies, and consumer products.
3. The usefulness of a project drawing when it becomes the plan you will use for a shop project in your other industrial arts classes or your home.
4. Standard material sizes that are used in the design of objects.
5. Drawing assignments that represent several areas of industrial arts, such as woodworking, metalworking, graphic arts, and plastics.

In this chapter you will be applying the skills learned in Chapters 3, 4, and 5. Your drawing assignments will progress from simple to more complex ones, such as assembly drawings. You will be able to select the assignments most appealing to you. This chapter will show the need to express your ideas clearly as you draw orthographic projections and use the conventional practices.

Orthographic projection is the best and most often used system for drawing plans for products. In Chapter 3, *Drafting: Conventional Practices*, the orthographic system for drawing is fully explained.

This chapter provides an opportunity for you to learn how to systematically make an orthographic projection drawing quickly and accurately. To do this you need to learn to use drafting tools, materials, terms and procedures with speed, accuracy and understanding. By learning these fundamentals you will be better able to express and understand technical ideas.

Select and draw the problems that are of most interest to you. The useful objects to be drawn are of three kinds: (1) square shapes, (2) round shapes, (3) assemblies of parts. The drawings are of engineered and tooling (jigs, fixtures, gages, and dies) products. Engineered or manufactured products are usually produced in large quantities as consumer items and used by many people. Tooling products are normally built in single units or small quantities and used for mass producing parts.

A six-step procedure is shown for making the first two drawings in both the square object and the round object portions of the chapter. The six-step procedure shows the most efficient way of drawing the object. According to the object's shape, select the best procedure to be used in making the orthographic projection drawings. In learning the procedure you will find it helpful to draw the same drawing more than once.

> **REMEMBER!**
>
> The purpose of this chapter is to learn to make an orthographic projection drawing quickly and accurately.

Refer to each of the previous reference chapters as needed in accomplishing this purpose. After learning this purpose, you may want to create drawings of other useful objects.

All of the drawings you will make are of useful products that you can make in the school shop or your home workshop. The drawings are arranged to provide for a gradual increase in the use of more drafting tools, conventions, and skills.

There is an adequate quantity of drawings presented so you can choose the projects that interest you most at each level of difficulty.

Square Objects

Square objects are basically *rectangular solids*. They are the easiest shapes to draw. In several of the projects, the angles to be drawn will provide you with learning experiences in using triangles.

Before you begin drawing, review "Sheet Layout", "How to Select Views" and "Placement of Dimensions" in Chapter 3. Also review "How to Draw Lines" in Chapter 5. You should follow these conventional practices when drawing orthographically.

SANDING BLOCKS are used to support sheets of abrasive material as it is used to shape and smooth surfaces for finishing. This sanding block is made of maple in a standard ¾" thickness. Its size is for ⅙ of a standard 9" X 11" sheet of abrasive material since most sheets are divided into six parts. This size of paper and the resulting sanding block are easy to handle.

The sanding block is a basic square or rectangular solid shape. It requires a two-view orthographic projection drawing. This is the easiest shape for you to begin drawing. The drawing requires use of a parallel straight-edge or a T-square, triangle, scale, pencil, eraser, erasing shield, and duster. The object is drawn on an "A" size (8½" X 11") sheet of paper.

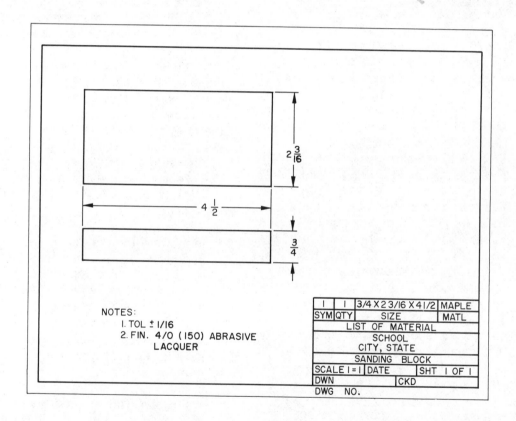

NOTES:
1. TOL ± 1/16
2. FIN. 4/0 (150) ABRASIVE
   LACQUER

I	I	3/4 X 2 3/16 X 4 1/2	MAPLE
SYM	QTY	SIZE	MATL
		LIST OF MATERIAL	
		SCHOOL	
		CITY, STATE	
		SANDING BLOCK	
SCALE I = I	DATE		SHT I OF I
DWN		CKD	
DWG NO.			

The front view of the drawing will show the ¾" thickness and 4½" length of the block. The top view of the drawing will show the mass of the object and provide the 2³⁄₁₆" width dimension. Notice that most of the lines in the drawing are horizontal. Therefore, the vertical lines are drawn very lightly first. The horizontal lines are then located and drawn dark. The *six-step basic procedure* for drawing orthographically should be practiced when completing all similar square objects. It is the best method for making drawings with more horizontal lines than vertical lines.

187

Six-Step Procedure for Drawing the Sanding Block

Study the photograph and orthographic drawing of the SANDING BLOCK. You are going to use the *six-step procedure* to draw the two views of the drawing. The top view and side view of the sanding block are drawn step-by-step in the example on the right hand page. Notice that the orthographic projection has been finished. When you complete the following description of the six-step procedure, your drawing should look exactly like the orthographic projection that is seen on page 187.

The six-step procedure is an efficient method that will enable you to record any object in orthographic projection form in a rapid, accurate manner. You will follow the instructions to become familiar with the six-step procedure, shown on page 189.

Step One:

In this step you will lay out the border line, locate the 4½" length of the object so that you can later scribe the outline of the object.

a. Lay out the border line with a margin of ¼" on all sides except for the top border, which is ½" from the top.

b. From the lefthand border line you will locate three points. Place your scale into position and measure 1" from the left border line. After locating that point, measure 4½" from the point you just located and locate your next point. Now you are 5½" from the left border line. From the last location point, measure ½" and mark your point. You are now 6" from the lefthand border line. At this point you have marked the 4½" length of the object and you have located what will become the dimension lines that will record the width of the top view and the thickness of the front view.

Step Two:

In this step you will draw the vertical lines and locate the next points that will become the horizontal lines of the object.

a. Make three very light vertical lines through the points that you have located.

You will now measure from the top border line and mark five points that will locate the object from the top border line. This will become the 2³⁄₁₆" measurement for the width of the top view and the ¾" thickness measurement of the front view. You will also locate the distance between the top view and the front view with the spacing for the 4½" dimension.

b. Locate the first point 1" from the top border line. From that point measure 2³⁄₁₆" and locate your next point. Now locate a point ½" from the last mark for the dimension line position. *At this point you are now 3¹¹⁄₁₆" away from the top border line.* Locate your next point ½" from your last point to identify the position of the top object line in the front view. Now you are 4³⁄₁₆" from the top border line. From the last location point, measure the next point ¾" to form the thickness of the front view. You are now 4¹⁵⁄₁₆" away from the top border line.

Step Three:

In this step you will draw dark horizontal lines as illustrated in the example. Four of the horizontal lines will be drawn wide and dark; these will be the object lines for the top view width and the front view thickness. The other horizontal lines will become extension lines and dimension lines.

Step Four:

In this step you are going to draw the dark vertical lines.

a. Start from the left side of the paper (working toward the right side) and draw dark vertical lines. You will have four wide, dark object lines representing the end lines of the front view and top view. You will also draw the narrow dark extension and dimension lines.

Now you have analyzed the example drawing, located, and drawn the necessary horizontal and vertical lines for the sanding block.

Step Five:

In this step you will add the *arrowheads* to your drawing, locate and draw the necessary *guidelines* for lettering, and make the *title block* and *list of material*.

a. Draw the arrowheads as located in the example.

b. Measure the points for locating the guidelines for the general notes on the drawing.

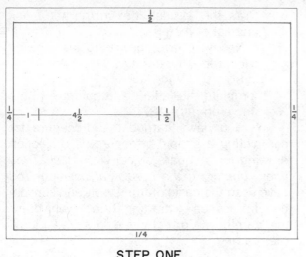

STEP ONE

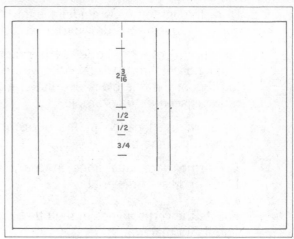

STEP TWO

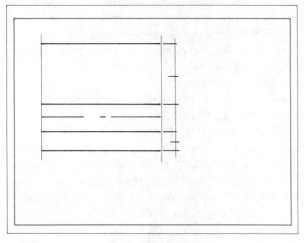

STEP THREE

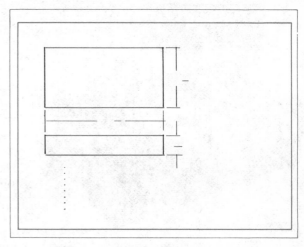

STEP FOUR

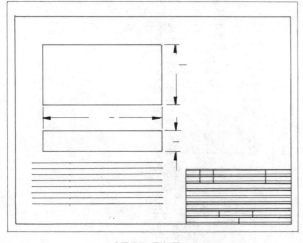

STEP FIVE

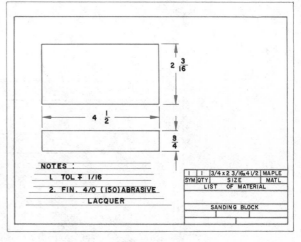

STEP SIX

189

c. Draw the light, narrow guidelines for the *general notes* on the drawing.

d. Measure 4″ over to the left of the right-hand border line to locate the vertical left line of the title block and list of material as seen in the example.

e. Measure the location of the horizontal lines in the title block.

f. Draw the horizontal lines in the title block and list of material.

g. Locate the vertical lines in the title block and list of material.

h. Draw the vertical lines in the title block and list of material.

Now you have completed the drawing except for all lettering.

Step Six:

Complete the lettering to conform to the example on page 187.

Now you have learned the procedure for completing a simple orthographic projection drawing for a square object *with most of the lines running in the horizontal position*. You have used the basic drafting tools and conventional practices of drafting. Check your drawing carefully. Correct all errors and clarify the drawing.

Problem 24
V-Block

V-BLOCKS are used to hold round or cylindrical shapes while work is being performed on them. The V-BLOCK in this drawing is made of wood and is used to hold wood or plastic parts. It is considered a type of tooling called a *jig*. Jigs are portable and hold parts during machining operations.

The new drafting experiences provided in this drawing project include the use of the 45° triangle, compass, hidden lines, and leader lines. This drawing should be done on an "A" size (8½″ X 11″) sheet. The six-step procedure on page 191 is best for drawings with more vertical lines than horizontal lines. Notice the horizontal lines are located and drawn light. Then the vertical lines are located and drawn dark.

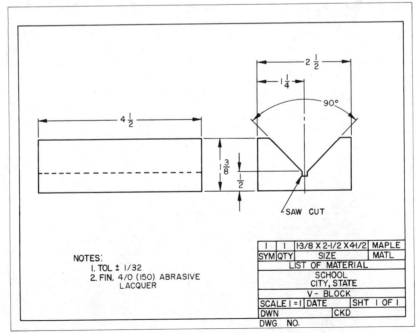

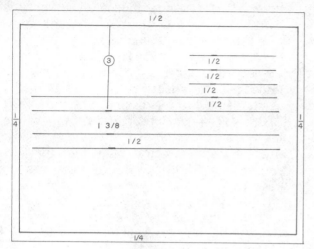

STEP ONE

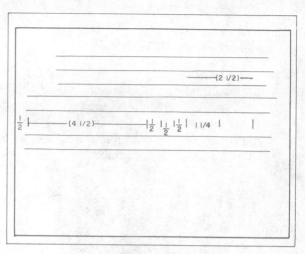

STEP TWO

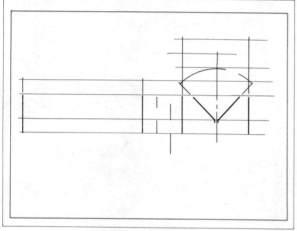

STEP THREE

STEP FOUR

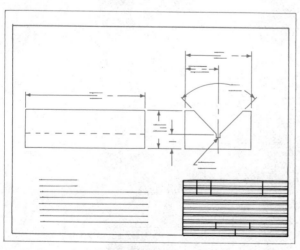

STEP FIVE

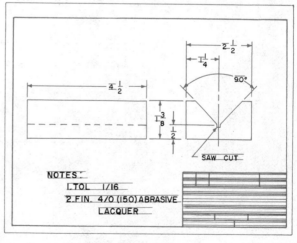

NOTES:
1. TOL 1/16
2. FIN. 4/0 (150) ABRASIVE
   LACQUER

STEP SIX

A DOOR STOP is a wedge-shaped object used to hold doors open at a desired position. This is considered to be an engineering item that has possible consumer appeal. This type of product can be manufactured in large quantities for mass distribution.

In this drawing, the angle is formed by locating the two points which the inclined line intersects at the top and side surfaces to form a wedge shape. Then the inclined line is drawn through the two points. The line is drawn with the use of a straightedge or a triangle. Most of the lines in this drawing are horizontal. *Remember* to locate and draw the light vertical lines; then locate and draw the dark horizontal lines. Use an "A" size (8½" X 11") sheet. Place the views 1¾" from the left edge and the top view 1½" from the top edge of the sheet.

After studying the example of the DOOR STOP, you should observe that most of the lines are horizontal. Therefore, you should use the same six-step procedure that describes the SANDING BLOCK drawings on page 188.

Step One:

Draw the border line first. Locate the position of each vertical line.

Step Two:

Draw the vertical lines narrow and light. Locate the positions of the horizontal lines.

Step Three:

Make the horizontal lines wide and dark.

Step Four:

Draw the vertical lines wide and dark.

Step Five:

First add the arrowheads to the dimension lines. Now locate the narrow, light guidelines to be used when lettering the general notes.

Step Six:

Now add the dimensions and lettering. Check your drawing carefully and correct all errors.

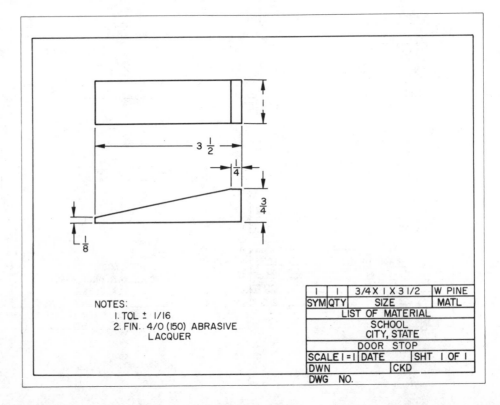

NOTES:
1. TOL ± 1/16
2. FIN. 4/0 (150) ABRASIVE LACQUER

		3/4 X 1 X 3 1/2	W PINE
SYM	QTY	SIZE	MATL
		LIST OF MATERIAL	
		SCHOOL	
		CITY, STATE	
		DOOR STOP	
SCALE 1 = 1	DATE		SHT 1 OF 1
DWN		CKD	
DWG NO.			

Study the SANDING BLOCK drawing on page 187 and compare it to the SANDING BLOCK GAGE drawing. Compare the width of the sanding block to the gage. The sanding block gage is used to check the width (2 3/16″ dimension) of the sanding block and allows a tolerance of ± 1/16″. This type of tooling is called a *go*, *no-go*, or *high-limit*, *low-limit gage*. The part being checked should fit into the *go* side (this means the width is less than 2 1/4″) but should

not fit into the *no-go* portion (the part should be larger than 2 1/8″) of the gage. Gages are a type of tooling used to check measurements.

When products are mass-produced, inspection gages are used to check the dimensions. As the production line inspector checks parts, he can determine if the tools, materials, and machines are performing properly. If a production product does not pass the inspection test, it is reworked or rejected. When too many parts fail the inspection test, the production line is "shut down" until corrections have been made. A *fixed* or *limit* inspection gage allows the parts to be checked quickly and accurately.

New learning experiences include the use of the circle guide and special tolerances which are specified on certain dimensions. Use an "A" size drawing sheet, start the views 1 1/4″ from the left edge and the top view 2 1/2″ from the top edge of the sheet.

┌─ REMEMBER!

Use the appropriate six-step procedure in making each drawing.

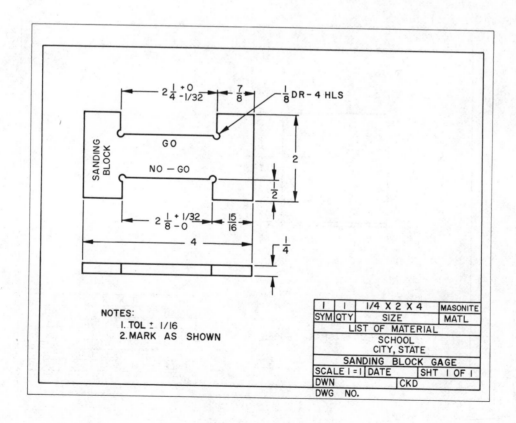

Such woodworking tools as chisels, gouges, plane irons, and lathe tools have cutting edges which have been ground to a 30° angle. This WOOD TOOL GAGE is used for checking that angle as it is ground.

In the drawing the 30°–60° triangle is used in making the 30° angle. The top view should be drawn lightly first. Next, all of the ¹⁄₁₆″ radii are drawn dark with a pencil, using a circle template to draw the correct size radius. Remember, a radius is one-half the size of a diameter. Finally, straight, dark lines should be drawn. Use an "A" size drawing sheet. The placement of the views should be judged by the drawer. Proper placement is a skill that develops through practice.

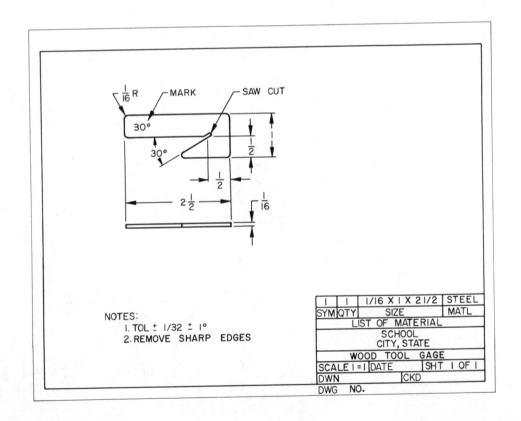

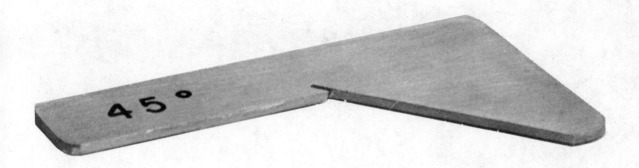

The MITER GAGE is used to check the angle of parts used in making square corners with miter joints. It can also be used for checking 45° chamfers. The 45° angle is understood in the following ways:

$$180° - 135° = 45° \quad or \quad 135° - 90° = 45°$$

The purpose of this drawing is to develop skill, speed and confidence through repeated use of previously used drawing practices.

Use an "A" size drawing sheet.

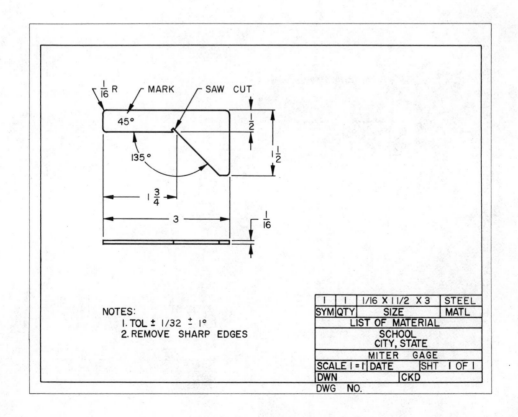

NOTES:
1. TOL ± 1/32 ± 1°
2. REMOVE SHARP EDGES

		1/16 X 1 1/2 X 3	STEEL
SYM	QTY	SIZE	MATL
LIST OF MATERIAL			
SCHOOL CITY, STATE			
MITER GAGE			
SCALE 1 = 1	DATE		SHT 1 OF 1
DWN		CKD	
DWG NO.			

Problem 29
Cold Chisel Gage

Cold chisels are driven with a hammer to cut metal. This COLD CHISEL GAGE is used to check the accuracy of the angle ground on the chisel's cutting edge. It is a type of go, no-go gage.

On this drawing, a protractor or an adjustable triangle is used to make the 70° angle. The 60° angle can be measured with the same tools or a 30°–60° triangle.

Use an "A" size drawing sheet.

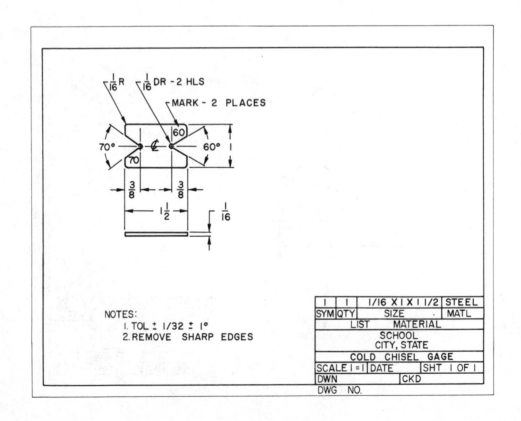

NOTES:
1. TOL ± 1/32 ± 1°
2. REMOVE SHARP EDGES

I	I	1/16 X I X I 1/2	STEEL
SYM	QTY	SIZE	MATL
	LIST	MATERIAL	

SCHOOL
CITY, STATE

COLD CHISEL GAGE

SCALE I = I	DATE		SHT I OF I
DWN		CKD	

DWG NO.

Problem 30
Making Orthographic Projections from Pictorials

Make orthographic projection drawings of as many of the following problems as necessary to reinforce your ability to understand and draw square objects. The purpose of this problem is to provide you with the opportunity to develop further skill in the use of the six-step procedure. This also gives you an opportunity to see if you understand (1) orthographic projection drawing, (2) the selection of views, (3) placement of dimensions. (4) labeling, and (5) completing the sheet layout for making drawings of square objects. Each drawing should be checked and corrected before proceeding with the next problem. *Remember, drawing with speed and accuracy is very important.*

SQUARE OBJECTS

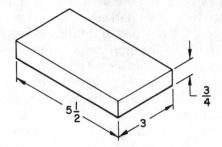

SANDING BLOCK (1/4 SHEET)

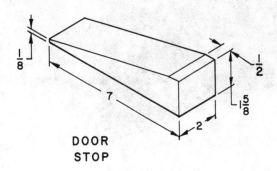

DOOR STOP

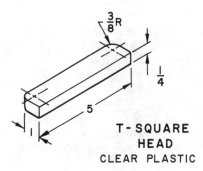

T-SQUARE HEAD
CLEAR PLASTIC

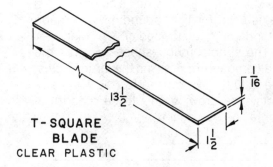

T-SQUARE BLADE
CLEAR PLASTIC

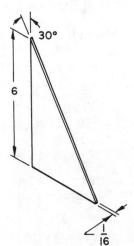

30°-60° TRIANGLE
CLEAR PLASTIC

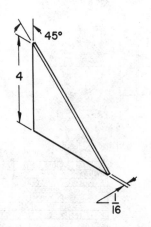

45° TRIANGLE
CLEAR PLASTIC

Round Objects

Before drawing the following round parts, study the information about circles, arcs, circle templates, and compasses in Chapter 5, *Drawing Mechanically*. Material about conventional lines should also be reviewed in Chapter 3, *Drafting: Conventional Practices*.

Problem 31
Mallet Head

This MALLET HEAD, when attached to a handle, is used for light pounding. It is made from standard 2″ thick wood or 1 ¾″ diameter stock. The simple round shape requires the use of a compass for drawing the large circles. A circle guide may be used for the ½″ diameter hole. The drawing should be made full-scale on a "A" size sheet.

Study the *six-step procedure* on page 199 for drawing round objects. By practicing this procedure, circular objects can be drawn successfully. Notice that center lines are located with light lines first; then the circles and arcs are drawn wider and darker. Finally, the center lines are drawn darker.

Analyze the completed drawing of the MALLET HEAD. In the front view, you will see a horizontal and vertical center line that locates the center of the ½″ diameter hole. When drawing round objects, the center of a circle should be drawn first. After the circles have been drawn, the straight lines are added.

Six-Step Procedure for Drawing Round Objects

Step One:
Begin by locating and drawing a light layout line to the position of the horizontal center line.

Step Two:
Measure from the left border line and locate the vertical object and center lines. Draw them as light layout lines. Also draw the circles and the arc with wide, dark object lines.

Step Three:
Draw the horizontal and hidden lines with wide, dark lines. Locate and draw the dimension lines with narrow, dark lines.

Step Four:
Draw the vertical lines with wide, dark lines. Draw narrow, dark leader lines. Locate the guidelines.

Step Five:
Draw the guidelines and form the title block. Add the arrowheads.

Step Six:
Complete the drawing with the necessary lettering. Check and correct your drawing.

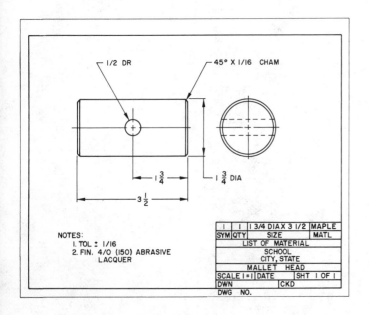

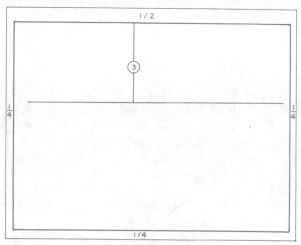

STEP ONE

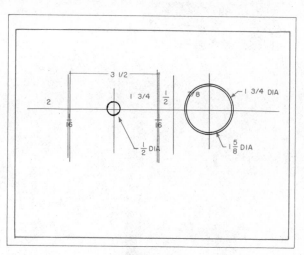

STEP TWO

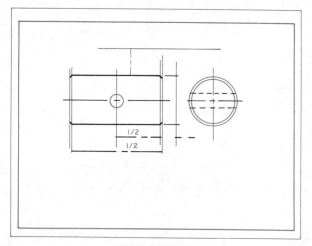

STEP THREE

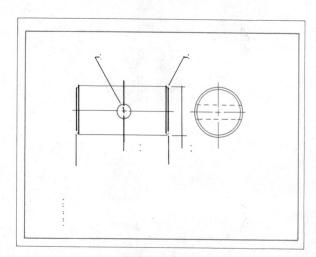

STEP FOUR

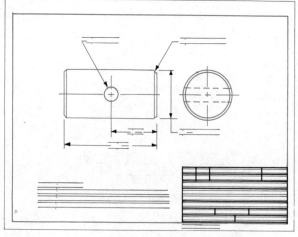

STEP FIVE

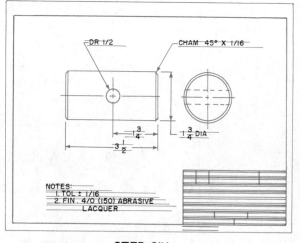

STEP SIX

199

The CANDLEHOLDER is a simple, attractive shape that is drawn with the use of a compass.

Notice in the *six-step procedure* that drawings of round parts are started with light lines representing the center lines. These are followed by the circles which should be drawn with dark object lines. The straight lines are projected from the circles after the thickness measurements are completed.

Use an "A" size sheet for this drawing. Make sure you check and correct your drawing carefully.

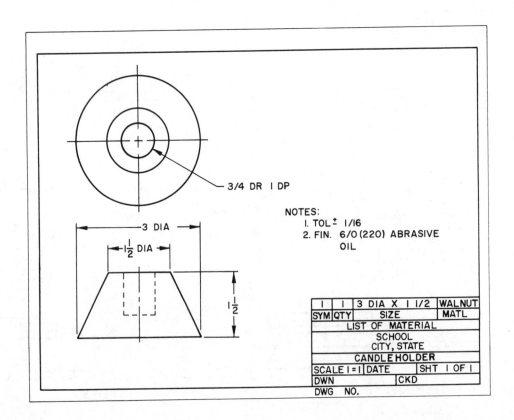

3/4 DR 1 DP

3 DIA

1½ DIA

1½

NOTES:
1. TOL ± 1/16
2. FIN. 6/0 (220) ABRASIVE
   OIL

1	1	3 DIA X 1 1/2	WALNUT
SYM	QTY	SIZE	MATL
LIST OF MATERIAL			
SCHOOL			
CITY, STATE			
CANDLEHOLDER			
SCALE 1 = 1	DATE		SHT 1 OF 1
DWN		CKD	
DWG NO.			

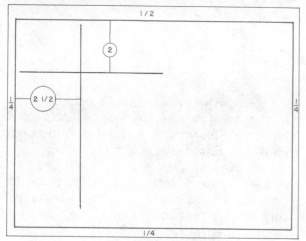

STEP ONE

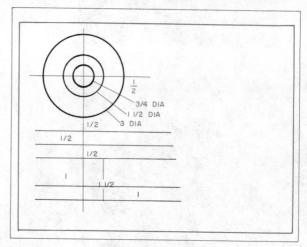

STEP TWO

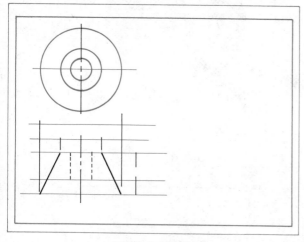

STEP THREE

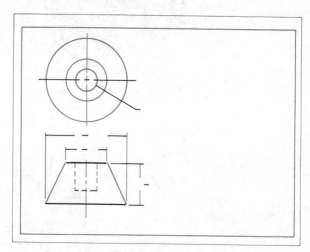

STEP FOUR

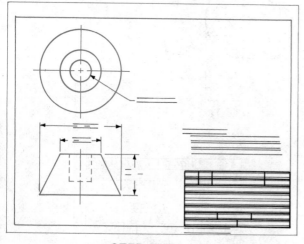

STEP FIVE

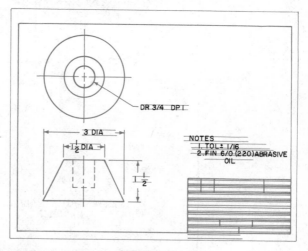

STEP SIX

The ROUND-FACE MALLET HEAD is attached to a handle; the unit is used as a hammer. This mallet is used to form sheet metal into round shapes such as bowls.

This drawing provides additional practice in the use of a compass. It is important to draw the circles and arcs before making the connecting straight object lines. The front view has a spherical radius (SPHER R). This surface is formed on a lathe. The lefthand view was used to eliminate the hidden line of the 45° X 1/16" chamfer that would result if a righthand view were drawn.

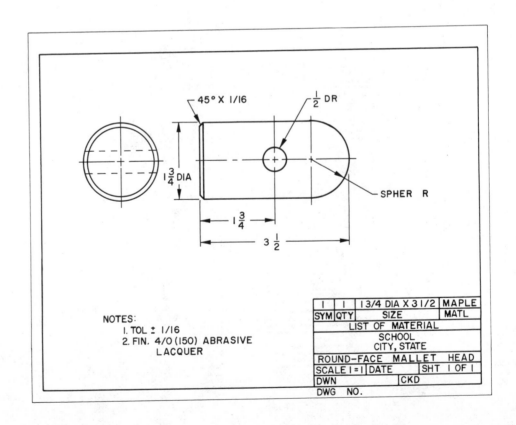

45° X 1/16

$\frac{1}{2}$ DR

$1\frac{3}{4}$ DIA

SPHER R

$1\frac{3}{4}$

$3\frac{1}{2}$

NOTES:
1. TOL ± 1/16
2. FIN. 4/0 (150) ABRASIVE
   LACQUER

		1 3/4 DIA X 3 1/2	MAPLE
SYM	QTY	SIZE	MATL
LIST OF MATERIAL			
SCHOOL CITY, STATE			
ROUND-FACE MALLET HEAD			
SCALE 1 = 1	DATE		SHT 1 OF 1
DWN		CKD	
DWG NO.			

COASTERS are used under drinking glasses to contain the moisture and protect table tops. This drawing of a basically square object involving circles should be started by drawing light center lines. These are followed by drawing the 2½" diameter circle with dark lines. A full-section view is used in the front view to make the lines of the round cavity visible for dimensioning. The spacing of section lines is judged by sight.

In making the WOOD COASTER, the cavity can be shaped rather easily on a wood lathe if you make a special square-socket chucking device to hold the 3" square stock. The square-socket chucking device is attached to the faceplate of a wood lathe. The special chuck is a good design problem for beginning tool design drafting. Ask your teacher to help you understand and solve this design problem.

Use an "A" size sheet.

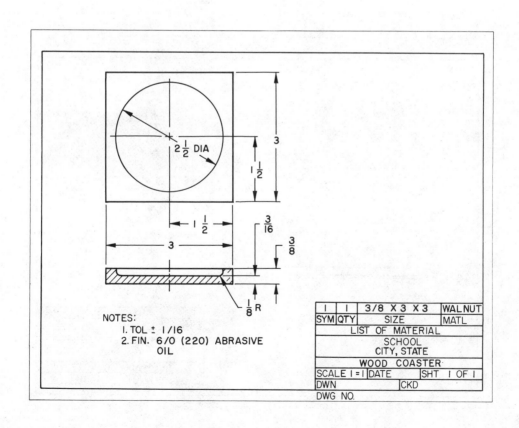

NOTES:
1. TOL ± 1/16
2. FIN. 6/0 (220) ABRASIVE OIL

I	I	3/8 X 3 X 3	WALNUT
SYM	QTY	SIZE	MATL
LIST OF MATERIAL			
SCHOOL CITY, STATE			
WOOD COASTER			
SCALE 1 = 1	DATE		SHT I OF I
DWN		CKD	
DWG NO.			

This metalworking project provides added experience in the use of the compass. The drawing also requires the use of section lines which are drawn with a 45° triangle. Spacing of these section lines is judged by sight. These section lines should be evenly spaced between 1/16" and 1/8" apart.

Use an "A" size sheet.

This coaster is formed by the coaster punch (page 205) and coaster die (page 206) in a vise or press. It is checked for size with the coaster plug gage (page 207).

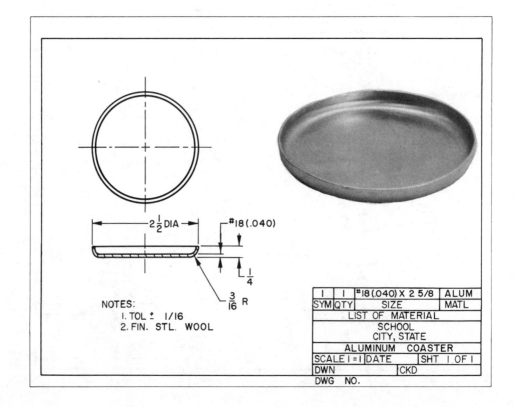

$2\frac{1}{2}$ DIA   #18(.040)

$\frac{1}{4}$

$\frac{3}{16}$ R

NOTES:
1. TOL ± 1/16
2. FIN. STL. WOOL

		#18(.040) X 2 5/8	ALUM
SYM	QTY	SIZE	MATL
LIST OF MATERIAL			
SCHOOL CITY, STATE			
ALUMINUM COASTER			
SCALE I = I	DATE		SHT I OF I
DWN		CKD	
DWG NO.			

The COASTER PUNCH is used with a coaster die in a press or vise to form an aluminum coaster. The punch forms the inside surface of the coaster. Punches are usually made of tool steel. They can be made of wood and plastic materials for limited production requirements. Forming punches and dies are a type of tooling.

The 5/16″ drilled hole is a tooling hole used to align the punch with the die in mounting them in the vise or press. Metal punch and die sets use alignment pins for proper mating. Alignment pins may be added to improve the design of this punch and the die in the next drawing.

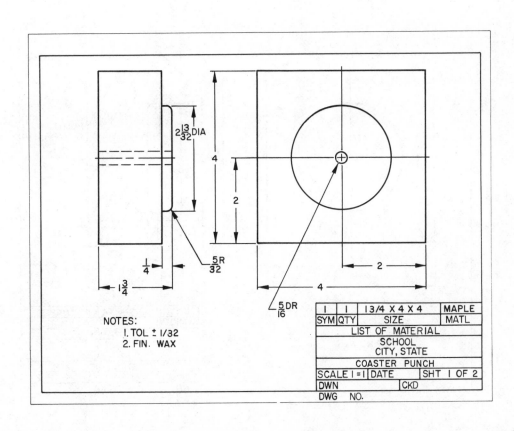

NOTES:
1. TOL ± 1/32
2. FIN. WAX

SYM	QTY	SIZE	MATL
I	I	1 3/4 X 4 X 4	MAPLE
LIST OF MATERIAL			
SCHOOL CITY, STATE			
COASTER PUNCH			
SCALE I = I	DATE		SHT I OF 2
DWN		CKD	
DWG NO.			

The COASTER DIE forms the outside surface of the aluminum coaster when used with the coaster punch in a press or vise.

The 2⅝″ diameter cavity holds the metal disc as the forming operation begins. The ⁵⁄₁₆″ drilled hole acts as a tooling hole and a place to knock the part out of the die after it is formed. Some punches and dies cut the blank for the part from a sheet of material as the part is being formed. Dies are most often made of tool steel, but in certain uses wood and/or plastic materials are best. Some parts require several dies for forming the complete shape.

Use an "A" size sheet.

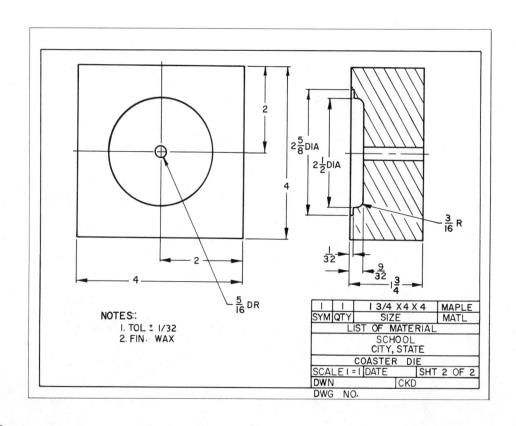

NOTES::
1. TOL ± 1/32
2. FIN. WAX

		1 3/4 X 4 X 4	MAPLE
SYM	QTY	SIZE	MATL
LIST OF MATERIAL			
SCHOOL CITY, STATE			
COASTER DIE			
SCALE 1 = 1	DATE		SHT 2 OF 2
DWN		CKD	
DWG NO.			

Problem 38
Coaster Plug Gage

This piece of tooling is used to check the size of the cavity in the *wood coaster* and the *metal coaster*. Plug gages are a type of go-no-go gage. The purpose of this drawing is to help you gain additional skill in the use of the compass.

Use an "A" size sheet.

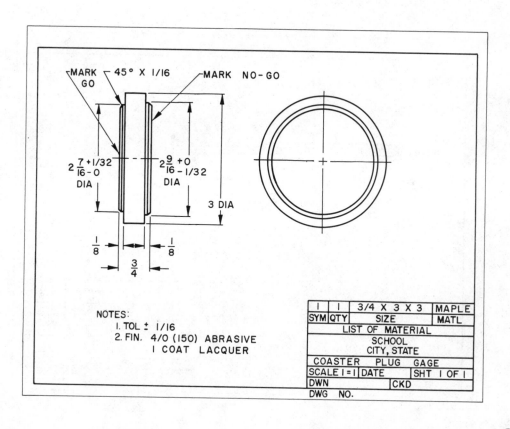

NOTES:
1. TOL ± 1/16
2. FIN. 4/0 (150) ABRASIVE
   1 COAT LACQUER

SYM	QTY	SIZE	MATL
I	I	3/4 X 3 X 3	MAPLE

LIST OF MATERIAL

SCHOOL
CITY, STATE

COASTER PLUG GAGE

SCALE I = I	DATE	SHT I OF I
DWN		CKD

DWG NO.

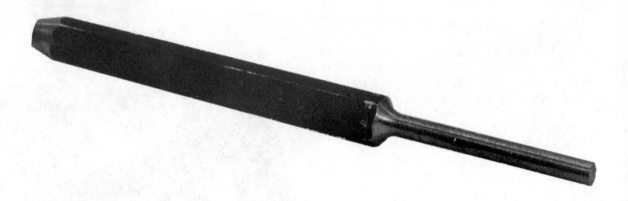

PIN PUNCHES are used to drive pins out of metal assemblies. This consumer product requires the drawing of an octagon. It also has 15° angles to be drawn by combining the 30°–60° and 45° triangles or using a protractor or adjustable triangle. The procedure for drawing this angle with triangles is shown in Chapter 5, page 162. By using a letter "A" for the diameter of the punch and a chart for the dimensions, three different-size punches can be specified on one drawing. This technique is called indexing dimensions.

Use an "A" size sheet.

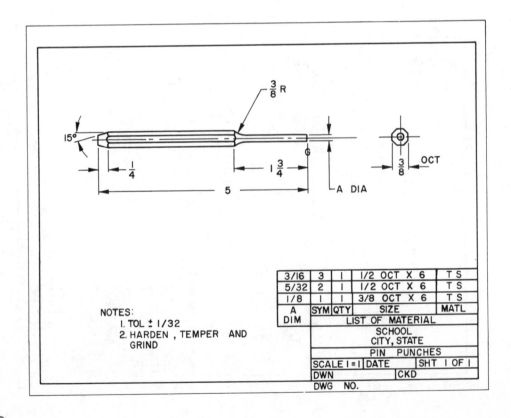

3/16	3	I	1/2 OCT X 6	T S
5/32	2	I	1/2 OCT X 6	T S
1/8	I	I	3/8 OCT X 6	T S
A DIM	SYM	QTY	SIZE	MATL

LIST OF MATERIAL

SCHOOL
CITY, STATE

PIN   PUNCHES

| SCALE I = I | DATE | | SHT I OF I |
| DWN | | CKD | |

DWG   NO.

NOTES:
 I. TOL ± I/32
 2. HARDEN , TEMPER AND
    GRIND

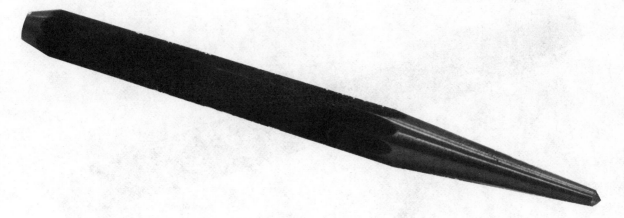

CENTER PUNCHES are used to score or dent metal and other materials at the location of a hole that is to be drilled. This drawing gives added experience in the use of tools that measure angles and more use of a dimension indexing chart in showing measurements.

Use an "A" size sheet.

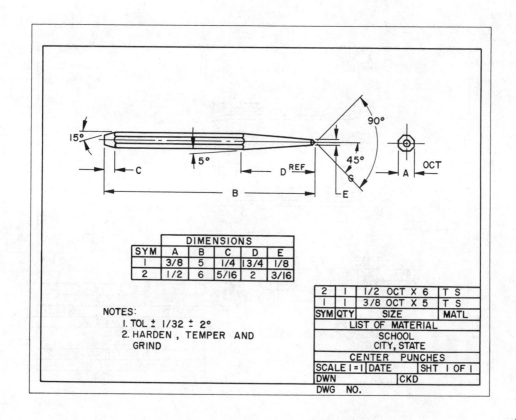

DIMENSIONS				
SYM	A	B	C	D	E

SYM	A	B	C	D	E
1	3/8	5	1/4	1 3/4	1/8
2	1/2	6	5/16	2	3/16

NOTES:
1. TOL ± 1/32 ± 2°
2. HARDEN, TEMPER AND GRIND

2	1	1/2 OCT X 6	T S
1	1	3/8 OCT X 5	T S
SYM	QTY	SIZE	MATL

LIST OF MATERIAL

SCHOOL
CITY, STATE

CENTER PUNCHES

SCALE 1 = 1	DATE	SHT 1 OF 1
DWN		CKD

DWG NO.

209

COLD CHISELS are driven by hammers to cut metal. In this drawing two methods of measuring angles are used. One method uses two linear measurements, *D* and *E*. The second method involves angles by degrees, 60° and 15°.

Use an "A" size sheet.

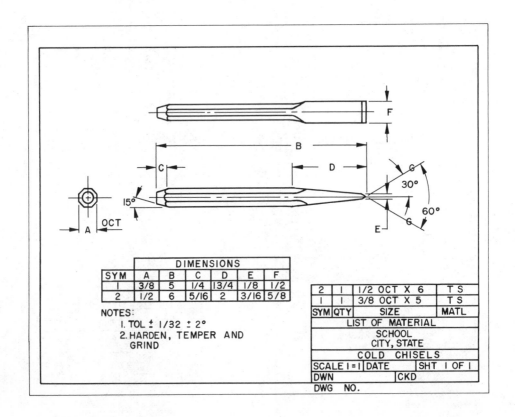

DIMENSIONS						
SYM	A	B	C	D	E	F
I	3/8	5	1/4	13/4	1/8	1/2
2	1/2	6	5/16	2	3/16	5/8

NOTES:
1. TOL ± 1/32 ± 2°
2. HARDEN, TEMPER AND GRIND

2	I	1/2 OCT X 6	T S
I	I	3/8 OCT X 5	T S
SYM	QTY	SIZE	MATL
LIST OF MATERIAL			
SCHOOL CITY, STATE			
COLD CHISELS			
SCALE I = I	DATE		SHT I OF I
DWN		CKD	
DWG NO.			

Problem 42
Mallet Handle

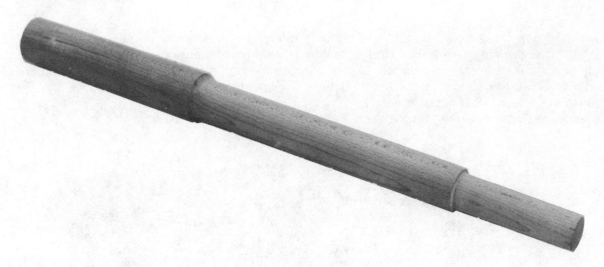

The MALLET HANDLE (used with the MALLET HEAD on page 198) forms a complete mallet. This drawing requires the use of a conventional break (refer to page 130 of Chapter 3) and the drop-bow compass. The compass should be used for the three concentric circles in the end view. If a circle template is used for this purpose, extreme care must be taken to keep the three circles on a common center (see pages 165–166 in Chapter 5). It is best to draw the smallest circle first, followed with each larger circle.

Use an "A" size sheet.

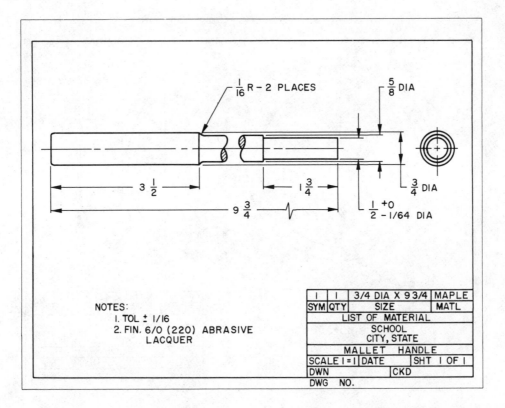

211

This woodworking project is made on a wood lathe. The drawing has a REF (reference) dimension. A *reference dimension* is used only to show the size of stock required to make the product. It is not used as a working dimension when making the product. The reference dimension is approximate. This means the dimension is used to get proper size piece of stock but is not used in machining operations in making the product.

Use an "A" size sheet.

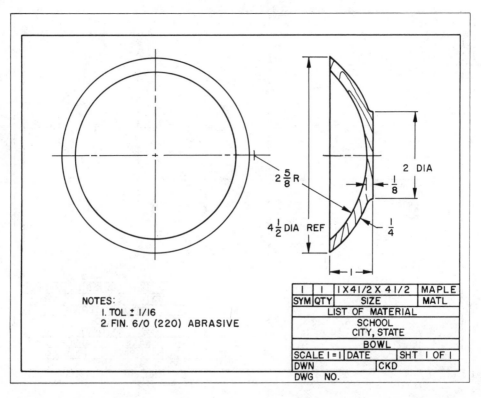

NOTES:
1. TOL ± 1/16
2. FIN. 6/0 (220) ABRASIVE

SYM	QTY	SIZE	MATL
I	I	I X 4 1/2 X 4 1/2	MAPLE

LIST OF MATERIAL

SCHOOL
CITY, STATE

BOWL

SCALE I = I	DATE		SHT I OF I
DWN		CKD	
DWG NO.			

Problem 44
Making Orthographic Projections from Pictorials

Make orthographic projection drawings of as many of the following problems as necessary to reinforce your ability to understand and draw round objects. The purpose of this problem is to provide you with the opportunity to develop further skill in the use of the six-step procedure. This also gives you an opportunity to see if you understand (1) orthographic projection drawing, (2) the selection of views, (3) placement of dimensions, (4) labeling, and (5) completing the sheet layout for making drawing of round objects. Each drawing should be checked and corrected before proceeding with the next problem. *Remember drawing with speed and accuracy is very important*.

ROUND OBJECTS

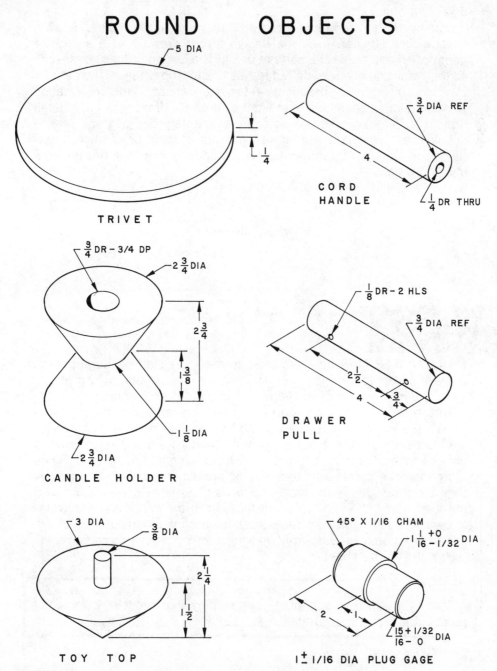

5 DIA

1/4

TRIVET

3/4 DIA REF

4

1/4 DR THRU

CORD HANDLE

3/4 DR – 3/4 DP

2 3/4 DIA

2 3/4

1 3/8

1 1/8 DIA

2 3/4 DIA

CANDLE HOLDER

1/8 DR – 2 HLS

3/4 DIA REF

2 1/2

4

3/4

DRAWER PULL

3 DIA

3/8 DIA

2 1/4

1 1/2

TOY TOP

45° X 1/16 CHAM

1 1/16 +0 −1/32 DIA

2

1

15/16 +1/32 −0 DIA

1 ± 1/16 DIA PLUG GAGE

Assemblies

Assembly drawings show devices that have more than one part. When a drawing has dimensioned parts, it is called a *detailed drawing*. Simple devices are often drawn as detailed assembly drawings. Complex devices are drawn as assemblies without detail dimensions. This type of drawing is called a *design* or *layout assembly drawing*. When design or layout assembly drawings are used, detail or individual drawings are made of each part to be built. This is called *detailing* or *detail drafting*. Drawing these assemblies provides several basic learning experiences for detail drawing.

Usually, the new employee in a drafting room will work as a *detailer*. The detail draftsman uses the design layout drawing as a source of information and draws the parts in detail. The designer does not specify all the details on his drawing but leaves this for the detailer. The detailer will use conventional practices, reference catalogs, and information from production engineers to make the complete drawing. A good detail draftsman may be asked to do some elementary design work. After a detailer has developed a broad understanding about production, materials, and design requirements, he can advance to the design level of drafting.

Problem 45
Track Step Marker

TRACK STEP MARKERS are used to mark the start of the approach in track and field jumping events. They are used in one or two places along the runway to indicate where certain steps should fall.

This project uses such standard materials as ¾" diameter birch doweling and a nail in its design. The *reference dimension* of ¾" diameter is used to show the size of the standard stock. The reference dimension means that no production machining will be needed. Since more than one part is used to make the project, it is called an *assembly drawing*. In assembly drawings, balloons (⅜" diameter) are used with numbers as symbols to represent the part in the *list of material* (refer to page 112 of Chapter 3). Because all necessary dimensions are given, it is called a *detailed assembly drawing*.

Use an "A" size sheet.

┌─ REMEMBER! ───

Study the drawing and plan your step-by-step procedure for completing this drawing accurately and quickly.

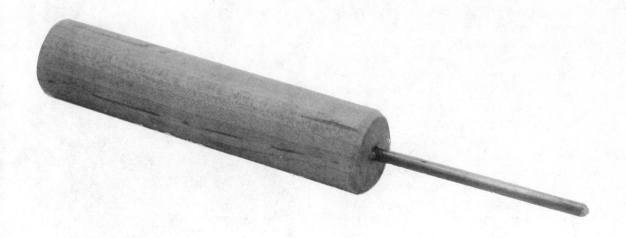

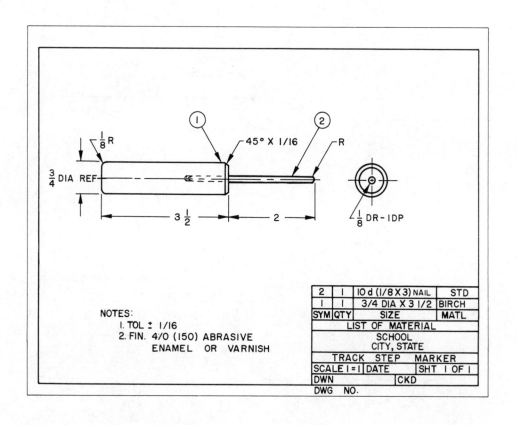

$\frac{1}{8}$ R

45° X 1/16

①   ②   R

$\frac{3}{4}$ DIA REF

$\frac{1}{8}$ DR-1DP

3 $\frac{1}{2}$ 2

NOTES:
1. TOL ± 1/16
2. FIN. 4/0 (150) ABRASIVE
   ENAMEL OR VARNISH

2	1	10 d (1/8 X 3) NAIL	STD
1	1	3/4 DIA X 3 1/2	BIRCH
SYM	QTY	SIZE	MATL
LIST OF MATERIAL			
SCHOOL CITY, STATE			
TRACK STEP MARKER			
SCALE 1=1	DATE		SHT 1 OF 1
DWN		CKD	
DWG NO.			

Problem 46
Book Rack

The BOOK RACK is used to hold several books on a desk top or table. It can also be turned over and used to hold one book in an open position for reading. This design uses materials of standard thickness and diameter. The fastening of parts is done by drilling holes and gluing parts in them to form a strong joint.

Use ½" scale to make this drawing on an "A" size sheet. This is the first scale drawing that you have been required to draw. Refer to Chapter 5 on page 156 for an explanation of scale drawing. If you use the ½" portion of your scale, you can read the full size dimensions and the scale will automatically change the reduction for you. This drawing is being reduced to one-half scale so it will fit on an "A" size sheet.

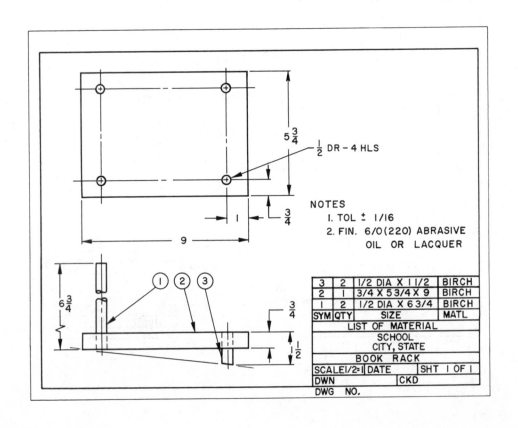

$\frac{1}{2}$ DR – 4 HLS

NOTES
1. TOL ± 1/16
2. FIN. 6/0 (220) ABRASIVE
   OIL OR LACQUER

SYM	QTY	SIZE	MATL
3	2	1/2 DIA X 1 1/2	BIRCH
2	1	3/4 X 5 3/4 X 9	BIRCH
1	2	1/2 DIA X 6 3/4	BIRCH

LIST OF MATERIAL

SCHOOL
CITY, STATE

BOOK RACK

SCALE1/2=1	DATE		SHT I OF I
DWN		CKD	
DWG NO.			

216

This COASTERHOLDER holds the wood coasters in Problem 34. The note "TO SUIT" in the end view means to make *part 2* long enough to hold the desired number of coasters (Refer to page 127 in Chapter 3). Allowance should be made for clearance when the coasters are stored and removed.

Use an "A" size sheet.

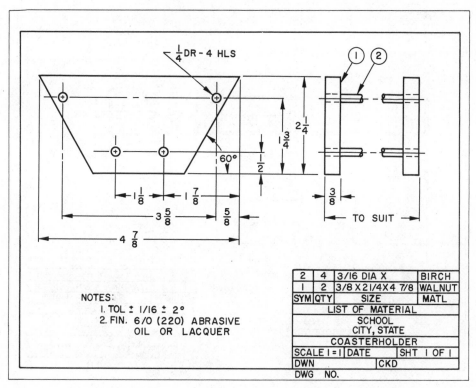

NOTES:
1. TOL ± 1/16 ± 2°
2. FIN. 6/0 (220) ABRASIVE
   OIL OR LACQUER

SYM	QTY	SIZE	MATL
2	4	3/16 DIA X	BIRCH
1	2	3/8 X 2 1/4 X 4 7/8	WALNUT

LIST OF MATERIAL

SCHOOL
CITY, STATE

COASTERHOLDER

SCALE 1 = 1	DATE		SHT 1 OF 1
DWN		CKD	
DWG NO.			

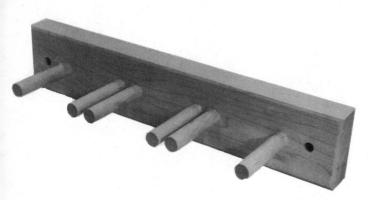

This BAT RACK will hold three softball or baseball bats in a safe position. It should be mounted at a proper height on a wall.

This drawing is to be done half-scale on an "A" size sheet.

The 1$^{15}/_{16}$" dimension represents the slot to hold the bat handle. If you study the tinted color area you will see that these three dowel rods represent one total unit of the holding device. If you wanted to expand the length of the bat rack so that more bats can be held, increase the units (in the colored area) and the overall length of the rack.

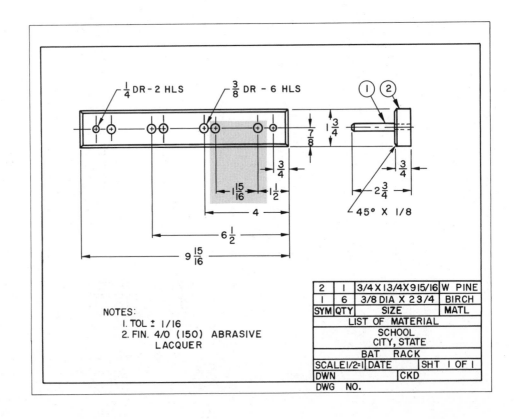

NOTES:
1. TOL $\pm$ 1/16
2. FIN. 4/0 (150) ABRASIVE
   LACQUER

SYM	QTY	SIZE	MATL
2	1	3/4 X 13/4 X 915/16	W PINE
1	6	3/8 DIA X 23/4	BIRCH
SYM	QTY	SIZE	MATL
		LIST OF MATERIAL	
		SCHOOL CITY, STATE	
		BAT RACK	
SCALE 1/2=1	DATE		SHT 1 OF 1
DWN		CKD	
DWG NO.			

A KICKING TEE is used in football to hold the ball during the kickoff. A 45° × ⅛″ chamfer is specified by the note extended with a leader from the front view. By using chamfers, sharp edges are removed and chipping of the wood along corners is reduced.

Use an "A" size sheet.

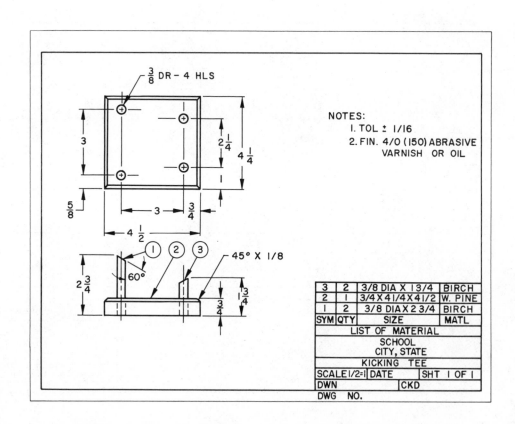

⅜ DR – 4 HLS

NOTES:
1. TOL ± 1/16
2. FIN. 4/0 (150) ABRASIVE VARNISH OR OIL

3

2 ¼

4 ¼

1

5/8

3

¾

4 ½

60°

2 ¾

1 2 3

45° X 1/8

1 ¾

¾

3	2	3/8 DIA X 1 3/4	BIRCH
2	1	3/4 X 4 1/4 X 4 1/2	W. PINE
1	2	3/8 DIA X 2 3/4	BIRCH
SYM	QTY	SIZE	MATL
LIST OF MATERIAL			
SCHOOL CITY, STATE			
KICKING TEE			
SCALE 1/2=1	DATE		SHT 1 OF 1
DWN		CKD	
DWG NO.			

The FRUIT TRAY holds a display of fruit on a table. A bowl shape is formed by uniformly spaced dowel rods (part 2) and two end boards (part 1). The various angles required in the end pieces should be located with a protractor, adjustable triangle, or the combined use of the 45° and 30°–60° triangles. Review page 162 in Chapter 5.

Use a "B" size sheet (11" x 17").

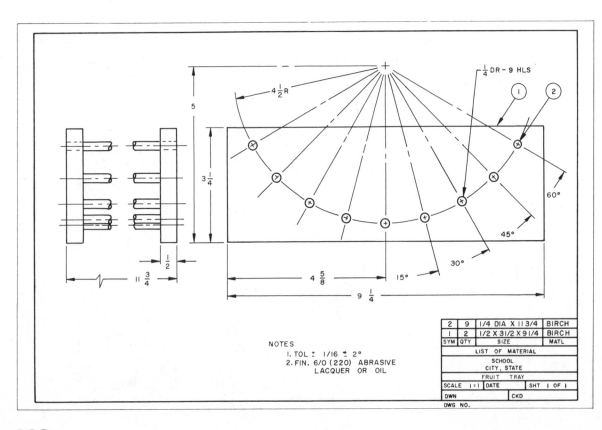

NOTES
1. TOL ± 1/16 ± 2°
2. FIN. 6/0 (220) ABRASIVE
   LACQUER OR OIL

SYM	QTY	SIZE	MATL
2	9	1/4 DIA X 11 3/4	BIRCH
1	2	1/2 X 3 1/2 X 9 1/4	BIRCH

LIST OF MATERIAL

SCHOOL
CITY, STATE

FRUIT TRAY

SCALE 1 = 1	DATE	SHT 1 OF 1
DWN		CKD
DWG NO.		

The PICTURE FRAME is a project combining woodworking and plastics. Extensive use of the 30°–60° triangle is required in this drawing.

Draw the right-side view first on a "B" size sheet (11" x 17"). The horizontal lines in the front view are projected from the right side view.

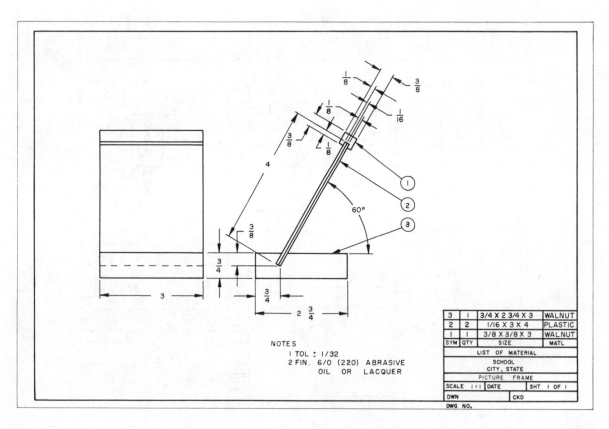

| $\frac{1}{8}$ | $\frac{3}{8}$ |
| $\frac{1}{8}$ | $\frac{1}{16}$ |

4

$\frac{3}{8}$ $\frac{1}{8}$

①
②
③

60°

$\frac{3}{8}$

$\frac{3}{4}$

3

$\frac{3}{4}$

2 $\frac{3}{4}$

NOTES
1 TOL ± 1/32
2 FIN. 6/0 (220) ABRASIVE
OIL OR LACQUER

3	1	3/4 X 2 3/4 X 3	WALNUT
2	2	1/16 X 3 X 4	PLASTIC
1	1	3/8 X 3/8 X 3	WALNUT
SYM	QTY	SIZE	MATL
LIST OF MATERIAL			
SCHOOL CITY, STATE			
PICTURE FRAME			
SCALE 1 = 1	DATE		SHT 1 OF 1
DWN		CKD	
DWG NO.			

This BEAM COMPASS can be used in drafting and shop work to draw large arcs and circles. A pencil is to be placed in the ⁵⁄₁₆″ drilled hole in part 1. Part 1 is shown in bottom view. The ¹⁄₈″ drilled hole in part 1 is for a pointed piece of steel to scribe lines on metal and plastic.

Use an "A" size sheet.

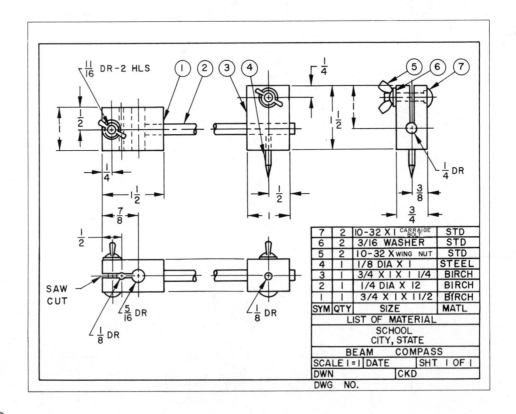

7	2	10-32 X 1 CARRAIGE BOLT	STD
6	2	3/16 WASHER	STD
5	2	10-32 X WING NUT	STD
4	1	1/8 DIA X 1	STEEL
3	1	3/4 X 1 X 1 1/4	BIRCH
2	1	1/4 DIA X 12	BIRCH
1	1	3/4 X 1 X 1 1/2	BIRCH
SYM	QTY	SIZE	MATL
LIST OF MATERIAL			
SCHOOL CITY, STATE			
BEAM COMPASS			
SCALE 1=1	DATE		SHT 1 OF 1
DWN		CKD	
DWG NO.			

Problem 53
Picture Frame

This PICTURE FRAME requires the use of a compass in making the 4⅜″ diameter circle. It is drawn half-scale on a "B" size sheet (11″ × 17″).

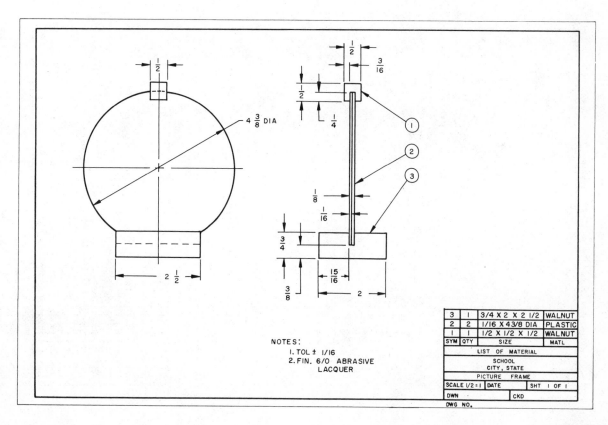

NOTES:
1. TOL ± 1/16
2. FIN. 6/0 ABRASIVE
   LACQUER

SYM	QTY	SIZE	MATL
3	I	3/4 X 2 X 2 1/2	WALNUT
2	2	1/16 X 43/8 DIA	PLASTIC
I	I	1/2 X 1/2 X 1/2	WALNUT

LIST OF MATERIAL

SCHOOL
CITY, STATE

PICTURE FRAME

SCALE 1/2 = 1	DATE		SHT I OF I
DWN		CKD	

DWG NO.

Extensive use of the 45° triangle is required in making the half-scale drawing of the WREN BIRDHOUSE on a "B" size sheet (11" x 17"). Draw the front view first. The horizontal lines in the right side view are projected from the front view.

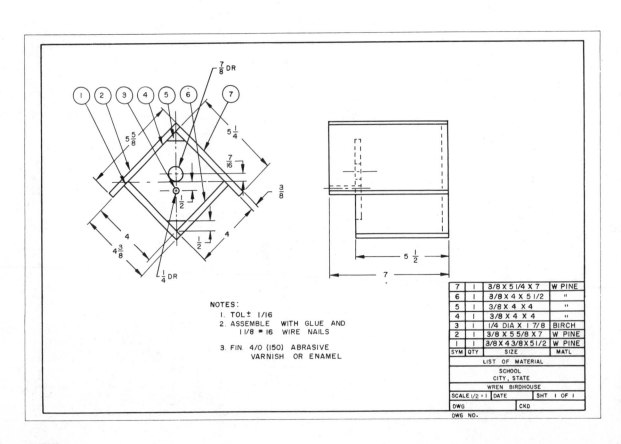

NOTES:

1. TOL ± 1/16
2. ASSEMBLE WITH GLUE AND 1 1/8 # 16 WIRE NAILS

3. FIN. 4/0 (150) ABRASIVE VARNISH OR ENAMEL

SYM	QTY	SIZE	MATL
7	1	3/8 X 5 1/4 X 7	W PINE
6	1	3/8 X 4 X 5 1/2	"
5	1	3/8 X 4 X 4	"
4	1	3/8 X 4 X 4	"
3	1	1/4 DIA X 1 7/8	BIRCH
2	1	3/8 X 5 5/8 X 7	W PINE
1	1	3/8 X 4 3/8 X 5 1/2	W PINE

LIST OF MATERIAL

SCHOOL
CITY, STATE

WREN BIRDHOUSE

SCALE 1/2 = 1	DATE		SHT 1 OF 1
DWG		CKD	
DWG NO.			

SPIRIT LEVELS are used in construction work to make surfaces level or vertical. Make a half-scale drawing on a "B" size sheet (11" X 17").

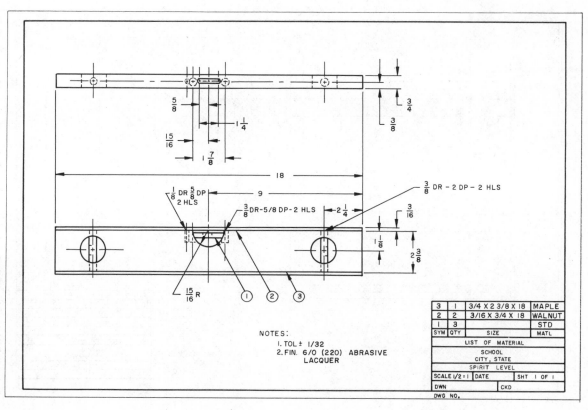

NOTES:
1. TOL ± 1/32
2. FIN. 6/0 (220) ABRASIVE LACQUER

3	1	3/4 X 2 3/8 X 18	MAPLE
2	2	3/16 X 3/4 X 18	WALNUT
1	3		STD
SYM	QTY	SIZE	MATL
LIST OF MATERIAL			
SCHOOL CITY, STATE			
SPIRIT LEVEL			
SCALE 1/2 = 1	DATE		SHT 1 OF 1
DWN		CKD	
DWG NO.			

225

Paper towels are held in this TOWEL RACK to be mounted on a cabinet or a wall. Make a half-scale drawing on a "B" size (11″ × 17″) sheet.

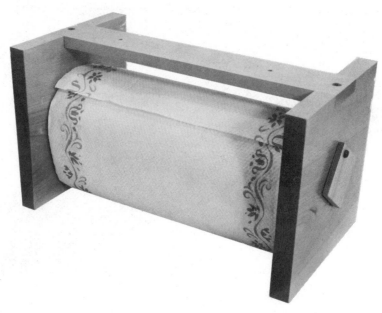

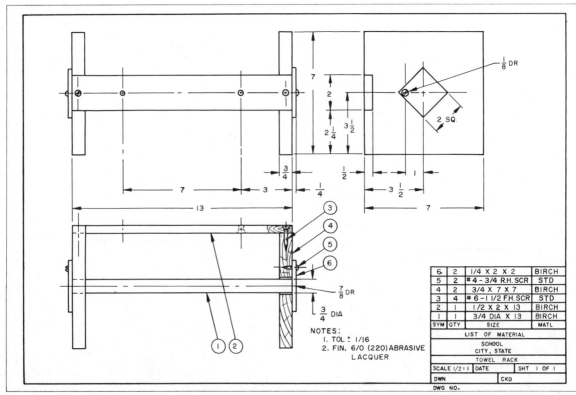

NOTES:
1. TOL ± 1/16
2. FIN. 6/0 (220) ABRASIVE
   LACQUER

6	2	1/4 X 2 X 2	BIRCH
5	2	#4 - 3/4 R.H. SCR	STD
4	2	3/4 X 7 X 7	BIRCH
3	4	#6 - 1 1/2 F.H. SCR	STD
2	1	1/2 X 2 X 13	BIRCH
1	1	3/4 DIA X 13	BIRCH
SYM	QTY	SIZE	MATL
		LIST OF MATERIAL	
		SCHOOL	
		CITY, STATE	
		TOWEL RACK	
SCALE 1/2=1	DATE		SHT 1 OF 1
DWN		CKD	
DWG NO.			

The TOOL TRAY is designed to hold an assortment of basic tools and materials used in household repairs and other work. This one-fourth scale drawing is done on an "A" size sheet.

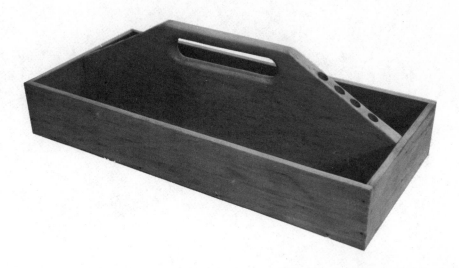

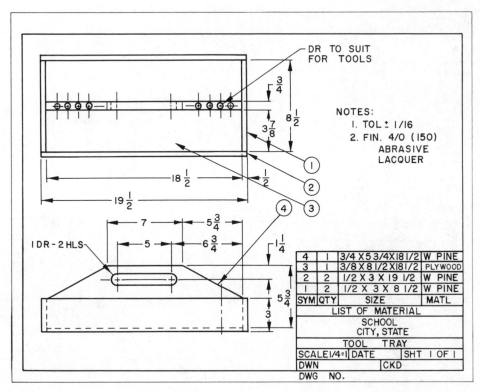

DR TO SUIT
FOR TOOLS

NOTES:
1. TOL ± 1/16
2. FIN. 4/0 (150)
   ABRASIVE
   LACQUER

SYM	QTY	SIZE	MATL
4	1	3/4 X 5 3/4 X 18 1/2	W PINE
3	1	3/8 X 8 1/2 X 18 1/2	PLYWOOD
2	2	1/2 X 3 X 19 1/2	W PINE
1	2	1/2 X 3 X 8 1/2	W PINE

LIST OF MATERIAL

SCHOOL
CITY, STATE

TOOL TRAY

SCALE 1/4=1	DATE		SHT 1 OF 1
DWN		CKD	
DWG NO.			

Problem 58
Screen Printing Frame

A SCREEN PRINTING FRAME is used in graphic arts work to print ink or other liquids on paper, metal, plastic, ceramics, glass, or other materials. Make a half-scale drawing on a "B" size (11″ X 17″) sheet.

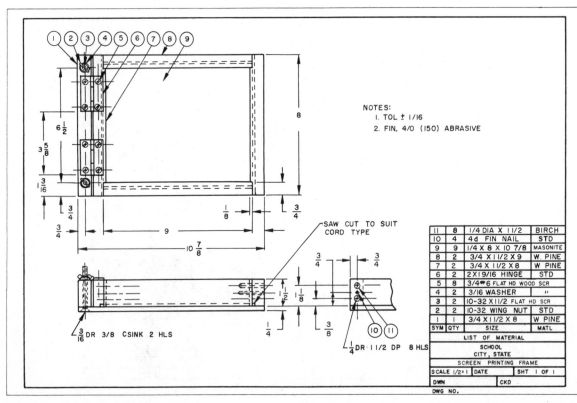

NOTES:
1. TOL ± 1/16
2. FIN, 4/0 (150) ABRASIVE

SAW CUT TO SUIT CORD TYPE

3/16 DR 3/8 CSINK 2 HLS

1/4 DR 11/2 DP 8 HLS

SYM	QTY	SIZE	MATL
11	8	1/4 DIA X 11/2	BIRCH
10	4	4d FIN NAIL	STD
9	9	1/4 X 8 X 10 7/8	MASONITE
8	2	3/4 X 11/2 X 9	W. PINE
7	2	3/4 X 11/2 X 8	W PINE
6	2	2 X 19/16 HINGE	STD
5	8	3/4 #6 FLAT HD WOOD SCR	
4	2	3/16 WASHER	''
3	2	10-32 X 11/2 FLAT HD SCR	
2	2	10-32 WING NUT	STD
1	1	3/4 X 11/2 X 8	W PINE
SYM	QTY	SIZE	MATL

LIST OF MATERIAL

SCHOOL
CITY, STATE

SCREEN PRINTING FRAME

SCALE 1/2=1	DATE		SHT 1 OF 1
DWN		CKD	

DWG NO.

Summary

You should understand the conventional practices and drawing techniques for making orthographic projections. Orthographic projections are used as working drawings to help plan and make products. You have studied the six-step drawing procedure and should be able to make orthographic views rapidly and accurately. In the next chapter you will learn how to make a pictorial view to show the relationship of the top, front, and end views. Often orthographic projections and pictorial views are used together to describe the object.

7

Drawing Pictorially

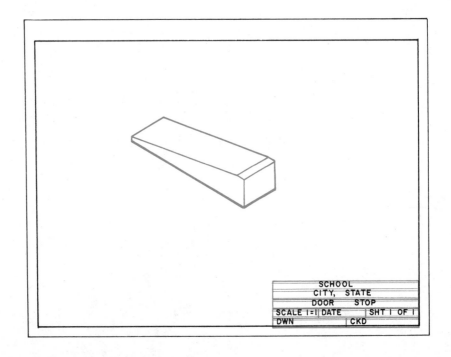

ISOMETRIC

PERSPECTIVE

OBLIQUE

Why Study This Chapter?

DRAWING PICTORIALLY will show you:
1. The isometric, perspective, and oblique views used in pictorial drawings.
2. The conventional practices and drawing procedures for making pictorial drawings.
3. The use of ellipse guides in making circles.
4. Diagrams and illustrations which help you understand pictorial drawings and how to make them.

In this chapter you will gain experience in making a different kind of drawing to show the shape of objects.

A pictorial drawing is a realistic representation of an object; that is, as it appears to the observer. By using standard drafting practices, drawings can be created in the likeness of an object.

The field of drafting dealing with pictorial drawing is known as *technical illustration*. Draftsmen that specialize in pictorial drawing are called technical illustrators.

SCHOOL		
CITY, STATE		
DOOR STOP		
SCALE 1=1	DATE	SHT 1 OF 1
DWN	CKD	

PICTORIAL   DRAWINGS

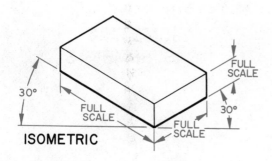

ISOMETRIC

30°

30°

FULL
SCALE

FULL
SCALE

FULL
SCALE

FULL
SCALE

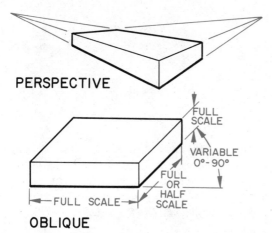

PERSPECTIVE

FULL
SCALE

VARIABLE
0° - 90°

FULL
OR
HALF
SCALE

FULL SCALE

OBLIQUE

ISOMETRIC   AXIS

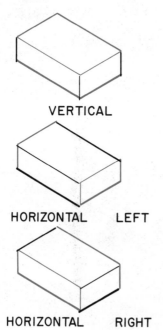

VERTICAL

HORIZONTAL   LEFT

HORIZONTAL   RIGHT

Pictorial drawings provide a clear understanding of the appearance of parts and assemblies. They are used as descriptive aids for selling and explaining the assembly, use, and maintenance of products. They are used in advertising literature and also repair-service manuals to explain operation, parts, assembly, service, and repair. As more complicated tools, machines, appliances, vehicles and other equipment are developed, the need for pictorial descriptions increases. Pictorial drawings are used very effectively in promoting learning.

In drafting, the three most-used types of pictorial drawing practices are the (1) *isometric*, (2) *perspective*, and (3) *oblique*.

Of these, isometric drawing is used most often by technical illustrators. An isometric view is easier to draw than a perspective view. Also, the results are more realistic than oblique drawings.

Isometric Drawing

Isometric drawings are made with the use of three axes. An axis can be thought of as a center line or a line of reference. Each axis represents one of the three primary directions in which lines of an object are to be drawn. These are:

1. Vertical axis lines.
2. Horizontal axis lines to the left.
3. Horizontal axis lines to the right.

Isometric ellipses are drawn on any of the three isometric planes. These planes are (1) horizontal, (2) left vertical, and (3) right vertical.

ISOMETRIC PLANES

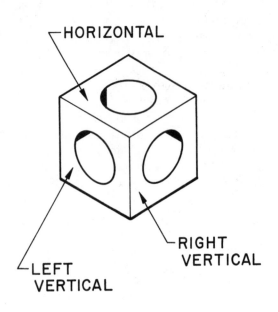

HORIZONTAL

LEFT VERTICAL

RIGHT VERTICAL

In the following pictorial drawing of a sand block, the normally horizontal lines are drawn at 30° angles above the horizontal to form three isometric angles of 120° each.

ISOMETRIC ANGLES

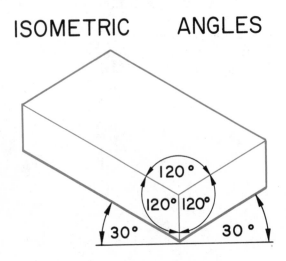

120°

120° 120°

30° 30°

All lines parallel to an isometric axis are full, actual dimensions. See the ISOMETRIC MEASUREMENTS illustration.

ISOMETRIC MEASUREMENTS

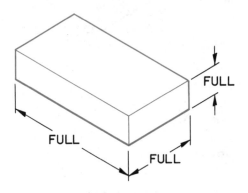

FULL

FULL

FULL

The length of a line which is not drawn parallel to an isometric axis is determined by projecting each of the two points at the ends of the line from the isometric axis as shown in the NONISOMETRIC MEASUREMENTS illustration.

NONISOMETRIC MEASUREMENTS

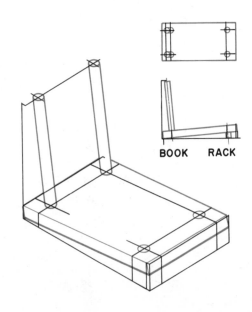

BOOK RACK

Angles are also drawn by locating their end points. Measurements are made on the isometric axis and then projected to locate the points of angle construction.

ANGLES   IN   ISOMETRIC

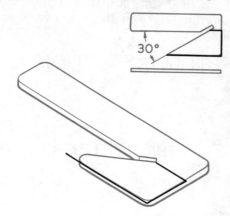

Circles and arcs are made with isometric ellipse templates or with a compass. The isometric ellipse template is much faster to use than a compass. Satisfactory ellipses can be drawn with a compass as shown below.

ISOMETRIC   CIRCLES
COMPASS

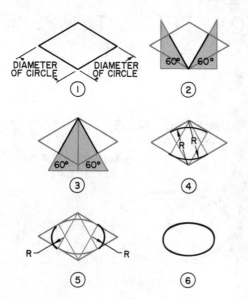

Ellipse Templates

Ellipse templates are made in many shapes and sizes. To use them correctly, some basic information should be understood. Ellipses are made at many angles for various positions. A few ellipse angles are shown.

ELLIPSE   ANGLES

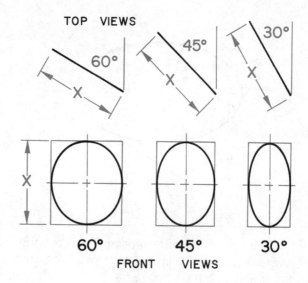

Isometric Ellipse Template

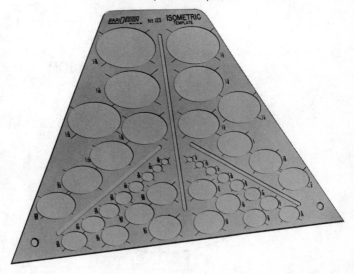

The isometric ellipses on a template are made at an angle that is correct for aligning and drawing ellipses on the isometric planes of drawings.

ISOMETRIC ELLIPSE SIZE

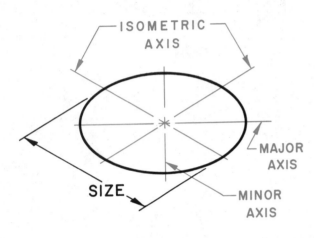

Isometric ellipses are measured across the isometric axis. All ellipses have two axes, the *minor* axis and the *major* axis.

MINOR AND MAJOR AXIS

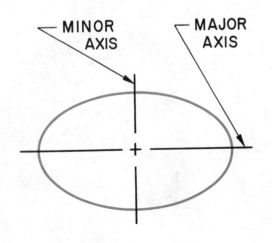

The *thrust line* and the minor axis of the ellipse template are important considerations in positioning an ellipse template for drawing. In isometric views, the *thrust line is the same as the center line* used in orthographic projections. The center line for orthographic projections and the thrust line for isometric views runs the length of either a hole or cylinder.

THRUST LINE

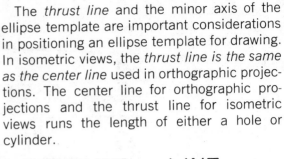

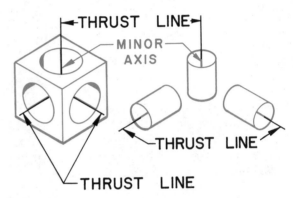

In drawing ellipses, the minor axis of the template should always be aligned with the thrust line. The isometric axes are used to locate the ellipse on the drawing.

ISOMETRIC TEMPLATE ALIGNMENT

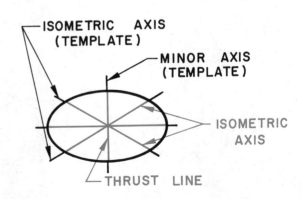

Irregular curves are developed in isometric drawing by following this procedure.

1. *Place a grid* over the orthographic projection view of the irregular curved line.
2. *Draw a scale isometric grid* in the correct position.
3. *Index both grids* with letters, and number respectively, as shown in the example.
4. *Follow the pattern* shown by the irregular curved line in the orthographic projection grid and draw the desired line in the isometric grid.

ISOMETRIC IRREGULAR CURVES

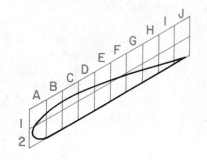

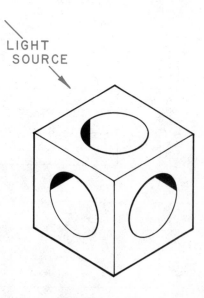

Line Width

The lines used in pictorial drawing should be of three *slightly* different widths as shown in this example. This is a conventional practice used in pictorial drawing. This practice is used to give the illusion of the third dimension (depth) in the drawing. The difference in line width should be very slight so the inexperienced observer does not see the difference in line width. However, the object should appear three-dimensional.

Shadows

The normal source of light in pictorial drawing should come from the upper left-hand side. Usually, small shadows are shown in the left or top of the holes, depending upon the plane where the ellipse appears. The shadow should extend about $\frac{1}{6}$ the distance across the major axis of the ellipse which indicates the hole. This is a conventional practice.

PICTORIAL SHADOWS

PICTORIAL LINE WIDTHS

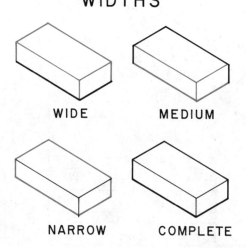

WIDE   MEDIUM

NARROW   COMPLETE

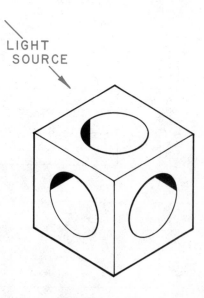

LIGHT SOURCE

Making Isometric Drawings

The following diagrams show a *step-by-step procedure* for making pictorial drawings of the isometric type.

These procedures can be practiced by using any orthographic projection problems and making isometric drawings of those parts.

Isometric Drawing Procedure

Study the orthographic projection drawing of the SANDING BLOCK to become familiar with the views, the dimensions, and the shape of the object. Now look at the step-by-step procedure for drawing isometrically as it is shown on the right-hand page. Follow the step-by-step procedure and draw the object in Problem 59 at full scale on an "A" size sheet of paper.

Step One:
Locate the position of the vertical axis 6½" from the left border and 3" from the bottom border. After this point is located, draw the vertical, the 30° right horizontal, and the 30° left horizontal axes. This completes the basic layout.

Step Two:
Measure and mark the length, width, and thickness of the object on these axes.

Step Three:
Darken the layout lines to the correct dimension of the object size. Draw vertical layout lines from the end of the horizontal axes.

Step Four:
Draw layout lines from the top of the vertical axes to form the top of the sanding block.

Step Five:
Draw wide, dark object lines of the object. The different line widths may be used to make the object appear to be three-dimensional. Draw the list of material and title block. Add guidelines for drawing notes.

Step Six:
Label the drawing. Check and correct the drawing.

You should understand the pictorial drawing procedure now. Select and draw pictorials for Problems 60, 61 and 62. Study the illustrations carefully.

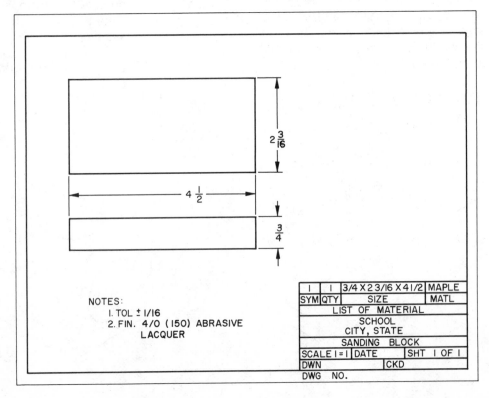

NOTES:
1. TOL ± 1/16
2. FIN. 4/0 (150) ABRASIVE
   LACQUER

I	I	3/4 X 2 3/16 X 4 1/2	MAPLE
SYM	QTY	SIZE	MATL
		LIST OF MATERIAL	
		SCHOOL	
		CITY, STATE	
		SANDING BLOCK	
SCALE I = I	DATE		SHT I OF I
DWN		CKD	
DWG	NO.		

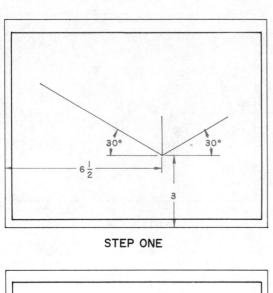

STEP ONE

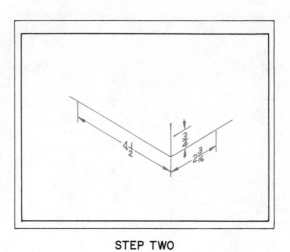

STEP TWO

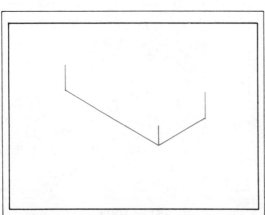

STEP THREE

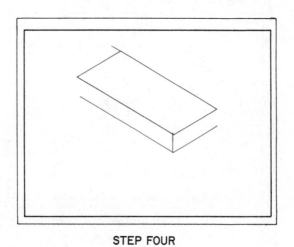

STEP FOUR

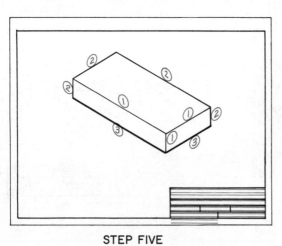

STEP FIVE

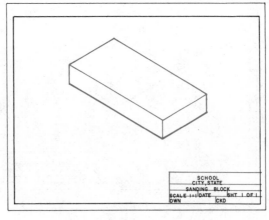

STEP SIX

Problem 60
Door Stop

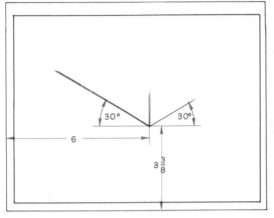

STEP ONE

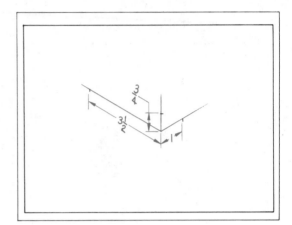

STEP TWO

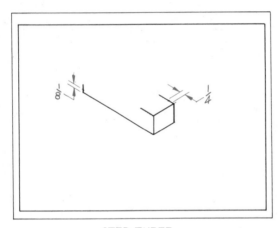

STEP THREE

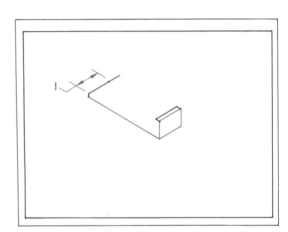

STEP FOUR

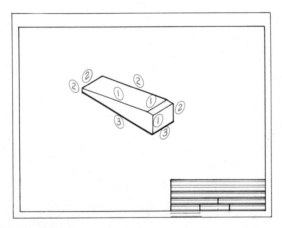

STEP FIVE

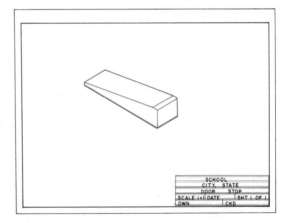

STEP SIX

Problem 61
Mallet Head

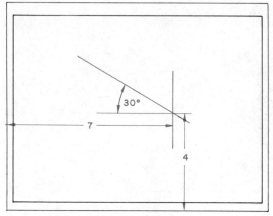

STEP ONE

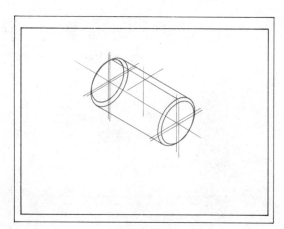

STEP TWO

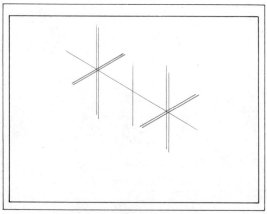

STEP THREE

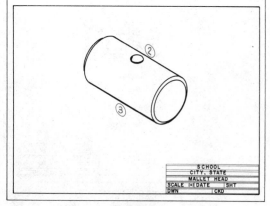

STEP FOUR

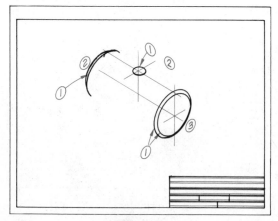

STEP FIVE

STEP SIX

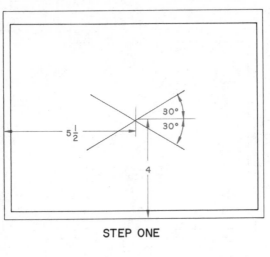

STEP ONE

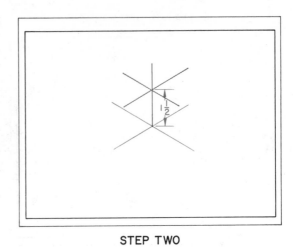

STEP TWO

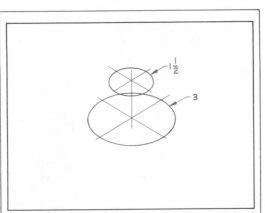

STEP THREE

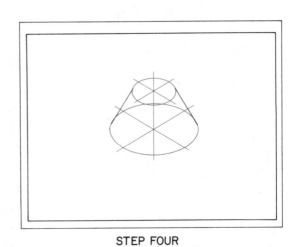

STEP FOUR

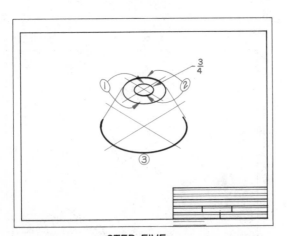

STEP FIVE

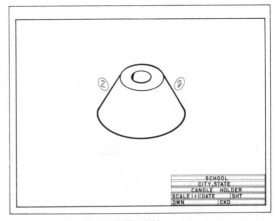

STEP SIX

Summary

You have studied the conventional practices and drawing techniques for making pictorial drawings. Isometric drawings are used frequently as a pictorial representation of an object. Isometric drawing is an easy method of drawing and has the appearance of a three-dimensional view.

8

Drawing Developments

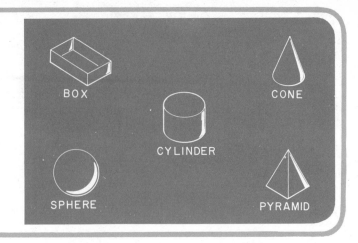

BOX   CONE

CYLINDER

SPHERE   PYRAMID

Why Study This Chapter?

DRAWING DEVELOPMENTS will explain how:

1. Drawing developments prove useful when you want to show how a flat piece of paper, metal, or plastic is folded, bent, or assembled to make a container.
2. The orthographic projection drawings relate to development drawings in describing products to be constructed in your other industrial arts classes.
3. Layout forms are developed for such objects as a file folder, envelope, box, cylinder, and cone.
4. Bends, folds, or assemblies are shown in drawings.

The information in this chapter will be helpful to you as you progress to drawing objects with increasingly more difficult shapes.

Developments are plans or patterns formed for products with sheet materials. Cartons, clothing, containers, storage cans, air ducts, tents, office furniture, and piping are examples of items made from sheet materials. The bodies of boats, automobiles, airplanes, spacecraft, and other vehicles are also formed with thin materials. Developments are also used in making chasses and enclosures for electronic equipment.

In planning the shapes for products made of sheet materials, there are two types of drawings used: (1) *orthographic projection* drawings and (2) *development* drawings. The development drawing indicates the shape and size the material is to be cut before the object is formed. Good design is essential when very strong, useful, lightweight, and economical shapes are developed for use with thin materials. On many products such as cans and cartons, the finishes can be applied to the article while it is still flat. Usually this is done on a printing or coating press.

Basic Shapes

The two types of surfaces developed with thin materials are the flat and the curved. Flat surfaces form folders, boxes, and pyramids. Curved surfaces are of two types, (1) the single curved (cylinders and cones) and (2) the double curved (spheres and irregular or free forms).

How to Draw Developments

These drawing projects are to be drawn in order to learn how sheet materials are developed into useful shapes. Envelopes, boxes, pyramids, cylinders and cones are basic shapes used for making many useful products. In some cases there are several ways these basic shapes can be drawn; however, the examples are the most useful. Each drawing may be done full size on drawing paper or card stock for use as a template or on the project material.

BASIC SHAPES OF SURFACE DEVELOPMENTS

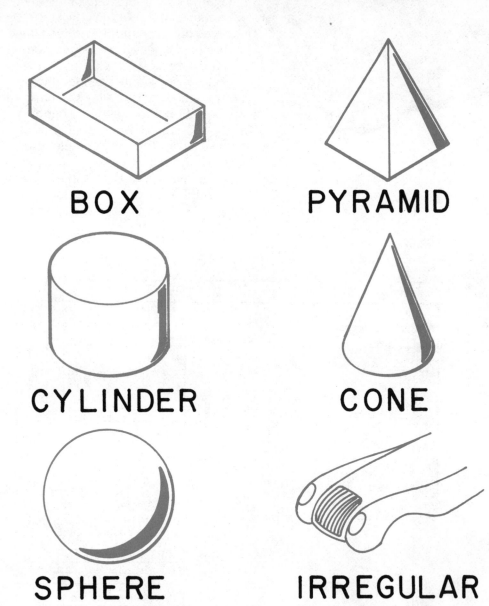

BOX

PYRAMID

CYLINDER

CONE

SPHERE

IRREGULAR

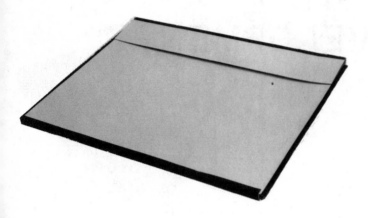

An envelope or folder is one of the easiest and most often used items to be drawn as a development. Each can be formed with one piece of material or by fastening several pieces together.

Study the photograph and orthographic projection of the DRAWING FOLDER. Use the plan as a source of information and draw the folder layout on heavy cardboard stock. Using one piece of stock will give you the experience of developing a full size development drawing. You may want to alter the basic dimensions (9″ × 11½″) to make a folder to hold "B" size or "C" size drawing sheets. This folder can be used to store your completed drawings. You may also individualize your folder by applying what you learned in Chapter 2, Drawing Freehand. The artwork on your folder should reflect your personal interest, such as your favorite hobby or sport.

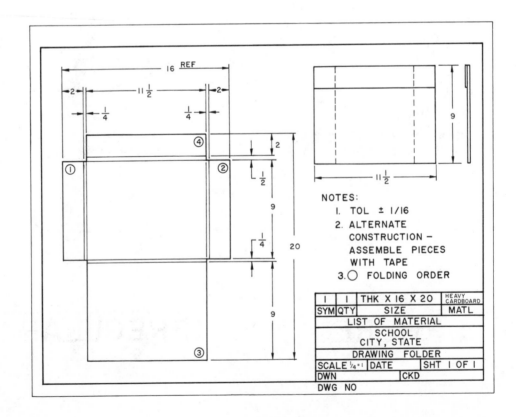

NOTES:
1. TOL ± 1/16
2. ALTERNATE CONSTRUCTION — ASSEMBLE PIECES WITH TAPE
3. ◯ FOLDING ORDER

		THK X 16 X 20	HEAVY CARDBOARD
SYM	QTY	SIZE	MATL
LIST OF MATERIAL			
SCHOOL CITY, STATE			
DRAWING FOLDER			
SCALE ¼"=1	DATE		SHT I OF I
DWN		CKD	
DWG NO			

Problem 64
Parts Tray

This tray is for storage of small parts such as nails, screws, bolts, etc. Similar trays may be designed for holding tools, cards, papers, or other items.

Draw the layout for the PARTS TRAY on thick paper or cardboard. Cut, fold, and tape this template to form the object. This method of checking the measurements and layout is an industrial practice to check accuracy. After the design and layout are approved, the template can be unfolded to a flat position and used to lay out the shape on sheet metal. This project can be made in your shop class.

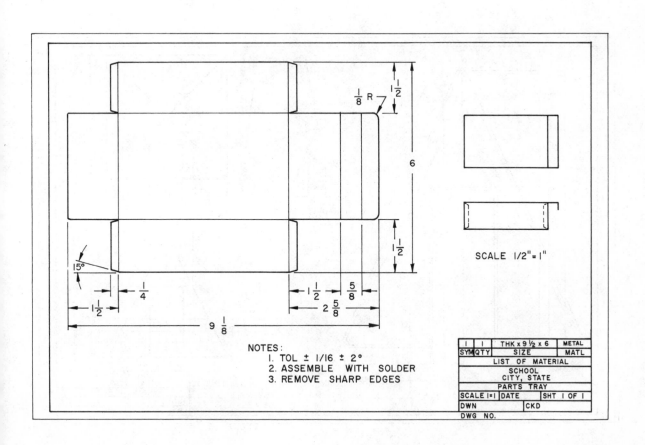

$\frac{1}{8}$ R

$1\frac{1}{2}$

6

$1\frac{1}{2}$

15°

$\frac{1}{4}$

$1\frac{1}{2}$

$1\frac{1}{2}$

$\frac{5}{8}$

$2\frac{5}{8}$

$9\frac{1}{8}$

SCALE 1/2" = 1"

NOTES:
1. TOL ± 1/16 ± 2°
2. ASSEMBLE WITH SOLDER
3. REMOVE SHARP EDGES

SYM	QTY	SIZE	MATL
I	I	THK x 9 ½ x 6	METAL

LIST OF MATERIAL

SCHOOL
CITY, STATE

PARTS TRAY

SCALE I=I	DATE		SHT I OF I
DWN		CKD	

DWG NO.

Problem 65
Pyramid

This PYRAMID TENT design is a good example for you to study and then draw. You should have a better understanding of the procedure for making a development drawing if you can do this drawing as explained below. The example drawing uses three different scales to illustrate the development

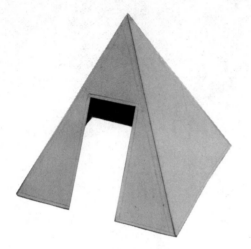

drawing for the tent. The ¼" = 1'-0", ½" = 1'-0", and 1" = 1'-0" scales are required so the drawing will fit on the paper.

As you can observe, the basic size of the tent is 7' wide × 7' deep × 7' high. The door is 2' × 4' and it is located 2'-6" from the corners.

The color overlay shows the profile layout The base of the triangle remains 7' square, but the height of 7' actually requires 7'-10". Also, this layout shows that the tent door height must be 4'-6" if the erected height is expected to be 4'-0". The ¼" = 1'-0" layout shows the complete development. Study this drawing and prepare to make a similar development.

Use a "B" size sheet to lay out a pyramid development. Use the following dimensions:
Base = 6'-0" × 6'-0"
Height = 6'-0"
Door = 1'-6" wide × 3'-6" high

Remember to do a layout for finding the true line lengths.

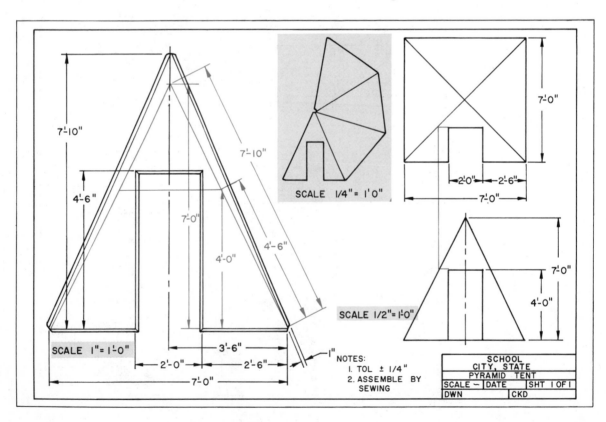

246

Cylinders are used in making pipes, cans, and other useful containers. This plan is for a cylinder in which game balls can be stored. The basic design can be adapted to any size ball.

Select the type of BALL HOLDER that you would like to make and draw a full scale lay-out on heavy paper or cardboard. After your drawing has been completed, cut out, roll, and tape the template into shape and check the clearance with a ball. If this template is func-tional, you can make the ball holder with sheet metal in your workshop.

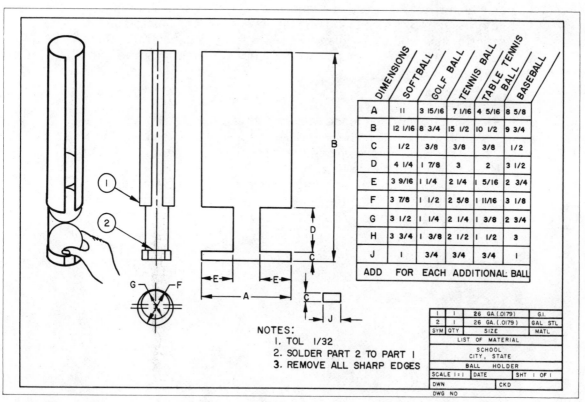

DIMENSIONS	SOFTBALL	GOLF BALL	TENNIS BALL	TABLE TENNIS BALL	BASEBALL
A	11	3 15/16	7 1/16	4 5/16	8 5/8
B	12 1/16	8 3/4	15 1/2	10 1/2	9 3/4
C	1/2	3/8	3/8	3/8	1/2
D	4 1/4	1 7/8	3	2	3 1/2
E	3 9/16	1 1/4	2 1/4	1 5/16	2 3/4
F	3 7/8	1 1/2	2 5/8	1 11/16	3 1/8
G	3 1/2	1 1/4	2 1/4	1 3/8	2 3/4
H	3 3/4	1 3/8	2 1/2	1 1/2	3
J	1	3/4	3/4	3/4	1
ADD	FOR	EACH	ADDITIONAL	BALL	

NOTES:
1. TOL 1/32
2. SOLDER PART 2 TO PART 1
3. REMOVE ALL SHARP EDGES

1	1	26 GA. (.0179)	G.I.
2	1	26 GA. (.0179)	GAL STL
SYM	QTY	SIZE	MATL

LIST OF MATERIAL

SCHOOL
CITY, STATE

BALL HOLDER

SCALE 1:1	DATE		SHT 1 OF 1
DWN		CKD	
DWG NO			

Party hats, birdhouse roofs, and some food containers are in the shape of cones. The dimensions of this roof for a tin can birdhouse may be changed to suit any size can.

Study the example orthographic drawing of the BIRD HOUSE. Part 2 is a tin can Part 1 (the roof) was designed to fit Part 2. The cone shape of Part 1 is a full scale development drawing in the left half of the example.

Step One:
The 7″ diameter illustrated in color represents the desired base diameter of the cone. After the 7″ diameter has been drawn, a pair of dividers (set at approximately ½″ space) is used to locate the division of the circumference. In this example, 46 divisions (45 marks) have been located. (When you make this drawing, you may have a few more or less divisions.) This number of divisions represents the total circumference of the desired (when finished) cone base.

Step Two:
Now observe that the slanted surface of the roof has a length of 4⅛″. This dimension represents the radius of the layout circle. The center of the 7″ diameter circle was used to draw the circle with a diameter of 8¼″. The same divider setting was used to transfer the 46 divisions (45 marks) to the 8¼″ diameter. The divisions end on the major portion of the 8¼″ diameter circle and a section of the circle remains unused. This section will be cut out of the layout to form the cone.

Step Three:
A ¼″ flap was added to the section between the first mark and the forty-sixth mark. This is the solder flap for a sheet metal cone.

You can make this development on a "B" size sheet of drawing paper. Select a tin can for Part 2.

Make the development drawing and cut out the template. Tape the cone together and fit it to the tin can. If the cone development is correct, you can construct this project in a workshop.

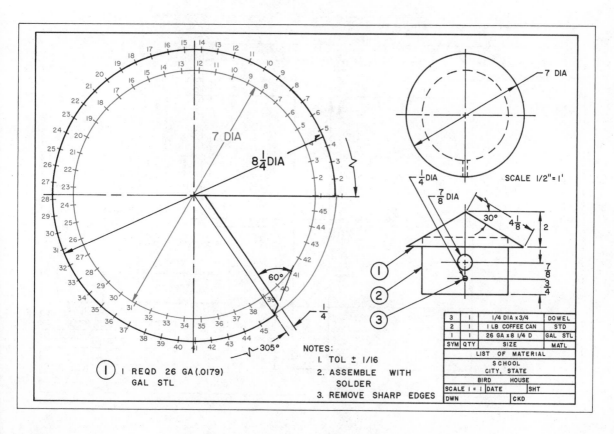

7 DIA

8¼ DIA

60°

305°

¼

1 REQD 26 GA (.0179)
GAL STL

7 DIA

SCALE 1/2"= 1'

¼ DIA

⅞ DIA

30°   4⅛

2

⅞

¾

① ② ③

NOTES:
1. TOL ± 1/16
2. ASSEMBLE WITH
   SOLDER
3. REMOVE SHARP EDGES

3	1	1/4 DIA x 3/4	DOWEL
2	1	1 LB COFFEE CAN	STD
1	1	26 GA x 8 1/4 D	GAL STL
SYM	QTY	SIZE	MATL

LIST OF MATERIAL

S C H O O L
CITY, STATE

BIRD   HOUSE

| SCALE 1 = 1 | DATE | | SHT |
| DWN | | CKD | |

249

This is a TRUNCATED (cut off at an angle) BOX for holding 3″ × 5″ index file cards. It is similar to the PARTS TRAY but it has a slanted top. The slanted surface is produced with the 1¾″ and the 3½″ height dimensions. The 7¾″ and 10¾″ REF (reference) dimensions represent the overall stock size needed for construction.

Make a template layout on heavy paper or cardboard. After the template layout is finished, cut and tape it to check dimensions. The finished template can be used when laying out the project on sheet steel.

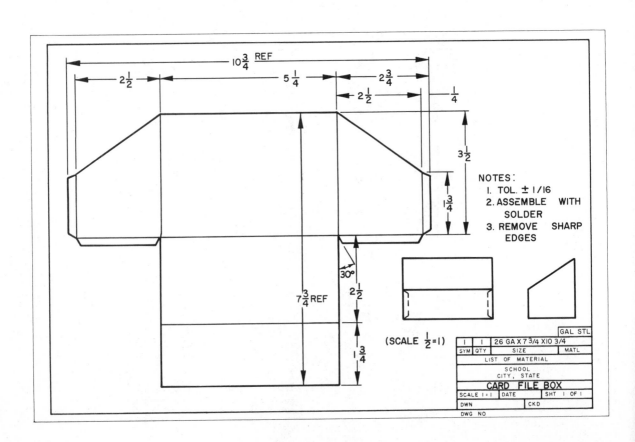

NOTES:
1. TOL. ± 1/16
2. ASSEMBLE WITH SOLDER
3. REMOVE SHARP EDGES

(SCALE ½ = 1)

		GAL STL
	26 GA X 7 3/4 X 10 3/4	
SYM	QTY	SIZE	MATL

LIST OF MATERIAL

SCHOOL
CITY, STATE

CARD FILE BOX

SCALE 1 = 1	DATE		SHT 1 OF 1
DWN		CKD	
DWG NO			

Funnels, parts of rockets, and pipe reducers are products using a section of cone. The part remaining when a cone has been cut off square to the center line of the cone is called a *frustum*. This plan for a model spacecraft shows how to develop a FRUSTUM OF A CONE.

Use a "B" size sheet and develop the frustum (Part 2) for the MODEL APOLLO. The base diameter for the frustum is 5¼".

Step One:

Draw a 5¼" diameter circle and divide it into several parts. The example was divided into 34 divisions (by the 33 marks).

Step Two:

Where the cone intersects the center line to the base of the frustum is 4⅝". Use the center of the 5¼" diameter circle and draw another circle with a radius of 4⅝".

Step Three:

Use the dividers (set at the same space per division) and transfer the divisions to the circle drawn in Step Two.

Step Four:

Set a compass at 3½" and locate the point on the circumference of the circle with a radius of 4⅝". Make an arc toward the original center of the circles to locate the top edge of the frustum. Now set the compass in the original center and adjust it to touch the arc. At this setting, scribe the circle to complete top edge of the frustum. Add the ¼" flap and cut out the template.

You can also use this procedure to make a megaphone or a funnel.

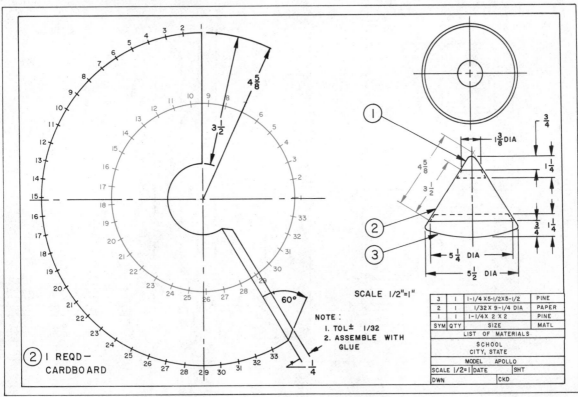

PERISCOPES are used for looking over or around objects. This design uses a box shape made of heavy cardboard. You may want to buy two standard mirrors at a variety store and develop your own design to suit the mirrors.

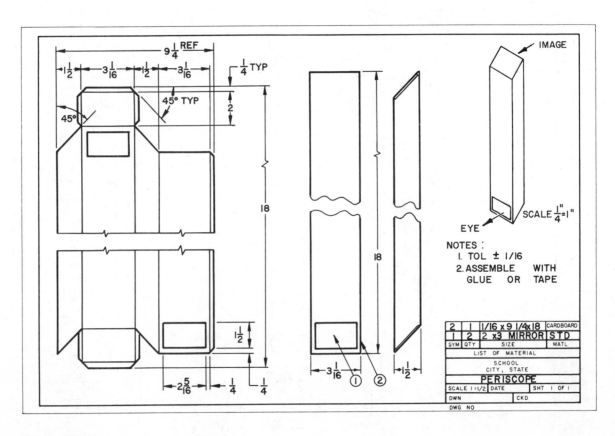

$9\frac{1}{4}$ REF

$1\frac{1}{2}$ $3\frac{1}{16}$ $1\frac{1}{2}$ $3\frac{1}{16}$

$\frac{1}{4}$ TYP

45° TYP

45°

2

18

18

$1\frac{1}{2}$

$2\frac{5}{16}$ $\frac{1}{4}$ $\frac{1}{4}$

$3\frac{1}{16}$ ① ② $1\frac{1}{2}$

IMAGE

SCALE $\frac{1}{4}'' = 1''$

EYE

NOTES :
1. TOL ± 1/16
2. ASSEMBLE WITH GLUE OR TAPE

SYM	QTY	SIZE	MATL
2	1	1/16 x 9 1/4x18	CARDBOARD
1	2	2 x3 MIRROR	STD

LIST OF MATERIAL

SCHOOL
CITY , STATE

PERISCOPE

SCALE 1=1/2	DATE		SHT 1 OF 1
DWN		CKD	
DWG NO			

Developments can also be drawn for making models of tents, rockets, and spacecraft as well as many useful boxes, containers, and trays for holding tools and supplies.

Summary

You should be able to make development drawings for simple, useful objects after drawing and studying this chapter. These techniques can be used in various combinations to develop surfaces for complex objects. Surfaces can be developed with freehand drawing, mechanical drawing, or by using grid paper. Remember that it is important to check and correct templates before cutting stock for product construction.

9

Drawing with Grids

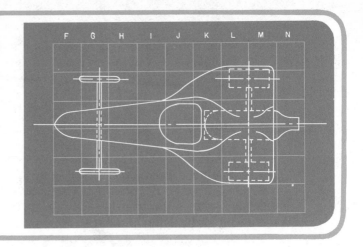

Why Study This Chapter?

DRAWING WITH GRIDS will explain how to:
1. Use the grid drawing method to make patterns or templates.
2. Draw irregularly shaped objects, such as animals, cars, and airplanes using grids.
3. Enlarge or reduce the size of an object on paper.

When you have learned how to use grid paper, you will be able to improve your skill at drawing curved and difficult shapes, such as model sailboats.

A grid is the pattern formed by a series of equally or proportionally spaced intersecting lines. The regular grid is a series of equal-sized squares running in horizontal and vertical columns. It is commonly called cross-sectioned paper, quadrille, or "squared" paper.

Some grids used in pictorial drawing and in making graphs are shown.

The use of grids reduces and sometimes eliminates the need for measuring tools in making some drawings. The grid may be drawn with drafting tools, or you may use commercially available grid paper.

Regular Grid

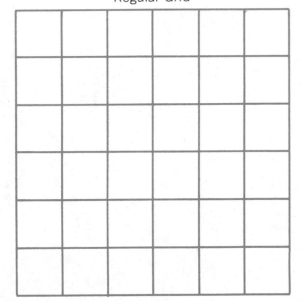

Isometric Grid

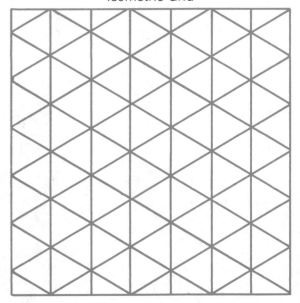

Grids are very useful for enlarging or reducing patterns and designs having curved lines. They are also helpful in making orthographic and pictorial mechanical drawings, charts, graphs, systems drawings, maps, and building plans.

Project patterns shown on grids are often printed in magazines and books. These include designs for ornamental projects of wood, metal, plastic, and paper as well as plans for model and full-size boats, airplanes, and cars. The use of a grid is very helpful in project planning.

Several ideas can be quickly drawn in a small size and the best design improved as desired. After selecting the best idea, a grid may be drawn over the design and the sketch enlarged to the required size. This practice is often used by artists in making large murals or sculptures.

Circular Grid

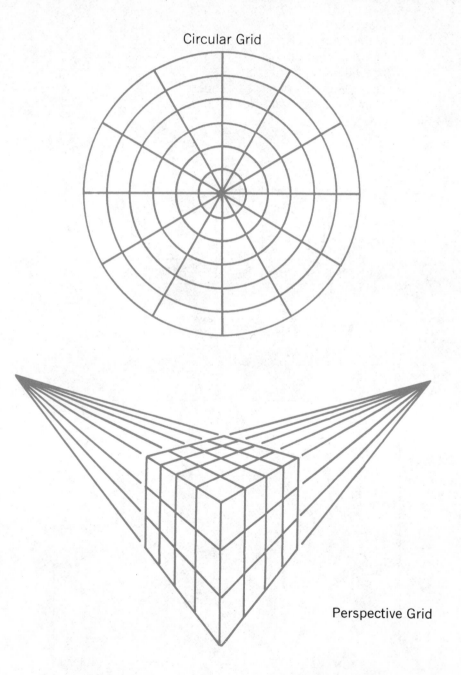

Perspective Grid

Drawing Procedure

With a little practice of the following procedure, very good results can be achieved in using grids to enlarge drawings.

1. Select the design pattern.
2. Determine the number of times the pattern will have to be increased to make the desired finished drawing. The plan for doubling the size of a pattern is shown below.
3. Prepare a grid for the finished drawing by making and indexing as explained in the following steps:
   a. Mark vertical spaces.
   b. Mark horizontal spaces.
   c. Draw light vertical lines.
   d. Draw light horizontal lines.
   e. Letter vertical columns of squares.
   f. Number horizontal columns of squares.

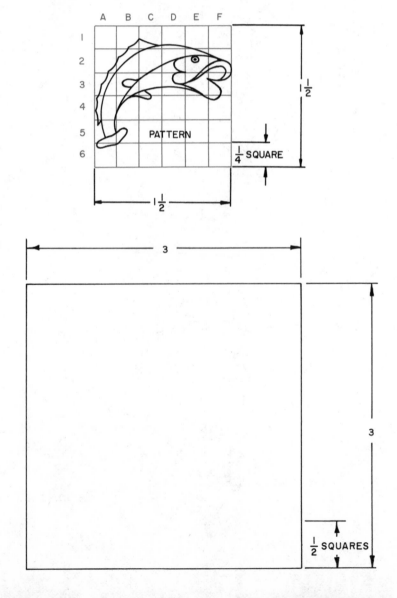

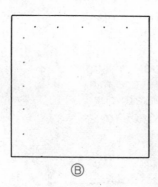
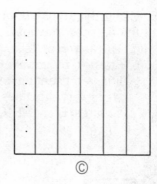

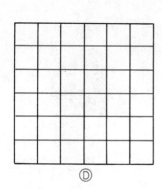
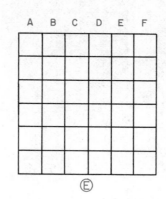
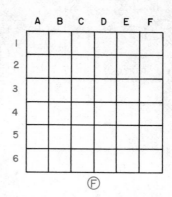

4. The actual-size grid will be as shown.

5. Using the steps shown below, complete the finished drawing.
   a. This is the pattern.
   b. Starting in square F-2, draw a light line representing the top of the fish. Using very light lines, continue through squares E-2, D-1, C-1, C-2, B-2, A-3, etc., to complete the drawing as shown in *Steps* B, C, and D.
   c. Check and correct the drawing until it is accurate.
   d. With an irregular curve and pencil, darken the lines as shown is step E.

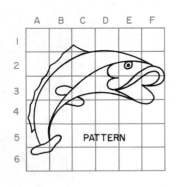

PATTERN

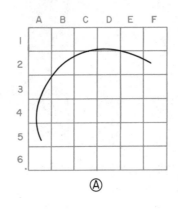

Ⓐ

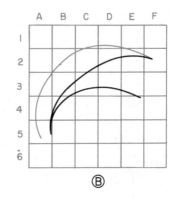

Ⓑ

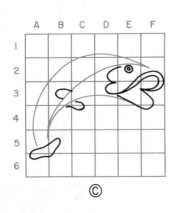

Ⓒ

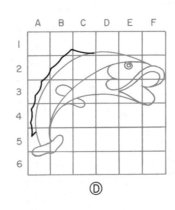

Ⓓ

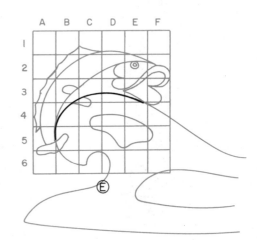

Ⓔ

Practice Grid Drawing

The following patterns may be enlarged to any size for making such projects as wood or plastic carvings, cutting boards, profile view of an object, wire sculpture, wall hangings, lawn ornaments, and models. Graphic artwork, crafts, and other projects can also be enlarged. One or more projects should be completed from each of the Groups 1, 2, and 3 to develop your ability to draw with grids. See pages 259–266.

Additional projects can be drawn by using pictures from newspapers, magazines, and books. By drawing squares on tracing paper and placing them over the pattern, you can avoid damaging the original picture. Drawing large squares will help you make the drawing faster.

Problem 71
Group 1 — Practice Grid Drawings

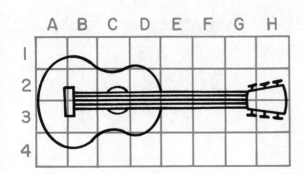

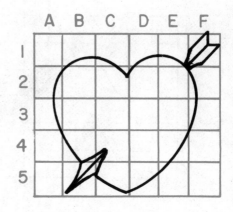

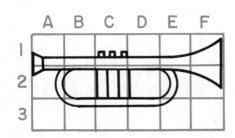

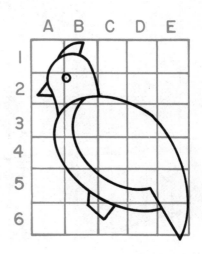

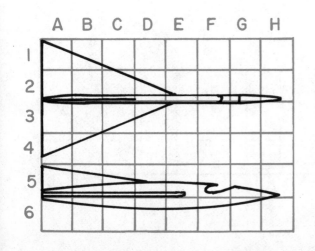

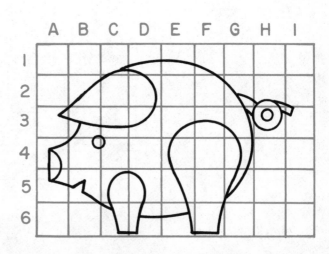

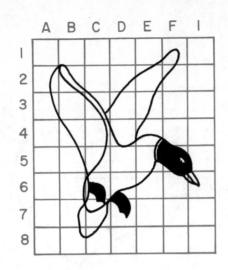

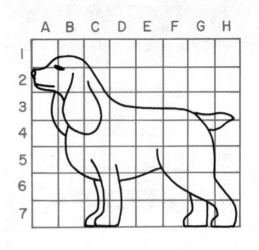

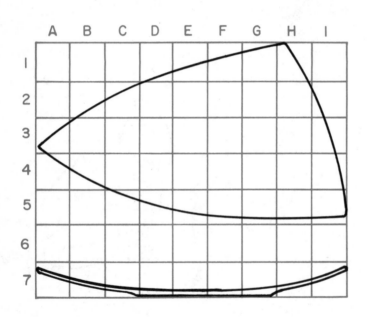

Tray

Bowl

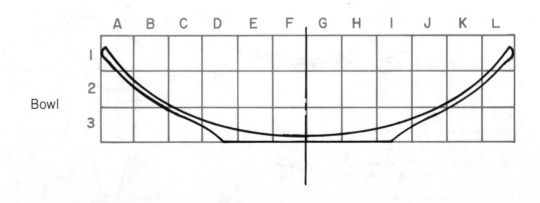

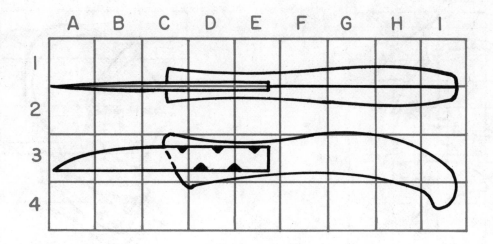

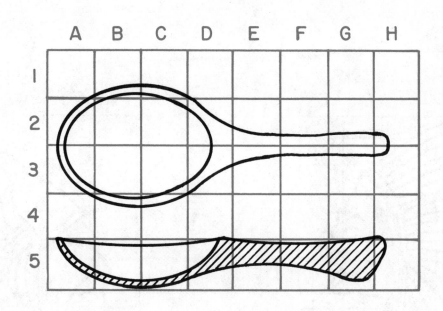

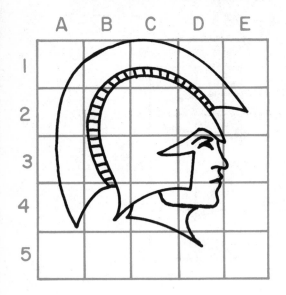

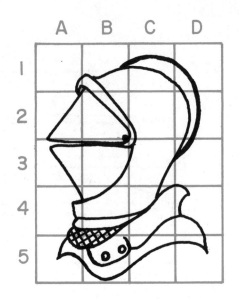

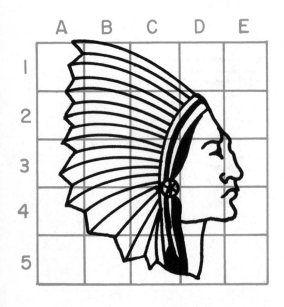

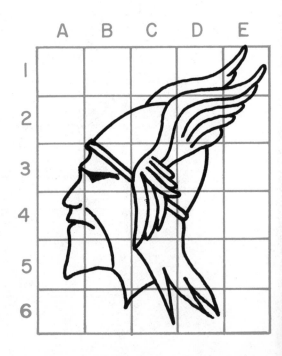

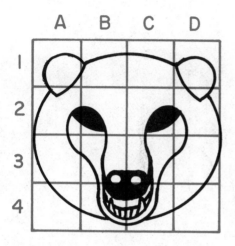

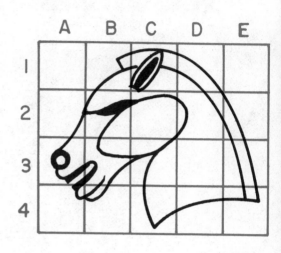

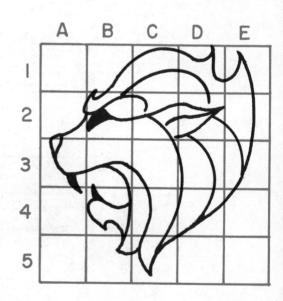

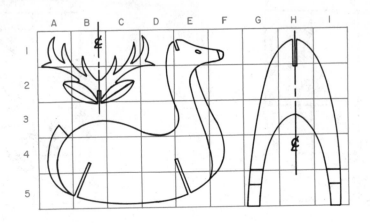

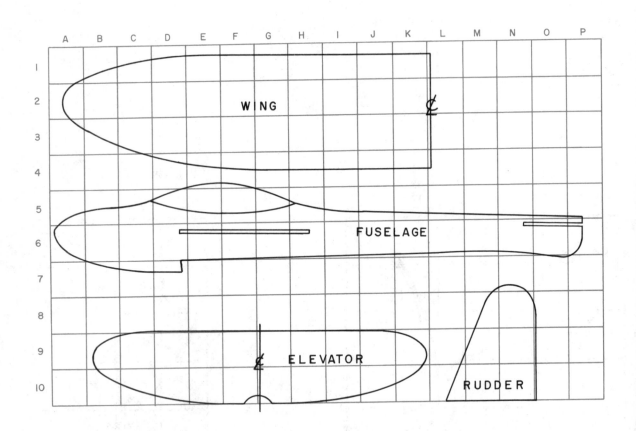

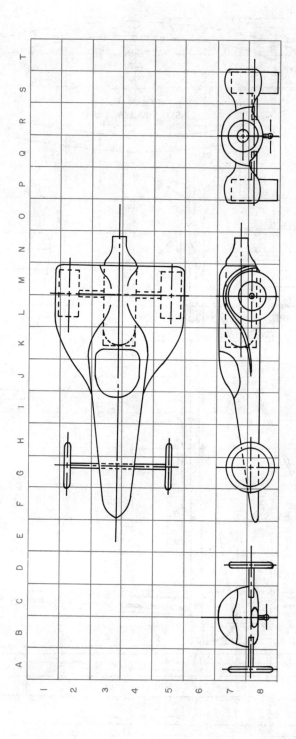

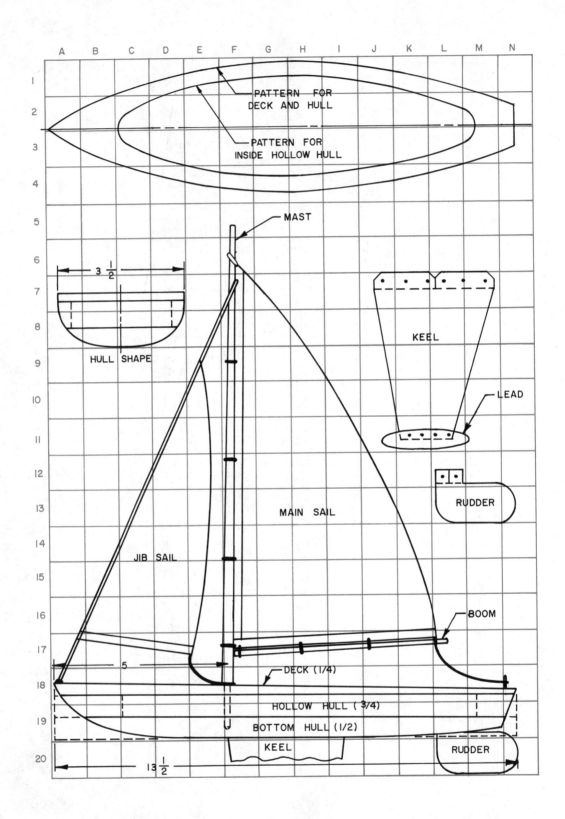

PATTERN FOR
DECK AND HULL

PATTERN FOR
INSIDE HOLLOW HULL

MAST

$3\frac{1}{2}$

HULL SHAPE

KEEL

LEAD

MAIN SAIL

JIB SAIL

RUDDER

BOOM

5

DECK (1/4)

HOLLOW HULL (3/4)

BOTTOM HULL (1/2)

KEEL

RUDDER

$13\frac{1}{2}$

Pantograph

A pantograph may be used for *reducing* or *enlarging* some types of drawings. By adjusting the pivot points on the arms, various size proportions can be selected. The location of the pencil or pointer can be reversed when you want to change from enlarging to reducing.

Summary

You have learned how to draw and index a grid for enlarging or reducing the size of irregular shaped objects. You have also learned how to use an irregular or "French" curve. By practicing the technique of indexing the grid, you have learned to locate points quickly and accurately within a grid system. In addition to learning a new drawing technique, you have developed several project drawings that you can make in your industrial arts classes.

10

Drawing a Building

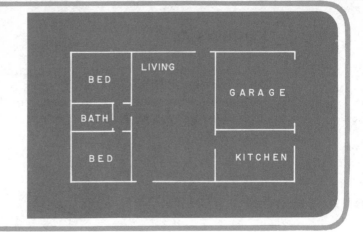

Why Study This Chapter?

DRAWING A BUILDING will show you how to:
1. Plan floor layouts for buildings, including the placement of walls, windows, doors, and furniture.
2. Plan floor layouts that meet your needs.
3. Communicate with an architect.
4. Use scale models (two-dimensional cutouts) to show the location of furniture and equipment on a floor plan.
5. Read an architect's scale.
6. Dimension architectural plans.

The information in this chapter will prove useful to you throughout your life as you plan places where you will live and work.

Buildings are structures such as houses, factories, offices, and stores. Buildings are made of wood, stone, concrete, metal, plastic, and glass. They offer shelter or protection from undesirable elements. The drawing of building plans is called *architectural drafting*. Draftsmen, known as architectural draftsmen, design and draw building plans. See page 269.

Shelter is one of the primary needs of people. People spend much of their money for buildings and live most of their lives in them. Because buildings last for a long time and are very important to people, they should be well planned.

When planning a building, many factors must be considered, such as weather, location, utilities, cost, and use. Of these, the use or function of the building is the most important factor.

A clear understanding of how a building will be used is the first step in good planning. The purpose and function of the building should be outlined before a floor plan is developed. Some of the considerations to be made in planning a building include:
1. *The people* who are to use the structure—the number, age, sex, interest, size, etc.
2. *The activities* such as working, playing, sleeping, eating, etc., that are to take place in the building.
3. *The equipment* needed by the people involved in the activities. Equipment may include tables, chairs, beds, television, cabinets, appliances, machines, etc.
4. *Future expansion* needs.
5. *The money* available for the building.

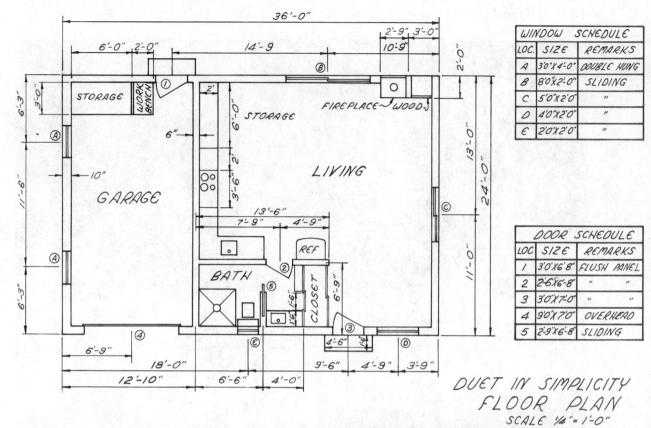

WINDOW SCHEDULE		
LOC.	SIZE	REMARKS
A	3'0"X4'-0"	DOUBLE HUNG
B	8'0"X2'-0"	SLIDING
C	5'0"X2'0"	"
D	4'0"X2'0"	"
E	2'0"X2'0"	"

DOOR SCHEDULE		
LOC	SIZE	REMARKS
1	3'0"X6'-8"	FLUSH PANEL
2	2'-6"X6'-8"	" "
3	3'0"X7'-0"	" "
4	9'0"X7'-0"	OVERHEAD
5	2'-9"X6'-8"	SLIDING

DUET IN SIMPLICITY
FLOOR PLAN
SCALE 1/4" = 1'-0"

Dimensions should be obtained for each item on the equipment list. The dimensions are found in catalogs and technical literature. By using these dimensions, scaled cutouts of the equipment can be made. Usually, two-dimensional cardboard cutouts showing the top view of each item are adequate for most building planning. There are well-prepared, three-dimensional kits available for planning houses, offices, stores, and factories.

A floor plan of a manufacturing plant layout is being developed in this example.

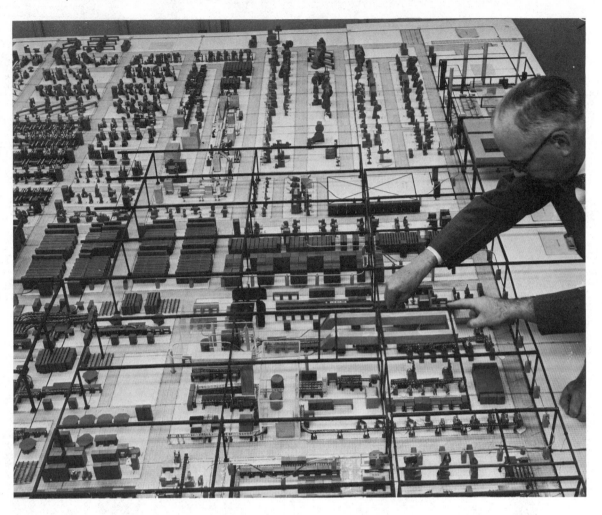

Basic Floor Plans

In a building plan, similar activities or equipment should be located in the same central area. In house planning, there are three basic activity areas. These basic areas are (1) *sleeping*, (2) *working*, and (3) *living*. The *sleeping area* normally includes bedrooms, bathrooms, and clothes and linen storage. *Working* areas are made up of the kitchen, laundry, and garage. The *living* area may include the living room, den, dining area, and family room. Each storage area is planned near the place of use within the activity area.

HOME FLOOR PLAN
ACTIVITY AREAS

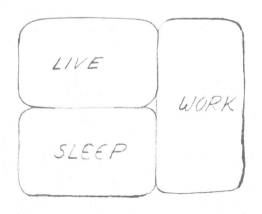

You should develop sketches of various arrangements for these general areas before working out the details of a building.

AREA   ARRANGEMENTS

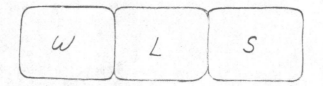

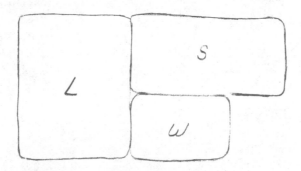

POOR BECAUSE PLUMBING AND RELATED ACTIVITIES OF WORKING AND SLEEPING AREAS (LAUNDRY, IRONING AND CHILD CARE) ARE WIDELY SEPARATED BY LIVING AREA.   LIVING AREA MAY EASILY BECOME A HEAVY TRAFFIC AREA.

GOOD FOR WORKING AND SLEEPING AREAS ARE NEXT TO EACH OTHER AND LIVING AREA WILL NOT NEED TO BECOME A HEAVY TRAFFIC AREA

Planning Considerations

Basic considerations for developing a building floor plan are the activity areas, traffic patterns, view lines of sight, and arrangement flexibility. A poorly planned living area may not be functional or attractive if the basic planning considerations are not analyzed.

Movement area is the space needed around equipment so it may easily be used. Using scale models of people is very helpful in planning enough area for their movement.

Traffic patterns are the paths along which people travel or where equipment is moved in a building. Generally, traffic patterns should be reduced both in distance and in number of

MOVEMENT   AREA

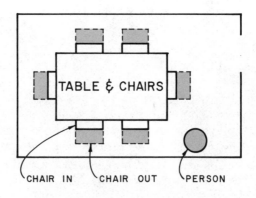

AREA TOO SMALL

routes. Traffic patterns are controlled by the location of equipment, walls and openings in walls. They are improved by placing "active," related equipment close together.

TRAFFIC PATTERN

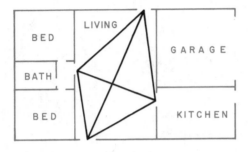

LIVING ROOM IS CUT UP WITH TRAFFIC PATTERN

VIEW LINES

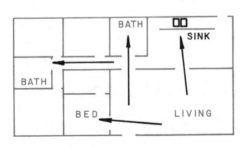

UNDESIRABLE VIEWS OF BEDROOM, BATH ROOMS AND SINK

To check traffic patterns, place a piece of tracing paper over the floor plan and draw lines between all "active" equipment and all wall openings. A very common traffic pattern problem is created when sleeping and working areas are separated by living areas.

View lines are lines of sight. They are controlled by the placement of walls, wall openings, and equipment. View lines are checked in the same manner as traffic patterns. Such view lines as landscape and fireplaces are desirable and may be designed into a plan. Undesirable view lines include views of bathrooms, kitchen sinks, and bedrooms.

Flexibility is the ability to rearrange the equipment or the floor plan of a room or building. In planning buildings, value is greatly increased when flexible arrangements are accommodated. The placement of equipment, utilities, walls, rooms, and openings, as well as possible room additions, all must be considered in planning for flexibility.

FLEXIBILITY

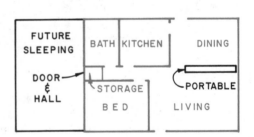

Layout Details

In developing details in a floor plan, the walls and equipment are placed into a variety of positions on the grid. When the desired arrangement has been decided, the scaled cutouts are fastened to the grid with glue or tape. Symbols are drawn for doors, windows, and electrical parts. Rooms are labeled according to function (kitchen, bath, bedroom, etc.) and sizes of each indicated (10' × 12', etc.). Sketches may be drawn or pictures obtained to show desired features (storage, entry, windows, furniture, etc.) for the building. These are placed around the plan or on other sheets of paper. This entire project becomes a package of ideas to be presented to an architect for further planning, page 273.

DUET IN SIMPLICITY

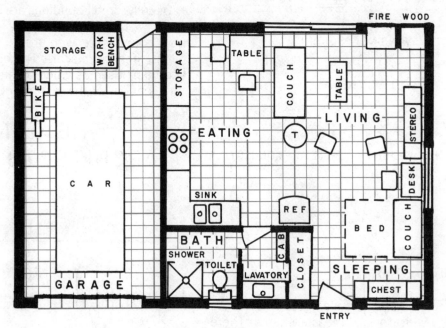

FIRE WOOD

STORAGE

WORK BENCH

BIKE

STORAGE

TABLE

COUCH

TABLE

LIVING

EATING

T

STEREO

CAR

DESK

SINK

REF

BED

COUCH

BATH

SHOWER

TOILET

CAB

CLOSET

LAVATORY

SLEEPING

GARAGE

CHEST

ENTRY

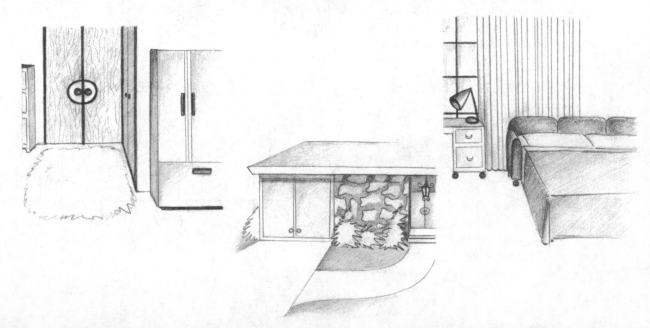

Use Symbols for Layout Plans

Many symbols are used in architectural drawing to represent various parts of a building. Some common symbols used in planning buildings are shown below.

ARCHITECTURAL SYMBOLS

STRUCTURAL

WALL   DOORS   WINDOW
SWINGING SLIDING

ELECTRICAL

SWITCH   LIGHT   OUTLET   CONNECTING SWITCH & LIGHT

Architect's Triangular Scale

Usually, small buildings are drawn to a scale of ¼″ = 1′0″. The following diagrams show how to measure with the ¼″ = 1′0″ portion of the architect's scale. The colored numbers should be used as guide points in memorizing the locations of the inch marks.

READING ARCHITECTS SCALE

Measuring Length

In drawing plans for buildings, an architect's scale is used to make measurements. There are two styles of architect's scales: (1) the flat and (2) the triangular. The flat scale is easier to use and the triangular scale costs less.

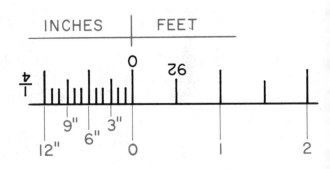

Architect's Flat Scale

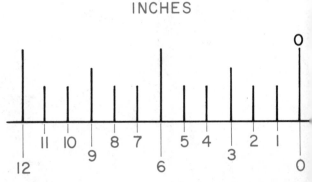

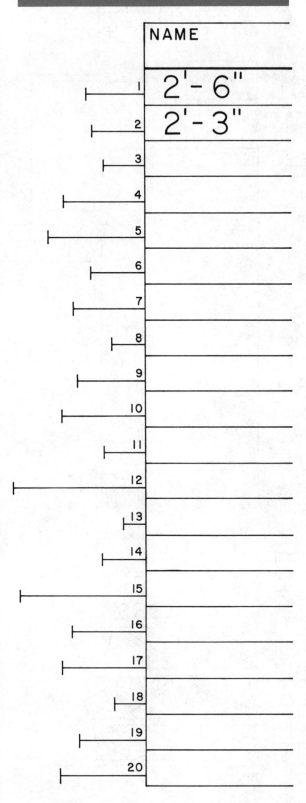

NAME

2'- 6"

2'- 3"

1
2
3
4
5
6
7
8
9
10
11
12
13
14
15
16
17
18
19
20

You should practice reading all the architectural scales. It may be helpful to check the answers for the first two measurements on the illustration.

After you have learned to read the architect's scale, practice measuring the following diagram. Measure the distance between the vertical lines and record the answers on the edge of a piece of lined writing paper. Use the ¼" = 1'-0" portion of your scale.

Use Scale Cutouts for Layout Plans

The scale used for making models of equipment varies with the designer's needs. Normally, a scale of ¼" = 1'-0" will work very well. The next two pages are examples of equipment used in planning houses, shops, offices, and stores. The examples are scaled to ¼" = 1'-0".

The scale of the models must be identical to the grid scale on the paper (¼" = 1'-0"). Walls of the structure are represented by strips of colored adhesive shelf paper or common colored paper which is cut to the width of the walls.

Inside walls are 6" and outside walls are usually 12". Therefore, when the scale of ¼" = 1'-0" is used, the inside walls become ⅛" and the outside wall becomes ¼".

HOME PLANNING CUTOUTS

SERVICING
SCALE 1/4" = 1'-0"

KITCHEN

| WASHER | DRYER | REFRIGERATOR | FREEZER | RANGE |

SOFT WATER

BUFFET DESK

TABLE AND CHAIRS

HOT WATER

SINGLE SINK DOUBLE SINK

STOVE TOP OVEN

BATH

TOILET TOILET LAVATORY SHOWER

LAVATORY

BATHINETTE

TUB

BATH

GARAGE

LARGE

MEDIUM

SMALL

CAR

MOWER

BICYCLE

WORK BENCH

LIVING

COUCH

ARM CHAIR ARM CHAIR ARM CHAIR

CORNER TABLE LOW TABLE LOW TABLE COFFEE TABLE TELEVISION

STEREO FLOOR LAMP FLOOR LAMP

ROCKER FIREPLACE FIREPLACE BOOKS

SIDE CHAIR SIDE CHAIR SIDE CHAIR PIANO DESK

SLEEPING

JUNIOR BED SINGLE BED SINGLE BED DOUBLE BED

CHAIR

CHAIR

CHAIR

QUEEN BED CRIB CHEST OF DRAWERS CHEST OF DRAWERS

CHAIR

SEWING MACHINE CHEST OF DRAWERS

NIGHT STAND NIGHT STAND NIGHT STAND

BOOKS

DOUBLE DRESSER MAKE UP TABLE

DOORS

3'-0"	2'-9"	2'-6"
3'-0"	2'-9"	2'-6"
3'-0"	2'-9"	2'-6"
3'-0"	2'-9"	2'-6"
2'-6"	2'-3"	2'-0"
2'-6"	2'-3"	2'-0"
2'-6"	2'-3"	PERSON	PERSON
2'-6"	2'-3"		

CLOSETS, CABINETS, OR STORAGE

BUILDING PLANNING CUTOUTS

SCALE 1/4" = 1'-0"

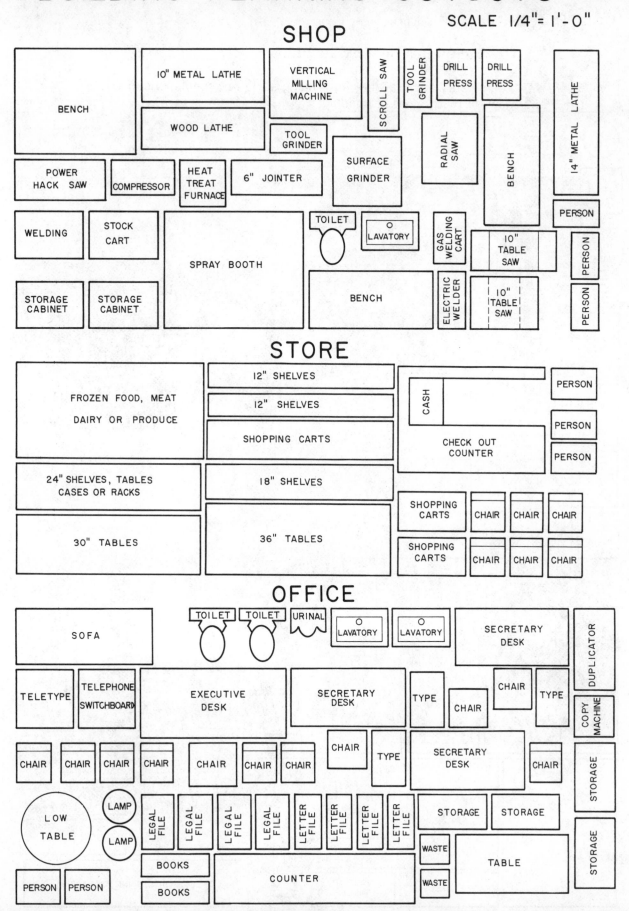

SHOP

BENCH · 10" METAL LATHE · WOOD LATHE · VERTICAL MILLING MACHINE · SCROLL SAW · TOOL GRINDER · DRILL PRESS · DRILL PRESS · 14" METAL LATHE · TOOL GRINDER · RADIAL SAW · BENCH · POWER HACK SAW · COMPRESSOR · HEAT TREAT FURNACE · 6" JOINTER · SURFACE GRINDER · PERSON · WELDING · STOCK CART · SPRAY BOOTH · TOILET · LAVATORY · GAS WELDING CART · 10" TABLE SAW · PERSON · PERSON · STORAGE CABINET · STORAGE CABINET · BENCH · ELECTRIC WELDER · 10" TABLE SAW · PERSON

STORE

FROZEN FOOD, MEAT DAIRY OR PRODUCE · 12" SHELVES · 12" SHELVES · SHOPPING CARTS · CASH · CHECK OUT COUNTER · PERSON · PERSON · PERSON · 24" SHELVES, TABLES CASES OR RACKS · 18" SHELVES · 30" TABLES · 36" TABLES · SHOPPING CARTS · CHAIR · CHAIR · CHAIR · SHOPPING CARTS · CHAIR · CHAIR · CHAIR

OFFICE

SOFA · TOILET · TOILET · URINAL · LAVATORY · LAVATORY · SECRETARY DESK · DUPLICATOR · TELETYPE · TELEPHONE SWITCHBOARD · EXECUTIVE DESK · SECRETARY DESK · TYPE · CHAIR · TYPE · CHAIR · COPY MACHINE · CHAIR · TYPE · SECRETARY DESK · CHAIR · CHAIR · CHAIR · CHAIR · CHAIR · CHAIR · CHAIR · CHAIR · TYPE · STORAGE · LOW TABLE · LAMP · LEGAL FILE · LEGAL FILE · LEGAL FILE · LEGAL FILE · LETTER FILE · LETTER FILE · LETTER FILE · LETTER FILE · STORAGE · STORAGE · STORAGE · LAMP · WASTE · BOOKS · COUNTER · WASTE · TABLE · PERSON · PERSON · BOOKS

Use Templates for Layout Plans

Templates are available for making scale representations of equipment for many types of buildings.

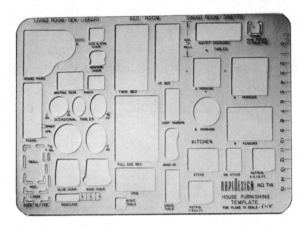

Home Template

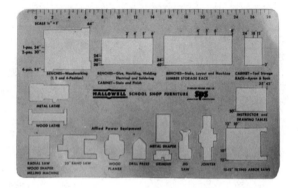

Shop Template

Store Template

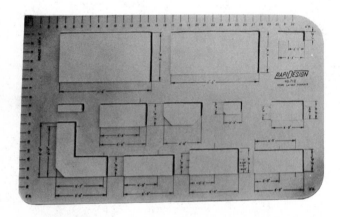

Office Template

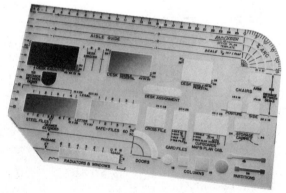

Books that include architectural standards are very useful sources of dimensions and information required in planning buildings.

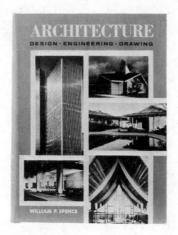

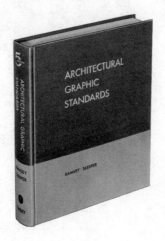

Dimensioning

In dimensioning architectural drawings, the sizes are shown in feet and inches (12'-3"). The dimension line is a continuous line. The dimension is usually placed above the dimension line.

ARCHITECTURAL DIMENSION

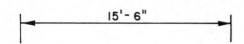

All dimensions placed horizontally on the drawing are positioned to read from the bottom of the drawing. Usually the vertical dimensions are placed to read from the right side of the sheet. This is the aligned method of dimensioning.

To dimension a building drawing, measurements are made from the outside edge of the exterior portions of the structure and from the center of interior members (walls, windows, doors, etc.).

ARCHITECTURAL DIMENSIONS

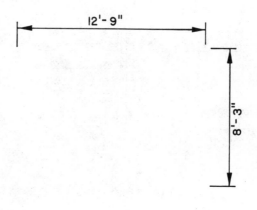

DIMENSIONING ARCHITECTURAL FLOOR PLANS

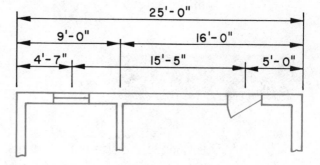

This simple set of plans for a small building will be helpful as an example in drawing architectural plans.

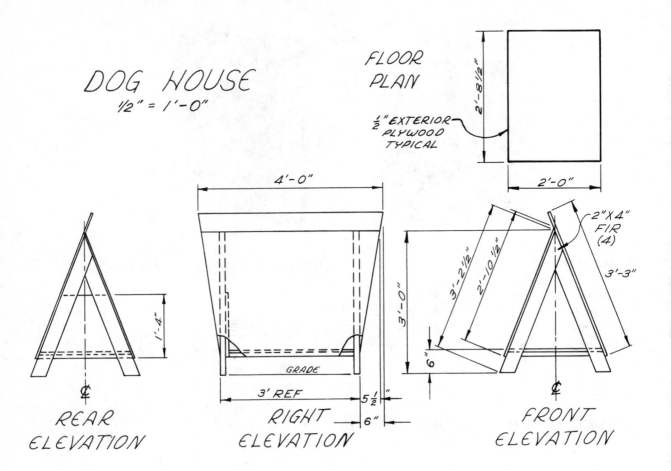

DOG HOUSE
1/2" = 1'-0"

FLOOR PLAN

1/2" EXTERIOR PLYWOOD TYPICAL

2'-8 1/2"

2'-0"

4'-0"

3'-0"

REAR ELEVATION

1'-4"

RIGHT ELEVATION

GRADE

3' REF

5 1/2"

6"

FRONT ELEVATION

2" X 4" FIR (4)

3'-2 1/2"

2'-10 1/2"

3'-3"

6"

Drawing Activities

Activities for learning to plan and draw buildings may include the following:

Develop an illustrated floor plan for a small home, office, store or shop using scaled cutouts (two dimensional cardboard) like those provided in this chapter.

Problem 75
Design Shelter for Pets

Draw plans for a doghouse or some other pet shelter giving consideration to the size requirements of the pet.

Problem 76
Design Small Storage or Play Area

Plan a small cabin, playhouse, or tool shed.

Problem 77
Design Small Building or Room

Design a vacation cabin, cottage, store, office, barn, or shop.

Problem 78
Design Large Building Plan

Develop plans for a house, service station, department store, or manufacturing plant.

Summary

You have learned the fundamentals of room arrangements, layout details, and basic architectural symbols for planning a building. You should be able to prepare a floor plan for a small building. You should also be able to talk to an architect about certain fundamental planning considerations.

11

Drawing Systems

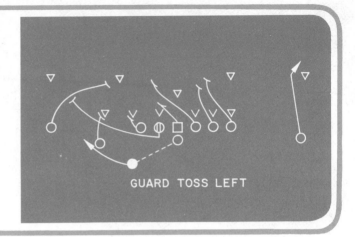

GUARD TOSS LEFT

Why Study This Chapter?

DRAWING SYSTEMS describes how:
1. The actions of people or machines are systems which you can draw and describe by the use of symbols.
2. Maps, production plans, electronic circuits, athletic plays and games, music, and the working relationship of people can be explained in terms of systems.
3. Different symbols can explain the action or various parts of a system in your drawing.
4. Three basic considerations are explained in a system—(1) the starting, (2) the stopping, and (3) the action that takes place in between these two points.

After you have studied the diagrams and symbols in this chapter and copied a system, you will be assigned drawing problems in which you plan simple systems. If you can learn to successfully plan and explain systems, many career opportunities will be open to you.

Systems are . . .
1. Complete work cycles or work flows.
2. Descriptive of organizations of people in teams or companies.
3. Operating sequences or schemes, as football plays, electronic plans.
4. Manufacturing or transportation plans.

A system may be a process, a chart, a scheme. A system drawing shows relationships, sequence, or relative values. It is conventionalized and abstract; not physically representative or exact.

Systems are arrangements of things so a task may be performed. Systems drawings are known as *schematics* or *network* drawings. In drawing systems, symbols are used to show how people, objects, or activities are organized to carry out a program.

The need for planning systems increases as a program or task becomes more involved. Systems drawings are used for planning and presenting such things as:
1. Personnel organization and athletic plays.
2. Distribution of money and manufacturing.
3. Scientific formulas and power flow.
4. Production and data processing.
5. Transportation.
6. Music and communication.

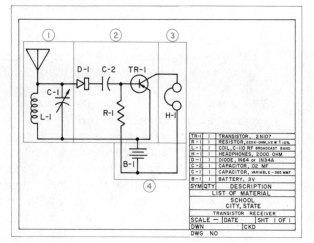

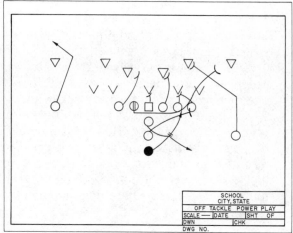

DRAFTING PERSONNEL
ORGANIZATION

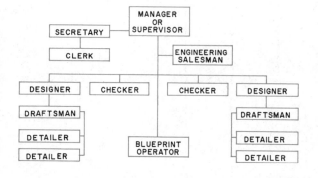

EXCERPTS: PIANO SONATA
BEETHOVEN

Drafting provides a graphic way of planning and showing complex ideas in a clear, brief form. Becoming familiar with the symbols and methods for drawing these types of systems is very helpful in planning technical activities.

In planning systems, individual pieces of cardboard representing each element of the total effort are often very useful. The pieces are labeled to identify the element and are easily moved from place to place as the plan is formed. This saves a great deal of erasing and drawing time. When the desired organization is developed, a drawing can be made. The final drawing is made with drafting tools and materials.

Maps

A city map is one of the most useful of system drawings. Transportations systems (streets, highways, railways, airways, and waterways) are shown on maps to describe direction or location from one place to another. A complete map shows all of the various transportation systems. However, it is helpful if a specific transportation system is described in detail on one map. Some maps describe the route to a specific address. They show only the primary streets where most of the traffic is located in the total city.

In planning simple maps, you should include the following:
1. Name and location of the specific place.
2. Numbers or names, direction and location of main highways leading to the area of the place.
3. Names, direction and location of the streets in the immediate area.

The map need not be drawn to scale. Careful placement of the lines and street names is necessary to make the map easily understood. Such maps can be reduced and duplicated for use as needed. There are many types of maps for various uses.

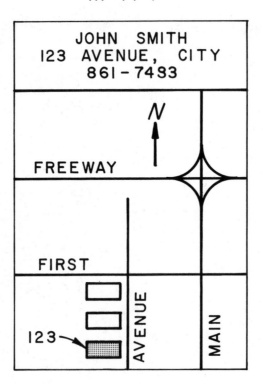

Problem 79
Draw a Map

Draw a map that describes the location of your house to someone that lives in another part of town or for someone from another town. Also, you could describe the directions from the city in which your home is located to the capital of your state.

Organization Charts of Personnel

Planning personnel organization charts is a very useful way of helping develop a better system of operation for groups of people. Systems help conserve human resources through greater efficiency. Personnel organization charts show lines of communication and responsibility. They group areas of similar activity and apply proven fundamentals of organizational management. Developing charts of responsibility or job descriptions can be very helpful in clubs, classes, schools, and businesses. Some important considerations in making a personnel organization chart are:

1. Mark individual cards with job titles and move the cards around until the proper relationships are developed.
2. Each leadership position should have 3 to 7 people directly responsible to it.
3. Similar activities should be grouped under the same leadership position.
4. The connecting lines show the paths of communication and responsibility.

CLUB ORGANIZATION CHART

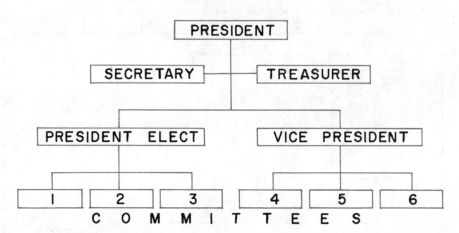

Problem 80
Draw a Personnel Chart

Draw a personnel chart describing the responsibilities that can be carried out by students in your class, club, school, or community.

Production Plans

Production plans are flow charts showing the order of the various operations in making a product. These can be developed in simple symbolic form by using cards with captions showing each activity in the production sequence. Cards are arranged in the most desirable order to reach the objective — a finished product, service, or design. The captions are connected with lines and arrows to show the flow of activity such as the example of the BOOK RACK given here.

Before production begins, a plant layout should be developed. A plant layout is made on a floor plan of the "shop." It shows how the work flows through the plant from operation to operation. Plant layouts help in the placement of machines and other equipment and are also useful in reducing the time and effort required in handling materials.

Study the orthographic projection example of a BOOK RACK and the PRODUCTION PLAN. On the orthographic projection, locate Part 2 and follow the production plan for an understanding of the relationship of these two drawings. In the production plan drawing, Part 2 is explained in the right-hand column. The first production operation for Part 2 is labeled *2A*. This means that the part is planed to a thickness of ¾". Now check the WOOD SHOP FLOOR PLAN drawing and observe the rectangle with the symbol *2A*. This symbol shows where the machine is located to plane Part 2 to a thickness of ¾".

Now follow the next step (2B) until you understand how these drawings explain the production system.

Problem 81
Draw a Simple Production Plan

Using the DOOR STOP plan on page 192, plan the flow of production for it as it would be mass-produced in your industrial arts class.

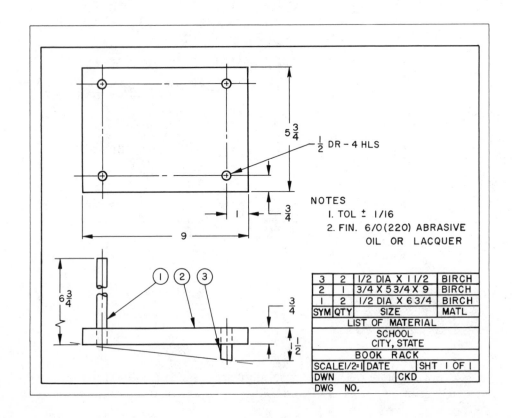

PRODUCTION PLAN - BOOK RACK

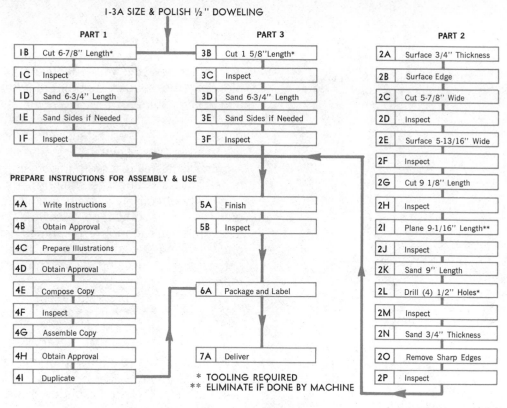

1-3A SIZE & POLISH ½" DOWELING

PART 1

IB	Cut 6-7/8" Length*
IC	Inspect
ID	Sand 6-3/4" Length
IE	Sand Sides if Needed
IF	Inspect

PREPARE INSTRUCTIONS FOR ASSEMBLY & USE

4A	Write Instructions
4B	Obtain Approval
4C	Prepare Illustrations
4D	Obtain Approval
4E	Compose Copy
4F	Inspect
4G	Assemble Copy
4H	Obtain Approval
4I	Duplicate

PART 3

3B	Cut 1 5/8" Length*
3C	Inspect
3D	Sand 6-3/4" Length
3E	Sand Sides if Needed
3F	Inspect

5A	Finish
5B	Inspect

6A	Package and Label

7A	Deliver

* TOOLING REQUIRED
** ELIMINATE IF DONE BY MACHINE

PART 2

2A	Surface 3/4" Thickness
2B	Surface Edge
2C	Cut 5-7/8" Wide
2D	Inspect
2E	Surface 5-13/16" Wide
2F	Inspect
2G	Cut 9 1/8" Length
2H	Inspect
2I	Plane 9-1/16" Length**
2J	Inspect
2K	Sand 9" Length
2L	Drill (4) 1/2" Holes*
2M	Inspect
2N	Sand 3/4" Thickness
2O	Remove Sharp Edges
2P	Inspect

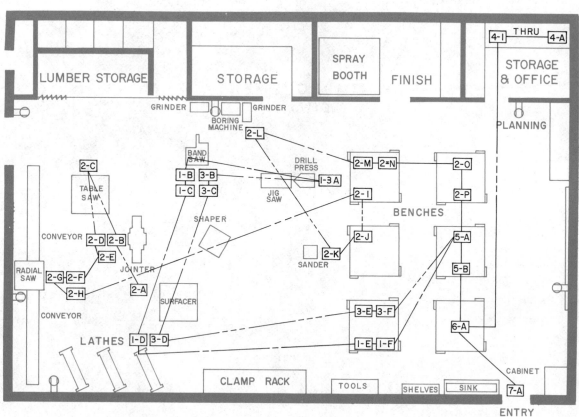

287

PERT NETWORK SYMBOLS

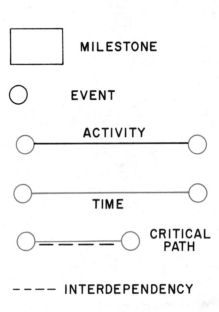

☐ MILESTONE

○ EVENT

○——————○ ACTIVITY

○——————○ TIME

○—·—·—·—○ CRITICAL PATH

– – – – INTERDEPENDENCY

PERT Planning

A rather new and very effective method for planning the sequence, time requirements, and relationships of task elements is called PERT (Program Evaluation Review Technique). PERT is used extensively in planning the relationships of events, activities, and time requirements for reaching objectives in business, industry, and the military. It can be used very effectively when planning the complex problems of schools and educational programs. Through PERT planning, tasks can often be more easily accomplished. PERT networks are developed in the following manner:

1. Establish the program objective.
2. Analyze the activities necessary to reach the objective.
3. Organize the activities into a network showing the relationship of each activity to the other.
4. Estimate the time required to complete each activity.
5. Identify the events from the start to the finish of an activity.

PROPERTY IMPROVEMENT PLAN
(PERT NETWORK)

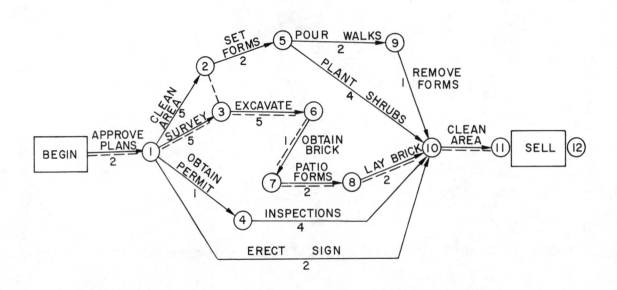

MANUFACTURING PLAN
(PERT NETWORK)

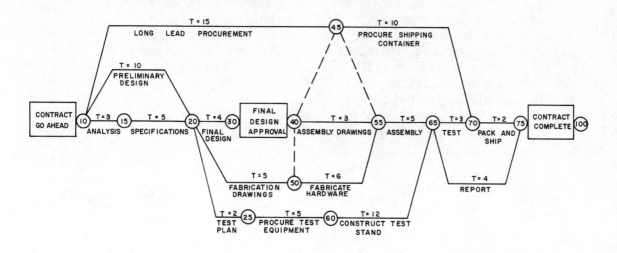

HOUSE CONSTRUCTION PLAN
(PERT NETWORK)

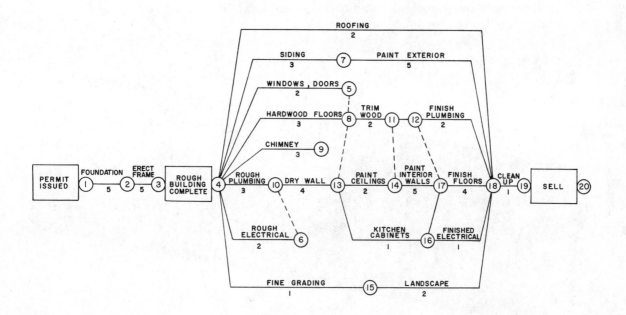

Select something that you are familiar with and plan the sequence of events. Diagram the events from start to finish and list the alternates that you can take between the starting event and the last event. For example, plan and draw a PERT plan for a camp-out involving four people, two tents, three meals and the necessary camp site improvements for a one night camp-out. Some planning considerations could be:

1. Who sets up the tent?
2. Who prepares the meals?
3. Who washes the dishes?
4. Will the group have recreational activities?
5. What procedure will be used to break camp?

Electronic Drawings

The biggest use of system drawings in industry is in electronics. It is important that each electronic circuit be diagramed properly so all the components are connected correctly.

Templates are used to draw the symbols in an electronic drawing.

There are many symbols used to describe the active components and types of connectors in an electronic device. The next page of symbols will show you some of the more important components used in electronic circuits.

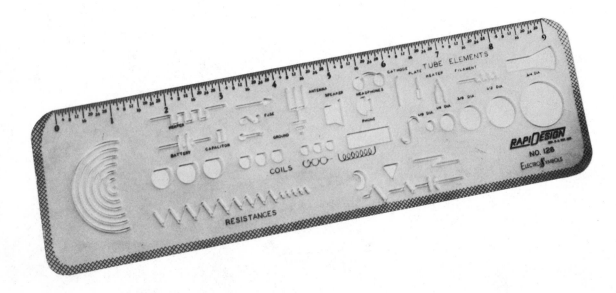

ELECTRONIC SYMBOLS

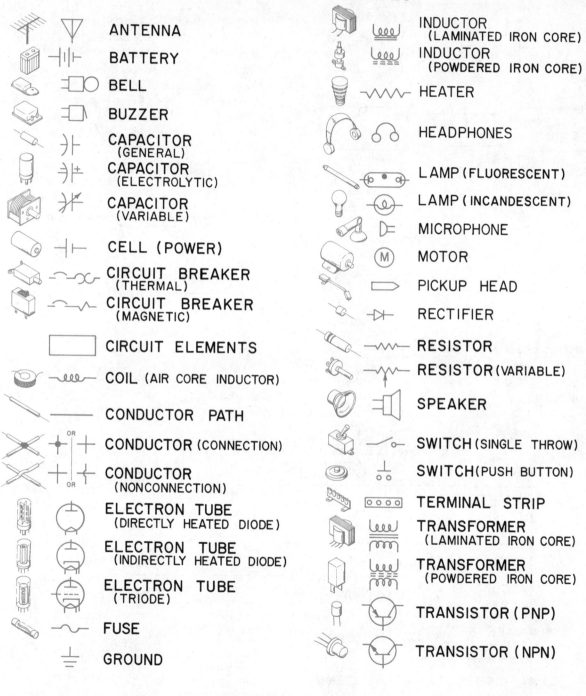

ANTENNA

BATTERY

BELL

BUZZER

CAPACITOR (GENERAL)

CAPACITOR (ELECTROLYTIC)

CAPACITOR (VARIABLE)

CELL (POWER)

CIRCUIT BREAKER (THERMAL)

CIRCUIT BREAKER (MAGNETIC)

CIRCUIT ELEMENTS

COIL (AIR CORE INDUCTOR)

CONDUCTOR PATH

CONDUCTOR (CONNECTION)

CONDUCTOR (NONCONNECTION)

ELECTRON TUBE (DIRECTLY HEATED DIODE)

ELECTRON TUBE (INDIRECTLY HEATED DIODE)

ELECTRON TUBE (TRIODE)

FUSE

GROUND

INDUCTOR (LAMINATED IRON CORE)

INDUCTOR (POWDERED IRON CORE)

HEATER

HEADPHONES

LAMP (FLUORESCENT)

LAMP (INCANDESCENT)

MICROPHONE

MOTOR

PICKUP HEAD

RECTIFIER

RESISTOR

RESISTOR (VARIABLE)

SPEAKER

SWITCH (SINGLE THROW)

SWITCH (PUSH BUTTON)

TERMINAL STRIP

TRANSFORMER (LAMINATED IRON CORE)

TRANSFORMER (POWDERED IRON CORE)

TRANSISTOR (PNP)

TRANSISTOR (NPN)

BLOCK DIAGRAM COMPLETE ELECTRICAL CIRCUIT

There are four main parts in an electronic circuit:

1. Source of Power,
2. Load,
3. Conductor Path, and
4. Control.

Parts of a circuit may be shown in block diagrams or schematic drawings.

The block diagram of a complete electrical circuit is used to express the major parts of a circuit. This circuit has a protective device to prevent overload. The block diagram is useful when describing the operation of a circuit; however, the *schematic* of the light circuit shows more detail for understanding.

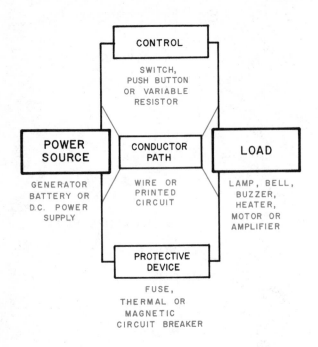

LIGHT CIRCUIT

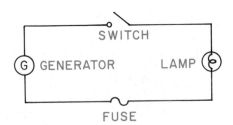

Drawings for Electronic Systems

Electronic drawings may describe a complete system or a section of the system. The chart below has a brief description of five different circuits. These circuits are (1) load control, (2) record or tape player, (3) record or tape recorder, (4) receiver, and (5) transmitter.

COMPLETE ELECTRONIC CIRCUITS

ELECTRONIC DEVICES	MODULES		
	INPUT	AMPLIFIERS	OUTPUT
LOAD CONTROL	PHOTOCELL	CONTROL AMPLIFIER	ALARM, LIGHT, HEATER, MOTOR, ETC.
RECORD PLAYER TAPE PLAYER	PICKUP HEAD	RECORDING-PLAYING AMPLIFIER	SPEAKER
TAPE RECORDER RECORD RECORDER	MICROPHONE		RECORDING HEAD
RECEIVER	ANTENNA	RECEIVER AMPLIFIER	SPEAKER
TRANSMITTER	MICROPHONE	TRANSMITTER AMPLIFIER	ANTENNA

The receiver circuit is actually a *transistor* receiver. The block diagram and schematic below show the relationship of these two types of drawings. The *antenna section* of the receiver block diagram, which is labeled No. 1, is explained in detail on the schematic drawing where it is also labeled No. 1. The other sections of the receiver (No. 2, 3, and 4) are also identified and explained.

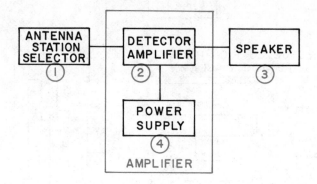

CRYSTAL & TRANSISTOR
RECEIVER
(BLOCK DIAGRAM)

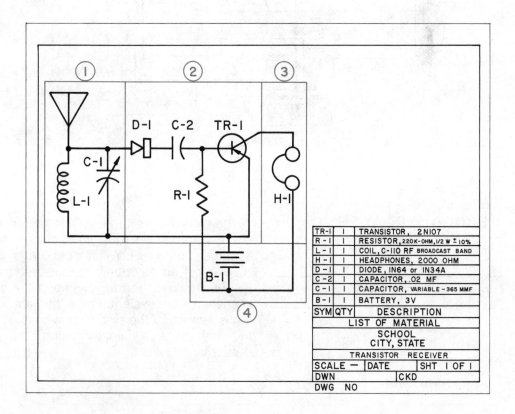

TR-1	1	TRANSISTOR, 2 N107
R-1	1	RESISTOR, 220K-OHM, 1/2 W ± 10%
L-1	1	COIL, C-110 RF BROADCAST BAND
H-1	1	HEADPHONES, 2000 OHM
D-1	1	DIODE, 1N64 or 1N34A
C-2	1	CAPACITOR, .02 MF
C-1	1	CAPACITOR, VARIABLE - 365 MMF
B-1	1	BATTERY, 3V
SYM	QTY	DESCRIPTION

LIST OF MATERIAL

SCHOOL
CITY, STATE

TRANSISTOR RECEIVER

| SCALE — | DATE | SHT 1 OF 1 |
| DWN | | CKD |

DWG NO

The *load control* circuit is also explained with a block diagram and a schematic diagram. Each major section of the block diagram is labeled to correspond to the specific description in the schematic drawing (No. 1, 2, 3, and 4).

ELECTRONIC LOAD CONTROL
(BLOCK DIAGRAM)

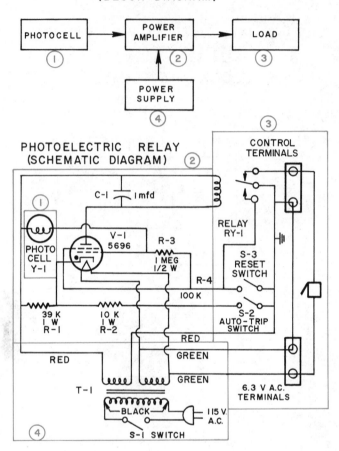

RECORD   PLAYER
(BLOCK   DIAGRAM)

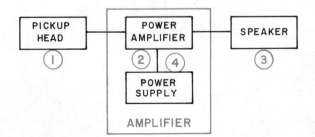

The record player, transmitter, and receiver circuits are shown with block diagrams and schematic drawings. You should draw a block diagram of an electronic circuit first so you will understand the relationship of the major sections of the system. The schematic drawing is required if the system is to be explained in detail to an engineer, technician, or a repairman.

RECORD PLAYER
AMPLIFIER
(SCHEMATIC DIAGRAM)

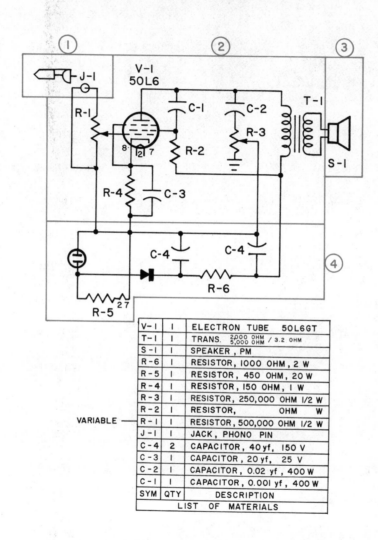

V-1	1	ELECTRON TUBE 50L6GT
T-1	1	TRANS. 2,000 OHM / 3.2 OHM (5,000 OHM)
S-1	1	SPEAKER , PM
R-6	1	RESISTOR, 1000 OHM, 2 W
R-5	1	RESISTOR, 450 OHM, 20 W
R-4	1	RESISTOR, 150 OHM, 1 W
R-3	1	RESISTOR, 250,000 OHM 1/2 W
R-2	1	RESISTOR, OHM W
R-1	1	RESISTOR, 500,000 OHM 1/2 W
J-1	1	JACK , PHONO PIN
C-4	2	CAPACITOR, 40 yf, 150 V
C-3	1	CAPACITOR, 20 yf, 25 V
C-2	1	CAPACITOR, 0.02 yf, 400 W
C-1	1	CAPACITOR, 0.001 yf, 400 W
SYM	QTY	DESCRIPTION
		LIST OF MATERIALS

VARIABLE (pointing to R-1 row)

Problem 83
Draw a Block Diagram and a
Schematic of an Electronic Circuit

Select a simple electrical or electronic device and describe it in a drawing. Make a block diagram to show the relationships of the parts. Label the major sections on the block diagram. Make a schematic drawing of the device that you selected and outline the major sections as related to the block drawing. A small battery-operated toy should not be too difficult.

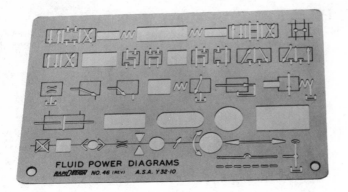

Fluid Power Drawings

The use of fluid power is growing rapidly and requires system drawings to give information to engineers, technicians, and repairmen. Fluid power uses a liquid (hydraulic) or a gas (pneumatic) to place pressure on an active component in the circuit. As with electricity, fluid power circuits require (1) a source of power, (2) a control device, (3) a load, and (4) conductor lines to allow the fluid to flow

FLUID POWER SYMBOLS

——————	WORKING LINE (MAIN)
— — — —	PILOT LINE (CONTROL)
- - - - - - -	DRAIN LINE
	LINES CROSSING
	LINES CONNECTED
	PNEUMATIC FLOW CONTROL
	HYDRAULIC FLOW CONTROL
	PLUGGED PORT
	VENTED RESERVOIR
	PRESSURIZED RESERVOIR
	ACCUMULATOR
	FLUID CONDITIONER
	HEATER
	COOLER
	FILTER
	SEPARATOR
	HYDRAULIC OR PNEUMATIC CYLINDER

	MANUAL CONTROL
	HYDRAULIC MOTOR
	HYDRAULIC PUMP
	PNEUMATIC MOTOR
	PNEUMATIC PUMP
	ELECTRIC MOTOR
	HEAT ENGINE
	PRESSURE INSTRUMENT
	TEMPERATURE INSTRUMENT
	FLOW METER
	PRESSURE SWITCH
	FLOW SWITCH
	VALVE ENVELOPE
	VALVE PORTS
	VALVE BLOCKED PORTS
	VALVE OPEN
	ON OFF VALVE (SIMPLIFIED)
	COMPONENT ENCLOSURE

within the circuit. The *source of power* is usually an electric motor which drives a pump to cause the fluid to flow. The *control devices* are usually one or more valves which restrict or allow the fluid to flow. The *load* may be a motor, pump, or piston that does work. The *connecting lines* are tubing.

A template can be used to draw the symbols in the schematic circuits. As you can see, there are many symbols used to describe the various parts of a fluid circuit.

Flow Control

The flow control of a fluid power circuit is part of the total system. A flow control circuit is shown on the right. The fluid is stored in the reservoir. In this circuit the motor drives the pump which causes the hydraulic fluid to flow through the circuit. The fluid in this circuit will not flow through the left-hand valve since it is not aligned with the fluid line. This circuit has symbols to show the following fluid parts:

1. Main lines
2. Pilot lines
3. Drain lines
4. Spring-operated valve
5. Regulator valve
6. Reservoir

Hydraulic Fluid System

A fluid power system is best described in a schematic drawing. In the lower drawing, you can clearly see the relationships of all the active components. If you were required to describe this system without using the symbols for hydraulic components, you would have a difficult task.

FLOW CONTROL

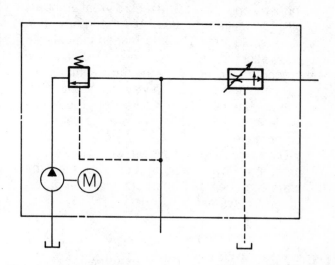

FLUID POWER CIRCUIT

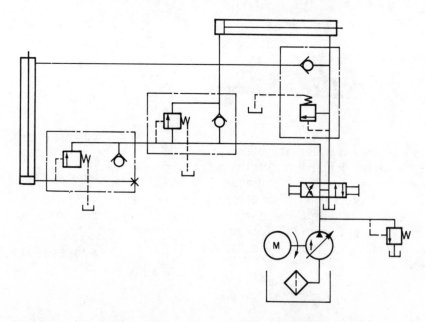

Analyze the FLUID POWER CIRCUIT and list the components that you can identify. If you have a book of hydraulic symbols, use it to identify the components in the circuit on page 297.

Select a fluid power system in your home, school, or community. After you have studied it thoroughly, make a schematic drawing.

Data Processing

Data processing is a technique used by industry and business to record great amounts of information and assemble the information in a usable form. The information is analyzed and recorded on cards, tapes, or discs. The procedure for recording the information must be established in such a way that you can recall it when necessary. The set of procedures is planned very carefully before the data may be processed.

Data processing is a system which is planned or charted by a programmer. Drawing templates can be used when planning the procedure with symbols.

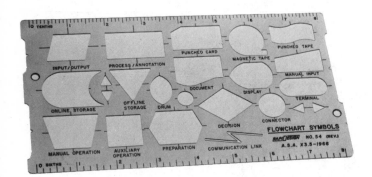

The following examples of different systems were planned carefully. Notice that the diagrams are very similar to PERT planning charts. However, data processing is an automated system, and the charted events normally take place in a short time. PERT plans are made for events that require weeks, months, or years.

DATA PROCESSING SYMBOLS

⬭	TERMINAL
▭	PROCESSING FUNCTION
⏢	INPUT / OUTPUT
◇	DECISION
○	SORTING
▱	DOCUMENT
○	CONNECTOR (ON PAGE)
▽	CONNECTOR (OFF PAGE)
▯	TRANSMITTAL TAPE
▱	CLERICAL OPERATION
◂ ▴ ▸ ▾	FLOW
▭	PUNCHED CARD
⌇	PERFORATED TAPE
▯	DISC OR DRUM
○	MAGNETIC TAPE

CUSTOMER ACCOUNTS
RECORD SYSTEM
(FLOW CHART)

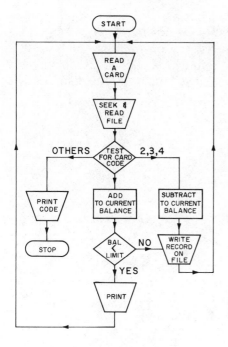

Select a simple system that you are familiar with and draw a flow chart. For example, you may be familiar with the operation of an automatic soft drink machine, a candy machine, automatic car wash, or a bowling alley with automatic pinsetters. There are many systems that you have used from time to time that you can draw.

RECORD PLAYER
SYSTEM

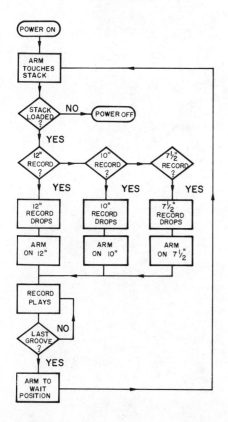

MARKETING CONTROL
SYSTEM

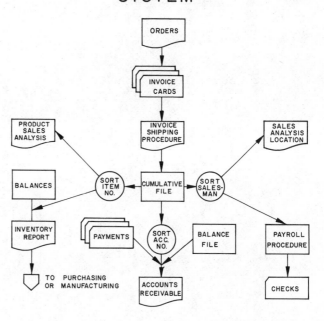

ATHLETIC PLAY SYMBOLS

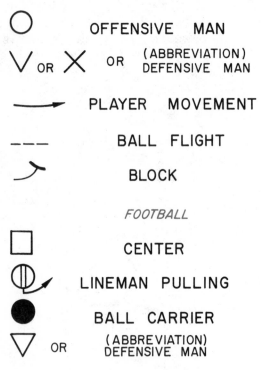

GENERAL

○   OFFENSIVE MAN

∨ OR ✕   OR   (ABBREVIATION) DEFENSIVE MAN

⟶   PLAYER MOVEMENT

— — —   BALL FLIGHT

⟩   BLOCK

FOOTBALL

▢   CENTER

⏀   LINEMAN PULLING

●   BALL CARRIER

▽ OR   (ABBREVIATION) DEFENSIVE MAN

Athletic Plays

Athletic plays are systems that organize the efforts of the players to accomplish an objective such as scoring (offense) or preventing a score (defense). Coaches use symbols to plan plays (systems) and explain them to the players.

BASKETBALL

〜〜   DRIBBLE

BASEBALL

— — —   BATTED BALL

—·—   THROWN BALL

‖   RELAY POSITION

—   INCOMPLETE THROW

⊗   CUT-OFF POSITION

Football

Football plays are concerned with scoring, keeping control of the ball, setting up other plays in an offensive or defensive series, and keeping the other team from scoring. You should study the following football plays and identify what each one of them will accomplish.

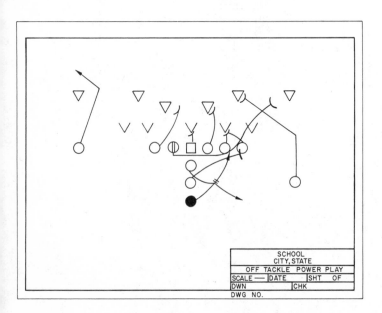

SCHOOL
CITY, STATE
OFF TACKLE POWER PLAY
SCALE — | DATE | SHT OF
DWN | CHK
DWG NO.

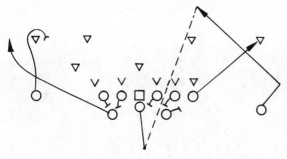

DROP-BACK PASS FLANKER DEEP

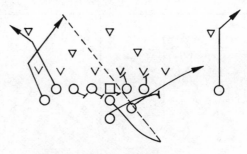

SPRINT RIGHT THROW
BACK WING BACK ACROSS

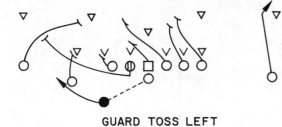

GUARD TOSS LEFT

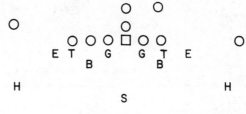

WIDE TACKLE SIX DEFENSE

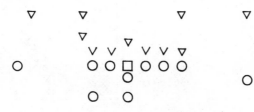

PRO FOUR-THREE DEFENSE

Basketball

Basketball plays are concerned with scoring, moving the ball, getting the ball in bounds, and preventing the other team from scoring. Study the plays and determine the objective of each.

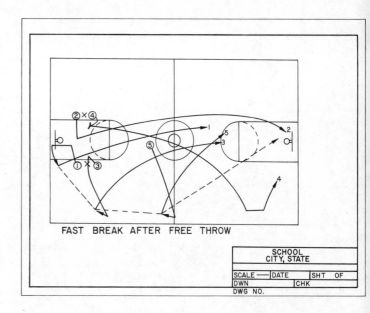

FAST BREAK AFTER FREE THROW

SCHOOL CITY, STATE		
SCALE ——	DATE	SHT OF
DWN	CHK	
DWG NO.		

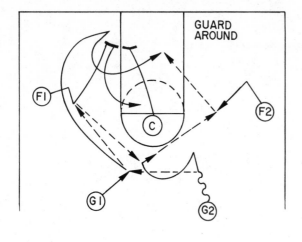

GUARD AROUND

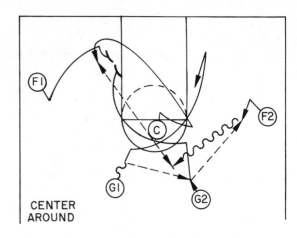

CENTER AROUND

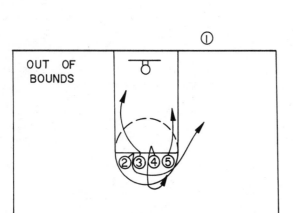

OUT OF BOUNDS

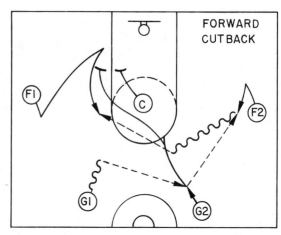

FORWARD CUTBACK

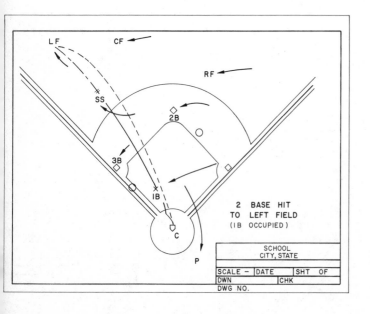

2 BASE HIT TO LEFT FIELD (IB OCCUPIED)

Baseball

Baseball plays are discussed before a game begins. Usually, like all athletic plays, the strengths and weaknesses are the main area of planning. Each player must know exactly what to do for each situation. Study the following baseball plays.

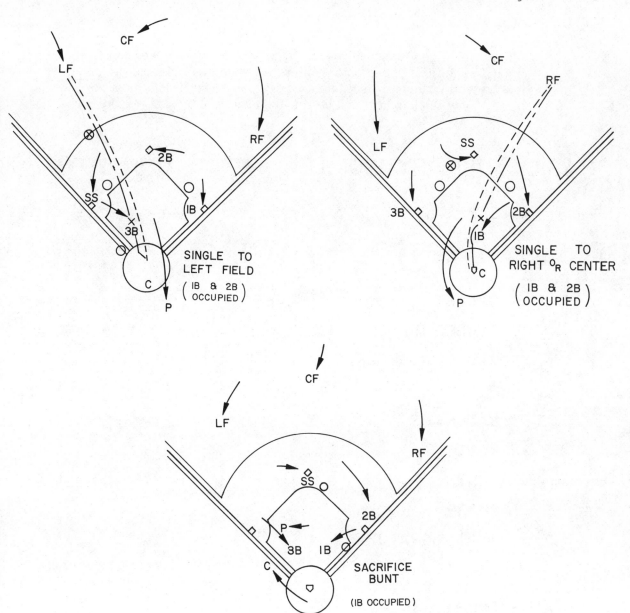

SINGLE TO
LEFT FIELD
(IB & 2B
OCCUPIED)

SINGLE TO
RIGHT OR CENTER
(IB & 2B
OCCUPIED)

SACRIFICE
BUNT
(IB OCCUPIED)

Problem 87
Draw Athletic Plays

Select a sport that you enjoy and design some plays. Each play should be designed to accomplish a specific objective. You may list a particular strength or weakness of your team and design the plays to give the team the best results.

Music

Long ago a very effective method of writing music was developed. It involves the use of standard symbols organized by the writer to be interpreted by others for specific musical results. Each note must be planned very carefully so that it fits into the total system (song or score).

BASIC MUSIC SYMBOLS

BAR LINES

BRACKETS

C CLEF

F CLEF (BASS)

G CLEF (TREBLE)

FLATS

NATURALS

NOTES

RESTS

SHARP

TIME SIGNATURE

STAFF

EXCERPTS : PIANO SONATA
BEETHOVEN

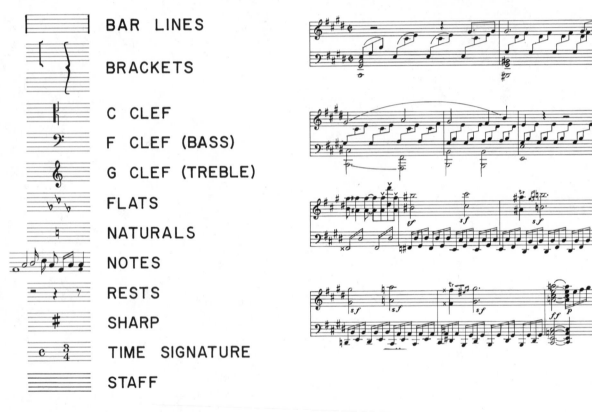

BAR GRAPH

EFFECTIVENESS OF LEARNING EXPERIENCES

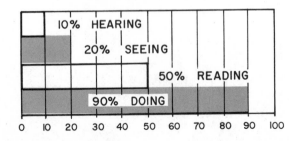

10% HEARING

20% SEEING

50% READING

90% DOING

0   10 20 30 40 50 60 70 80 90 100

Graphs

Graphs have symbols arranged to show relationships of various quantities to one another. They often involve both time and quantity comparisons which are shown in scale. Graphs are very useful in comparing related types of information.

ENERGY SUPPLIED BY

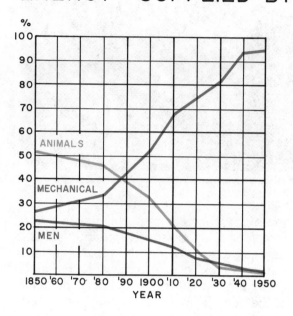

OWNERSHIP OF BUSINESSES

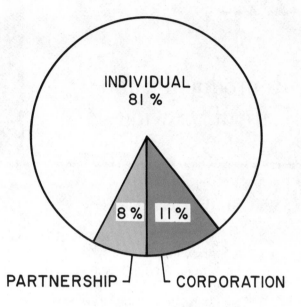

Make a graph that clearly explains something with which you are familiar. You could graph your performance or attendance in athletics, school, or church.

Summary

Now you have learned about the use of systematic planning and how it improves many of our everyday activities. In the beginning of this book you started learning a *system of drawing* or drafting. Now you have applied the things you have learned to planning and improving other systems that are used in business, manufacturing, servicing, and recreational activities. Through the study of systems, you have gained a familiarity with many occupational and recreational activities. You have learned something about the component parts of systems and the symbols used for the components in planning and drawing of systems. You have learned the importance of knowing the operation and function of components, and also the activities that make up systems. By learning to draw systems, you have gained an added way to record, plan and communicate ideas.

12

Reproduction and Care of Drawings

DRAWING ON TRACING PAPER

DIAZO PAPER

Why Study This Chapter?

REPRODUCTION AND CARE OF DRAWINGS will explain how to:
1. Use various methods to make copies of drawings.
2. Fold, store, and repair drawings.

If your school has copying equipment, you can use your drawings to gain experience in making prints.

Drawings are valuable documents, for they require much planning and drawing time to make and their replacement would be a costly process. For these reasons, extreme care should be taken when handling and storing drawings.

The following should be considered when storing or using drawings:
1. Develop a system for cataloging and storing drawings.
2. Handle drawings carefully so they are not damaged.
3. Never allow original drawings to leave the drafting room or storage area except for making prints.
4. Avoid folding original drawings; prints may be folded.

Reproductions of Drawings

Reproductions are copies or prints of drawings and are divided into two types: (1) checker prints and (2) production prints. *Checker prints* are made during the design and draw-

ing process for communication with the customer. They are also used as a communication between the checker and draftsman to insure the accuracy of the drawings. *Production prints* are made for use by the manufacturer of the item. Drawings are often reproduced in quantity so the original drawings can be kept on file in the drafting department. The copies are used by the several departments or companies who may be making the product. Usually several (six or eight) prints are made of a drawing, but sometimes hundreds of copies are produced.

Drawings are almost always made on tracing paper or plastic so that prints can be made economically. The tracing paper is translucent and permits light to pass through it easily. To make good prints, the lines and lettering on a drawing must be a dense black to stop light.

The lines and paper may be any of several colors, but prints are normally made with blue, black or brown lines on white paper or plastic. The most common method of making full-sized prints is the diazo process.

Diazo Printing Process

Paper used in making diazo prints is called *diazo paper*. It is coated with yellow colored chemicals which are sensitive to light. To make a print, a bright light is projected through the drawing onto the print paper. Where the light hits the diazo coating, the chemicals are broken down or neutralized. But where the lines of the drawing appear on tracing paper, the light does not penetrate and the diazo coating is not exposed. One type of diazo paper is developed in ammonia gas which is produced by the evaporation of liquid ammonia. Ammonia gas turns the unexposed yellow diazo coating lines to a dark color. The color may be blue, black, or brown. The other type of diazo paper is developed by moistening the sheet as it passes through rollers running in a special developing solution. The printing process can be done in an exposure frame or in a special diazo print machine. Diazo machines are available in many sizes.

Reproduction Techniques

A simple device for exposing diazo paper can be made with an appropriate-size piece of clear glass, heavy cardboard, and masking tape.

The diazo paper is placed on the cardboard with the coated side face up. The drawing is placed, face up, on the diazo paper. The glass is closed to hold the two pieces of paper securely. The glass face is then exposed to direct sunlight until the diazo coating disappears or is broken down. The correct length of time for this process varies with the brightness of the day. It can be determined by making several different trial exposures, recording the time required and evaluating or comparing the results.

DIAZO DEVELOPING WITH SPONGE

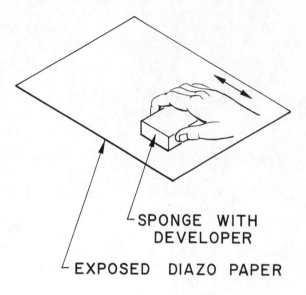

SPONGE WITH DEVELOPER

EXPOSED DIAZO PAPER

EXPOSURE FRAME

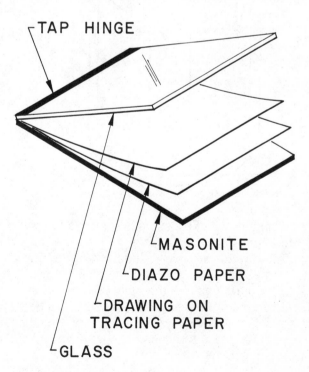

TAP HINGE

MASONITE

DIAZO PAPER

DRAWING ON TRACING PAPER

GLASS

To develop the print paper, a large glass container such as a wide-mouthed gallon pickle jar can be used. Place a piece of sponge or paper towel soaked in strong (26%) ammonia solution in the jar. Then put the exposed diazo material in the jar, leaving it there until the lines of the print darken.

The draftsman uses machines to accomplish the development process quickly. In using machines to make prints, the drawing is placed face up on top of the coated face of the diazo paper. By means of a conveyor belt the two pieces of paper are passed around a light source in the exposing section of the machine.

DIAZO DEVELOPING
AMMONIA JAR

EXPOSED DIAZO PAPER

SPONGE
(AMMONIA
SOAKED)

GLASS JAR
(GALLON)

EXPOSURE MACHINE

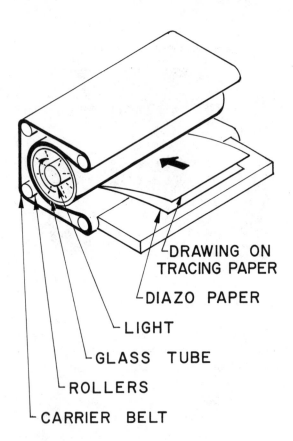

DRAWING ON
TRACING PAPER

DIAZO PAPER

LIGHT

GLASS TUBE

ROLLERS

CARRIER BELT

The amount of exposure is controlled by the speed of the conveyor belt. The slower the speed, the lighter the lines on the print will be. In a properly exposed and developed print, the background will have a very slight tint of the line color. When the two pieces of paper come out of the machine, the drawing is removed from the exposed diazo paper.

The diazo paper is then placed into the developing section of the machine. The paper is carried through the developing section by a conveyor belt and should come out completely developed. If the print shows any tint of yellow, it has not been completely developed. To fully develop the print, check the flow of the developing solution and/or put the print through the developing section again.

DEVELOPING MACHINE

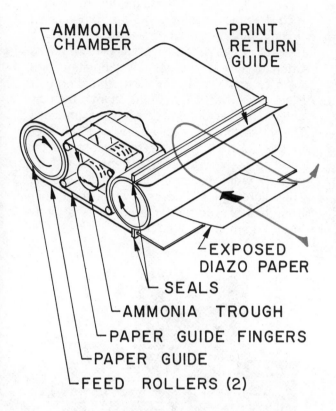

- AMMONIA CHAMBER
- PRINT RETURN GUIDE
- EXPOSED DIAZO PAPER
- SEALS
- AMMONIA TROUGH
- PAPER GUIDE FINGERS
- PAPER GUIDE
- FEED ROLLERS (2)

School Whiteprinter Machine

Professional Whiteprinter Machine

Folding Prints

Prints are folded for ease in handling and storage. The title block should show when a print is folded as shown in the illustration.

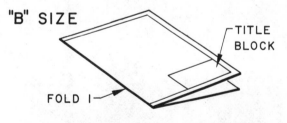

"B" SIZE

TITLE BLOCK

FOLD I

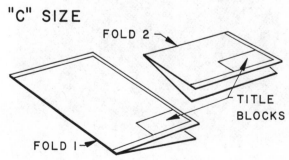

"C" SIZE

FOLD 2

TITLE BLOCKS

FOLD I

Microfilming

Microfilming is a photographic method of recording drawings and it is very widely used. In microfilming, drawings are reduced to about the size of two postage stamps or 35mm film. Often this film is mounted on a tabulating card.

An example of a microfilm tabulation card is shown in the illustration. The film is the dark portion on the bottom data processing card. The microfilm is easily filed and retrieved in this form. It may be retrieved from the data processing storage system for making prints, reading, or mailing to other locations. The microfilming process is very useful when it is necessary to file large numbers of drawings in a small storage area.

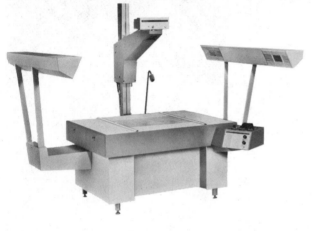

Storing Drawings

Drawings up to 34″ X 44″ in size are stored flat in drawers or cabinets. Larger drawings are rolled and stored in tubes.

Repairing Drawings

There are several ways of repairing damaged drawings. However, you should make every effort to avoid the need for repair. Drawings that have been torn can be successfully repaired by using a permanent-type transparent plastic tape.

Summary

You have learned how drawings can be reproduced with the diazo process and microfilm. You have learned to fold, store, and repair drawings. You have learned that drawings can be copied and distributed to many people so that the work and the materials can be planned accurately.

13

Drafting Design

Why Study This Chapter?

DRAFTING DESIGN will describe how:

1. You can use the knowledge and drawing skill you have acquired along with creativity to design products for industry.
2. The creative process is accomplished and used by a draftsman to develop and refine his ideas.
3. You can use standard parts, materials, and manufacturing practices in developing useful products.
4. The total drafting design includes:
   a. The creative process,
   b. Common objectives of design,
   c. Standard parts,
   d. Standard materials, and
   e. Basic manufacturing practices.

This chapter describes how you can think creatively. It encourages you to extend your thoughts and ideas in finding new and better ways of constructing products or tools. When you know how to record and refine your ideas, you will begin designing parts and assemblies for products. This chapter challenges you to think creatively.

Designing is an exciting, challenging, and fulfilling activity. It is exciting because in designing you can change things to help people. A new tool or machine can help many people perform work in a better way. The challenge of designing lies in trying to solve a problem without creating undesirable results. Pollution of our environment is an undesirable result from efforts to solve needs for greater

sources of power. Fulfillment is derived from design through application of people's total abilities in solving problems. People must use the senses, brain, and muscles of their bodies, as well as the resources of their surroundings to solve problems. The total use of one's human capabilities makes designing a complete human experience.

Drafting design is the blending of creative ability with the use of standard parts and materials in basic manufacturing practices to create useful products. Designing is planning the shape and treatment of materials to fulfill a need and therefore is a very interesting, challenging, and fundamental aspect of drafting. All draftsmen are involved in designing to varying degrees, but only the most capable and experienced draftsmen become full-time designers. Designers make a constant effort to improve products through the three goals of (1) simplicity, (2) performance, and (3) attraction.

Simplicity is to make a product as easily as possible, resulting in low cost. *Performance* means a product will serve satisfactorily. *Attraction* deals with the appeal a product has to the consumer.

You must be able to draw before you can do design work effectively. Your ideas need to be put on paper so they can be analyzed, evaluated, and refined. Study of the previous chapters has given you a variety of drafting abilities for expressing your ideas. In your study of this chapter you will learn what is involved in designing and how designing is a fundamental part of creative human beings.

Man Creates

Man is the only thing ever developed which *creates ideas* and, for this reason, is the most complete system known. Developed in man are four unique abilities:

1. *His mind* . . . which stores and processes vast experience information in a unique way to create ideas.
2. *His hands* . . . with thumbs and fingers positioned so their opposing forces are used to hold and use tools.
3. *His position* . . . in standing upright, allowing two limbs (arms) to be free for performing work.
4. *His refined communication systems* . . . including drawing, writing words and speaking.

Through the ages man has used his unique abilities with his common "animal" abilities to create or design new things. Even with all of modern technology, he has never been able to design anything that can create ideas. Much of what man has created *is an extension of his own abilities*. For example:

1. Hammers are an extension of the fist,
2. The computer extends his mind, and
3. Pliers enlarge the capacity of his grip.

Creative Process

With years of experience man has learned much about the creative or designing process he uses in developing products which may be expressed in six steps: (1) identifying problems, (2) applying resources, (3) formulating ideas, (4) recording ideas, (5) refining the product, and (6) presenting the product.

Identifying Problems

Identifying problems is done by man through the use of his senses and brain which are used in contact with surroundings to gain information: (1) seeing, (2) hearing, (3) touching, (4) tasting, and (5) smelling. The only way man can gain information is through his senses.

Man has extended the ability of his senses by designing sensitive instruments to find information. The information is carried to his brain as input for memory (storage) and reasoning (processing). He has extended the ability of his brain to store and process information by designing computers; *however,* computers can only process information according to a given program. The brain is capable of processing all of its stored information in any combination. It is with the combined use of his senses and brain, extended with instruments and computers, that man identifies problems.

You can develop greater use of your senses and your brain in identifying problems by developing the alertness of your senses and brain. Is it dark? Is it loud? Is it sharp? Is it sweet? Is it foul? Overall, is it a problem? Throughout the creative process it should be clearly understood what the problem is that needs to be solved.

Applying Resources

Man has found that problems can be solved by identifying and applying resources such as abilities or assets to the problem. Applicable resources are made up of your personal skills, as well as the abilities of other people. If you are not aware of an available resource, then perhaps you lack the knowledge to identify the best solution. This is one of the important reasons for learning all you can.

People develop the resources to solve problems through activity, study, and experience as they work. As people become knowledgeable in their work, the solution of problems becomes an easier task. For example: to solve problems related to space travel, experience or resources related to space must be developed and utilized. Similarly, manufacturing, chemistry, agriculture, electricity, and other technical fields must be studied thoroughly. If the answer requires abilities with certain materials and/or processes, then experiences should be gained in the use of those materials and/or processes. Applying resources can be done by using your own abilities or by involving other people who have the necessary skills to work on the identified problem. Other resources used in solving problems include information contained in books, films, and recordings. The application of resources involves research, tests, experiments, calculations, drawings, and models. Good ideas combined with ability, effort, and time produce excellent results!

Formulating Ideas

Formulating ideas is used to find the answer when resources have been applied to the problem. To formulate ideas, the work in solving problems should be broken with "change of pace" activities such as walks, rides, sports, rest, hobbies, recreation, or different work. Ideas are formulated by alternating periods of work with periods of rest in applying resources. Very often the idea "pops" or formulates in the brain during "change of pace" activities.

Recording Ideas

Recording ideas is necessary. Ideas are preserved by "capturing" them with notes, freehand drawings, or recordings. If materials and equipment are not available for recording ideas, the idea should be memorized.

Refining the Idea

Refining the product is important when improving the simplicity, performance, and appeal of the idea. It involves the repeated use of the first four steps in the creative process. In this step drawings and models are made, tested, corrected, retested, and redone until all the identified problems are solved.

Presenting the Idea

Presenting the product is the final step of making the item available for use. It may involve protecting the idea with a copyright or patent. Presenting products also involves the way new products are brought to the attention of other people by demonstrations and/or advertising. Products must gain an appealing exposure with people to become useful. Presenting products completes the creative process.

The creative process is learned through practice in using the many and varied abilities you possess as an individual. Your success in creativity will depend upon how well you develop your natural abilities and how you use previously acquired information. In drafting design, such information covers (1) standard (conventional) drafting practices, (2) the use of standard parts, materials, and manufacturing practices, and (3) the ability to develop useful new ones. You have learned to draw and use many standard (conventional) drafting practices. Now you will learn about other standard practices needed by the draftsmen in designing products.

In summary, man's only way of gaining information is through contact of his senses with his surroundings which include other people and the results of their work. Man can use his senses to find information for his mind by probing, seeking, and gathering like an elephant uses its trunk to probe, seek, and gather food for its hungry mouth. Man has developed instruments to extend the ability of his senses to gain information. Examples of such instruments are:

1. Television lens, transmission and picture systems extend man's *sight*.
2. Electronic microphone, amplifier and speaker systems extend man's *hearing*.
3. Thermometers extend man's *touch*.
4. Chemical tests or reactions extend man's ability to *taste* and *smell*.

The information gathered through the senses is transmitted or carried by the nerve system to the brain as *input* for *storage* and *processing*. With his brain, man has the unique ability to combine the stored information in many ways. This unique ability is basic to his capacity for creating products. The output of man's brain results in some type of muscular movement. For example: your voice, mouth, arms, hands, fingers, legs, feet, and toes all require muscles to move in doing anything. As a result, your productive capacity is dependent upon how well you develop the use of your senses to gather information, the capacity of your brain to store and process information, and the ability of your muscles to perform.

Standard Parts

Standard parts are ready-made items that are available at stores and other marketing businesses. Standard parts vary from simple items such as nails to complex items, including motors, transmissions, and controls. They perform similar functions in many different kinds of products and thus can be produced in large quantities, reducing costs through the efficiencies of mass production.

The use of standard parts provides several opportunities for conservation of time, ability, and materials. Usually, standard parts offer:
1. A reduction in the cost of producing the product,
2. A replacement of worn or damaged parts in the basic product with more ease and with less cost,
3. An elimination of the repetitive tasks involved in designing parts that have already been developed.

The use of standard parts allows the designer to use his talent in developing the unique features of the product.

Many thousands of types of standard parts are fully described in technical catalogs, specification sheets, charts, magazines, and books. Salesmen also provide a useful source of information. These information sources provide the designer with such information as specifications, capabilities, uses, and prices. One of the best sources of technical information used by designers is *Machinery's Handbook*.

As a consumer and worker in our technical world, you will find it very helpful to develop your ability to obtain and use technical information. You can obtain such literature through letters, telephone calls, or personal contacts with salesmen whose addresses and telephone numbers are easily available in telephone books, magazines, and directories in the public libraries.

Fasteners

Fasteners are one of the most commonly used standard parts. Only rarely is it necessary for a designer to create a special fastener to do a job. Technical information about basic fasteners is provided in the following diagrams and charts for your use in designing products. Additional information is available in *Machinery's Handbook*. The diagrams and charts also provide you with an opportunity to learn how to read the various forms of information. Charts offer a way of clearly presenting large amounts of information in relatively small areas.

Wood Fasteners • Wood Fasteners • Wood Fasteners

WIRE   BRADS AND NAILS

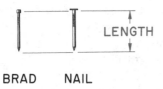

LENGTH

BRAD   NAIL

WIRE BRAD AND NAIL SIZES

LENGTH	GAGE	DIA.
3/16"	20	.0348"
	21	.0317"
	22	.0286"
1/4"	20	.0348"
	21	.0317"
	22	.0286"
3/8"	20	.0348"
	21	.0317"
	22	.0286"
1/2"	20	.0348"
	21	.0317"
	22	.0286"
5/8"	19	.0410"
	20	.0348"
	21	.0317"
3/4"	18	.0475"
	19	.0410"
	20	.0348"
7/8"	18	.0475"
	19	.0410"
	20	.0348"
1 & 1-1/8"	15	.0720"
	16	.0625"
	17	.0540"

LENGTH   SELECTION

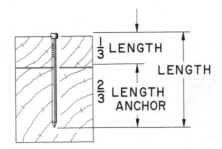

$\frac{1}{3}$ LENGTH

LENGTH

$\frac{2}{3}$ LENGTH
ANCHOR

SPECIFICATIONS

LENGTH GAGE   TYPE

EXAMPLE   1/2   #21(.0317) WIRE BRAD

Wood Fasteners • Wood Fasteners • Wood Fasteners

NAILS

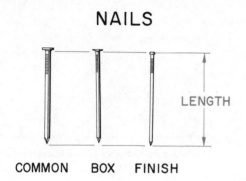

COMMON   BOX   FINISH

LENGTH SELECTION

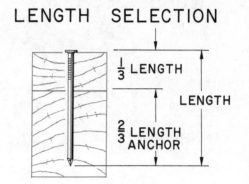

SPECIFICATIONS

	SIZE	TYPE
EXAMPLE	6 d (2)	COMMON NAIL

SPECIFICATIONS FOR COMMON, FINISHING, AND BOX NAILS

SIZE	LENGTH INCHES	COMMON NAIL		FINISHING NAIL		BOX NAIL	
		DIA	NO./LB	DIA	NO./LB	DIA	NO./LB
3 d	1-1/4"	.0800"	568	.0772"	807	.0760"	635
4 d	1-1/2"	.1065"	316	.0720"	584	.0800"	473
5 d	1-3/4"	.1065"	272	.0720"	500	.0800"	406
6 d	2"	.1130"	181	.0858"	309	.1065"	236
8 d	2-1/2"	.1314"	106	.1065"	189	.1130"	145
10 d	3"	.1483"	69	.1130"	121	.1277"	94
16 d	3-1/2"	.1620"	49	.1250"	90	.1350"	71
20 d	4"	.1920"	37	.1350"	62	.1483"	52

d IS THE SYMBOL FOR PENNY, A SPECIFICATION FOR NAIL SIZE.

■ Wood Fasteners • Wood Fasteners • Wood Fasteners ■

WOOD SCREWS

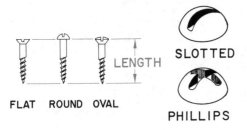

FLAT ROUND OVAL LENGTH

SLOTTED

PHILLIPS

SCREW HOLES

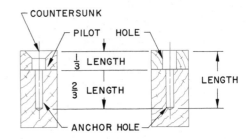

COUNTERSUNK

PILOT HOLE

$\frac{1}{3}$ LENGTH

$\frac{2}{3}$ LENGTH

LENGTH

ANCHOR HOLE

SPECIFICATIONS

DRILLING OPERATIONS

$\frac{3}{32}$ DR 2 1/4 DP   ANCHOR HOLE
7/32 DR 3/4 DP   PILOT HOLE
7/16 X 82° CSINK   COUNTERSINK
OR COUNTERBORE

LIST OF MATERIAL

LENGTH   TYPE
2 1/4 #12 FLAT HEAD PHILLIPS HEAD STYLE
            WOOD SCREW
DIAMETER

DRILL SIZES
(INCHES)

SCREW GAGE	ACTUAL SIZE SHANK	ANCHOR HOLE SOFT WOOD	ANCHOR HOLE HARD WOOD	PILOT HOLE	CSINK OR CBORE
4	.112	1/16	1/16	1/8	1/4
6	.138	1/16	3/32	9/64	5/16
8	.164	1/16	3/32	11/64	3/8
10	.190	3/32	1/8	13/64	3/8
12	.216	3/32	1/8	7/32	7/16
14	.242	1/8	1/8	1/4	1/2
18	.294	5/32	3/16	5/16	5/8

GAGES OBTAINABLE IN EACH LENGTH OF SCREW

LENGTH	GAGE
3/4"	2 - 14
1 - 1/2"	4 - 20
2 - 1/4"	6 - 20
3 -	8 - 24
5·	14 - 24

Other Wood Fasteners • Other Wood Fasteners

UPHOLSTERY   DOUBLE   ESCUTCHEON
    TACK   POINTED TACK   PIN

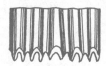

STAPLE   CORRUGATED
                    FASTENER

SCREW   HOOKS

SCREW EYE   POINTED   SQUARE BENT

  LAG   CUP   GATE HOOK & EYE
SCREW   HOOK

HEAD STYLES

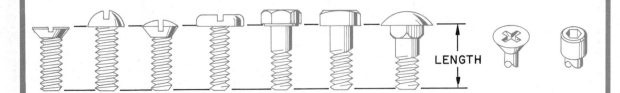

LENGTH

MACHINE SCREWS

STOVE BOLTS

SIZE = DIAMETER X LENGTH & HEAD TYPE

DIAMETERS
1/8 "
5/32"
3/16 "
1/4 "
5/16 "
3/8 "
1/2 "

ALL COARSE THREADS

LENGTHS	
NOMINAL SIZES	INCREMENT RATE
1/8" TO 1-1/2"	BY 1/8"
1-1/2" TO 3"	BY 1/4"
3" TO 6"	BY 1/2"

HEAD TYPES ARE ROUND AND FLAT

SPECIFICATIONS FOR MACHINE SCREWS

SIZE = DIAMETER & THREADS X LENGTH & HEAD TYPE

DIAMETERS		THREADS	
GAGES	EQUIVALENT	NF	NC
2	.086"	64	56
3	.099"	56	48
4	.112"	48	40
5	.125"	44	40
6	.138"	40	32
8	.164"	36	32
10	.190"	32	24
12	.216"	28	24
1/4	.250"	28	20
5/16	.3125"	24	18
3/8	.375"	24	16
1/2	.500"	20	13

LENGTHS	
NOMINAL SIZES	INCREMENT RATE
1/8" TO 5/8"	BY 1/16"
5/8" TO 1-1/4"	BY 1/8"
1-1/4" TO 3 "	BY 1/4"

HEAD TYPES ARE FLAT, ROUND,
OR OVAL WITHOUT NUTS.
MATERIAL – STEEL OR BRASS

═══ Metal Fasteners • Metal Fasteners • Metal Fasteners ═══

WASHERS

PLAIN FLAT   COMMON FLAT   TOOTH LOCK

NUTS

SQUARE   HEXAGON   WING

SHEET METAL SCREWS

TYPE A

SPECIFICATIONS FOR SHEET METAL SCREWS

SIZE = DIAMETER X LENGTH & HEAD TYPE

DIAMETERS	
GAGES	EQUIVALENT
4	.114"
6	.141"
7	.158"
8	.168"
10	.194"
14	.254"

LENGTHS	
NOMINAL SIZES	INCREMENT RATE
1/8" TO 3/8"	BY 1/16"
3/8" TO 1"	BY 1/8 "
1 " TO 2 "	BY 1/4 "

HEAD TYPES ARE <u>ROUND</u>, <u>PAN</u>, <u>TRUSS</u>, <u>FLAT</u>, <u>OVAL</u>, AND <u>HEXAGON</u>

SPECIFICATIONS FOR RIVETS

SIZE = DIAMETER X LENGTH & HEAD TYPE

DIAMETERS
1/8 "
5/32"
1/4 "
5/16 "
3/8 "

LENGTHS	
NOMINAL SIZES	INCREMENT RATE
3/16" TO 5/8"	BY 1/16"
5/8 " TO 3"	BY 1/8 "

MATERIAL - STEEL, BRASS, COPPER, OR ALUMINUM

RIVETS

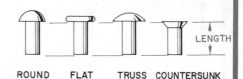

ROUND   FLAT   TRUSS   COUNTERSUNK

LENGTH

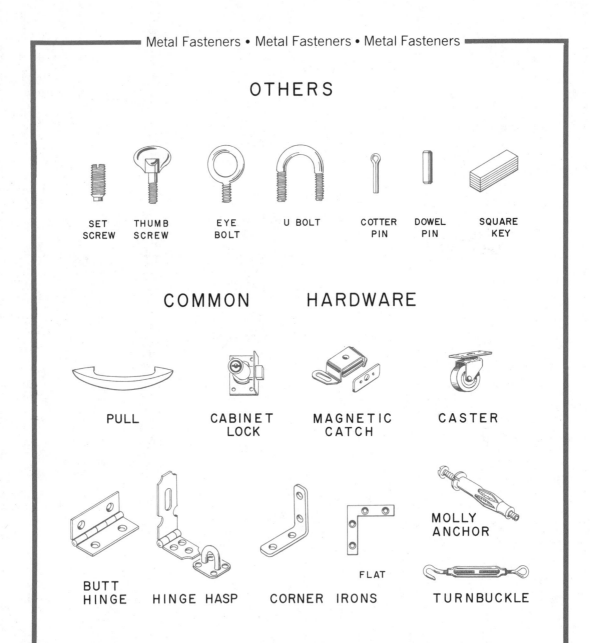

Metal Fasteners • Metal Fasteners • Metal Fasteners

OTHERS

| SET SCREW | THUMB SCREW | EYE BOLT | U BOLT | COTTER PIN | DOWEL PIN | SQUARE KEY |

COMMON   HARDWARE

| PULL | CABINET LOCK | MAGNETIC CATCH | CASTER |

BUTT HINGE   HINGE HASP   CORNER IRONS   MOLLY ANCHOR

FLAT

TURNBUCKLE

Standard Materials

Standard materials are those shapes, sizes, and qualities of substances that are sold for general use. All materials are marketed in standard shapes and/or sizes for many reasons. The most important reasons for standard shapes and sizes are: (1) mass consumption, (2) mass marketing, and (3) mass production. By producing materials in thousands of standard shapes, sizes, and qualities, their uses are increased and costs are reduced. Your ability to reduce costs, both as a designer and a consumer, will depend on how well you develop your ability to use standard materials.

In designing parts and in specifying materials, the following four factors of standard materials should be given consideration: (1) quality, (2) shape, (3) size, and (4) cost.

Quality, Shape, Size, and Cost

Quality of materials may be described by its properties or characteristics such as weight, strength, hardness, durability, and color. The consideration in selecting the best material for a part will require an analysis of the performance requirements of the various materials.

Shape is the form of the material. Standard materials are available in hundreds of shapes such as bars, rods, sheets, rolls, and tubes. It is often possible to purchase a standard material of a shape that very nearly fits the requirements for a particular part. Purchasing standard shaped material can reduce fabrication or "shaping" operations in making the part and thereby reduce the final cost to the consumer.

Size refers to the dimensions or measurements of material. For example: two standard sizes of lumber used in construction are 2″ X 4″ X 8′ (stud) and ¼″ X 4′ X 8′ (plywood). In designing, costly machining operations and material waste can often be reduced by designing parts that utilize the sizes of standard materials. For example: when parts are made by using all or some of the dimensions of a standard material, machining operations required to produce those dimensions are eliminated. Also, waste material is reduced when

parts are designed to be made from portions which totally equal the respective dimensions of standard materials. In designing such parts, be sure to allow material for necessary machining operations.

In utilizing the standard material sizes you should try to record the dimensions of parts in the following orders:

Square Parts	*Round Parts*
1. Thickness	1. Diameter
2. Width	2. Length
3. Length	

Example: ¼″ X 4′ X 8′   *Example*: ½″ Dia X 6½″

The dimensions should generally be considered in these orders because of the cost involved in removing material. Usually these are larger surfaces to be machined in making thickness or diameter dimensions for parts. Width and length sizes each require less stock removal. Therefore, if the thickness or diameter dimension is satisfied with a standard material size, *the most costly machining operation is eliminated*. For this reason the width should be considered after the thickness but before the length in designing parts.

Cost of materials involves buying the material and expense in producing the part. Material costs related to making products are affected by such manufacturing activities as: handling, controlling, treating, fabricating, assembling, and finishing materials.

The development of your ability to design will depend upon how well you learn to use reference sources in obtaining information about standard materials. Information about standard materials is obtained through the same procedure as described under "Standard Parts" involving the use of technical literature and resource people.

Types of Material

Qualities and shapes of some standard materials are provided in the following charts and diagrams. Only a few of the hundreds of materials, shapes and sizes are shown. For further information refer to material catalogs and resource people. This literature is provided to give you an opportunity to learn basic information about common standard materials. It also gives you a resource for needed information in selecting materials for products you may design. To be most effective in the selection of materials, you should gain experience in working with materials and tools in making products.

Woods are perhaps the most versatile material in terms of its uses and ease in making things of it. Study the Table and the illustration. Nominal sizes, shown in color on the Basic Shapes and Sizes of Woods chart, are specifications used in ordering standard materials and parts. *Nominal* means in name only, not in fact; as a 2″ × 4″ piece of wood is actually 1⅝″ × 3⅝″.

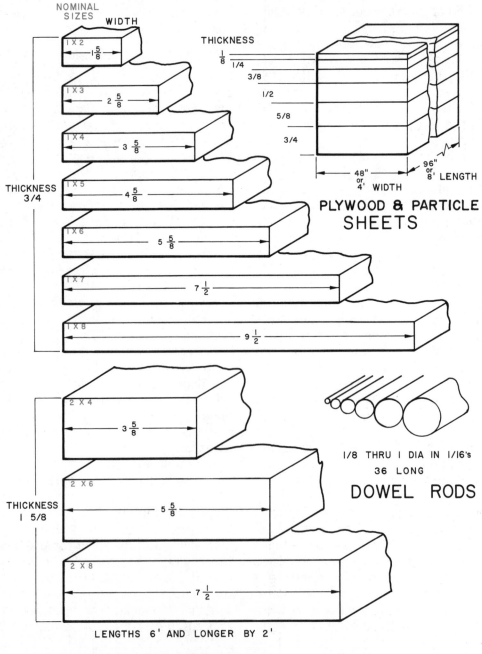

MOLDINGS

3/8 X 1 1/4	3/8 X 3/4	3/4 X 3/4	1/2 X 1/2	3/4 X 3/8	1 1/4 DIA	1 X 1	3/4 X 3/4
DOOR STOP	BASE SHOE	QUARTER ROUND		HALF ROUND	FULL ROUND	CORNER	COVE

QUALITIES AND USES OF WOODS

WOOD AND COLOR	COST PER BD. FT. (APPROX.)	HARDNESS	WEIGHT	STRENGTH	GRAIN	WEATHER	WORKING	RESISTS SPLITTING	FINISHING	USES
ASH – CREAM	.50	HARD	HEAVY	MEDIUM	OPEN		HARD	POOR	MEDIUM	HANDLES, BATS, BOAT FRAMING INTERIOR FINISH, FURNITURE
BIRCH – TAN TO BROWN	.60	HARD	HEAVY	STRONG	MEDIUM	POOR	MEDIUM	POOR	MEDIUM	DOWELS, FURNITURE, INTERIOR FINISH
CEDAR – RED	.40	MEDIUM	LIGHT	MEDIUM	CLOSE	GOOD	EASY	POOR	GOOD	CHESTS, BOXES, POSTS
CHERRY – RED BROWN	.80	HARD	MEDIUM	MEDIUM	MEDIUM		HARD	POOR	GOOD	FURNITURE, TURNINGS
CYPRESS – BROWN	.55	SOFT	MEDIUM	MEDIUM	MEDIUM	GOOD	HARD	POOR	GOOD	FLOWER BOXES, BOATS BIRDHOUSES
FIR – TAN TO BROWN	.30	MEDIUM	MEDIUM	STRONG	CLOSE	GOOD	MEDIUM	POOR	POOR	CONSTRUCTION, BOXES
MAHOGANY, HONDURAS – RED BROWN	1.00	MEDIUM	HEAVY	STRONG	MEDIUM	MEDIUM	EASY	GOOD	MEDIUM	FURNITURE, PATTERNS, BOATS, INTERIORS
MAHOGANY, PHILIPPINE – RED BROWN	.45	MEDIUM	MEDIUM	MEDIUM	OPEN	POOR	EASY	GOOD	MEDIUM	FURNITURE, BOATS, INTERIORS
MAPLE, EASTERN – WHITE TO BROWN	.60	HARD	HEAVY	STRONG	CLOSE	POOR	HARD	MEDIUM	GOOD	FURNITURE, TURNING, FLOORS
OAK – RED OR GRAY BROWN	.60	HARD	HEAVY	STRONG	OPEN	MEDIUM	HARD	MEDIUM	MEDIUM	FURNITURE, INTERIORS, BOATS, TIMBERS, FLOORS
PINE – CREAM	.30	SOFT	LIGHT	WEAK	CLOSE	MEDIUM	EASY	MEDIUM	GOOD	EXTERIORS, BOXES, PATTERNS, MOLDINGS
REDWOOD, – BROWN RED	.30	SOFT	LIGHT	MEDIUM	MEDIUM	GOOD	MEDIUM	GOOD	POOR	EXTERIORS, EXTERIOR FURNITURE
WALNUT – DARK BROWN	1.00	HARD	MEDIUM	MEDIUM	MEDIUM	GOOD	MEDIUM	MEDIUM	MEDIUM	FURNITURE, TURNINGS, INTERIORS

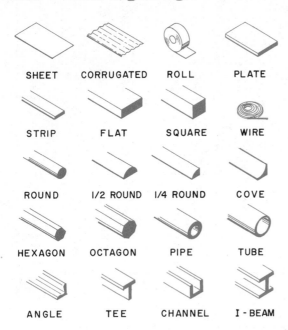

SHEET   CORRUGATED   ROLL   PLATE

STRIP   FLAT   SQUARE   WIRE

ROUND   1/2 ROUND   1/4 ROUND   COVE

HEXAGON   OCTAGON   PIPE   TUBE

ANGLE   TEE   CHANNEL   I-BEAM

Metals are of two basic types: (1) ferrous and (2) nonferrous. *Ferrous* metals contain iron, and *nonferrous* metals contain no iron. Both ferrous and nonferrous metals are manufactured in several basic shapes. Tables 1 and 2 should be studied for the basic differences and uses of these metals.

Table 1
Qualities and Uses of Ferrous Metals

Type & Specification	Qualities	Uses
Low-Carbon Steels 1018, 1020	Soft and easily welded, machined, and formed.	Sheet bodies, pipes, fasteners structural shapes, gears, forgings.
Medium-Carbon Steels 1040, 1042, 1045	More difficult to weld, machine, and form than low-carbon steel.	Tools, pins, shafts, rods.
High-Carbon Steels 1095	Very hard. Must be softened (annealed) to cut or form.	Cutting tools, forming dies.
Tool Steels 0-1, W-1	Easy to machine. Heat treat to improve toughness and hardness.	Cutting tools, forming dies.
Stainless Steels (Many types)	Corrosion resistant. Hard, strong, and tough.	Food and chemical processing equipment, exhaust systems, tableware, medical instruments.
Galvanized Steel Sheets	Corrosion resistant.	Roofing, siding, ducting.
Tin Plate Sheets	Mild steel with tin coating.	Containers and utensils.

Table 2
Qualities and Uses of Nonferrous Metals

Type and Specification	Qualities	Uses
Aluminum	Lightweight, excellent heat conductor, resists corrosion, easily machined and formed.	
1100	Excellent cold-working and welding, low hardness and strength.	Decorative.
2024	Good machinability, high strength, hard, not recommended for bending.	Structural shapes and machined parts.
6061	High tensile strength, good welding.	Structural shapes.
7075	High strength, good machinability, hard.	Aircraft.
Brass 42 (Sheets) 27L (Rods)	Easily machined or formed.	Hardware, small mechanical parts. decorative items.
Bronze 62	Good strength, fair machining, resists corrosion, takes heavy loads.	Bushings, bearings, guides, gears, pins, decorative items.
43 (Casting)	High strength.	Propellers, fittings.
Copper 100	Excellent electrical and heat conductor. Easily formed.	Electrical conductors, alloys, decorative items.
Silver (Sterling)	Easily formed and shaped; resists corrosion.	Jewelry, tableware.

Plastics are growing in use and development faster than any other material. The two basic types of plastics are *thermoplastic* (Table 3 — repeatedly softens with heat) and *thermoset* (Table 4 — hardens permanently after one heating). Plastics can be purchased in various basic forms.

LIQUIDS   **PARTICLES**   **SHEETS**

ROLLS   **RODS**   **TUBES**

Table 3
Qualities and Uses of Thermoplastics

Name	Qualities	Uses
Acetal	Very high strength, stable size, abrasive resistant, good electrical insulator, high resistance to solvents.	Zippers, moldings, plumbing, fixtures, bearings, appliances, machine parts.
Acrylic (Plexiglass or Lucite)	Transparent or opaque, average weight, rigid, high impact strength, stable (size), easily formed, high resistance to corrosion (attack by some solvents), scratch resistant.	Drafting tools, signs, decorations, food containers, lenses.
Cellulosics (Several types)	Very tough, withstands low temperature, expensive.	Handles, eyeglass frames.
Fluorocarbons CEF (Transparent) TEE (Opaque) (Teflon)	High impact strength, low friction, dense, electrical insulator, nonflammable, resists solvents, expensive.	Electrical insulators, pipes, bearings, coatings, coating on cooking utensils.
Polyamide (Nylon)	High tensile strength, wear resistant, low friction, resists heat, easily stained, resists solvents.	Fabric, gears, bearings, impellers, pipes.
Polyethylene	Lightweight, flexible, stretches, burns, not heat nor gas resistant, indoor uses.	Toys, kitchenware, packaging.
Polypropylene	Very lightweight, resists heat.	Toys, kitchenware
Styrene (Styrofoam)	Very lightweight, fairly hard and rigid, stable size, excellent electrical insulator, resists low temperatures, indoor uses.	Models, kitchenware, tile, paints, flotation, insulation, piping, bristles.
Vinyl	Stretches, good electrical insulator, fair abrasive resistance, low heat resistance, flexible, resists low temperatures, adhesives.	Glue, lighting panels, hose, floor tile, inflatable toys, fabric and sheeting.

Table 4
Qualities and Uses of Thermoset Plastics

Name	Qualities	Uses
Amino Urea	Excellent compressive and flexural strength, hard surface, indoor electrical insulator, heat resistant, good resistance to cleaners and solvents, light defusing.	Glue
Melamine (Melmac, Formica)		Dishes, table and cabinet tops, electrical controls, light fixtures.
Casein	Strong, flexible, transparent; does not resist moisture.	Glue, knitting needles, buttons.
Epoxy	High strength, very resistant to abrasion, very adhesive, excellent electrical resistance, high resistance to acids and solvents.	Glue, honeycomb, coating, fiberglassing, tooling, aerospace parts.
Phenolic	Very hard, high compression strength, stable size, poor heat conductor, resists water and household liquids.	Handles, electrical parts, appliance parts, flotation.
Polyester	High strength and flexibility, hard surface, weathers well, resists water and oil, bonds well.	Paint, molding, fabric, bonding fiberglass, bodies, panels, roads, film, repair and customizing of bodies.
Silicone	High heat resistance, dense, strong, flexible, good electrical insulator, resists acids and alkalies.	Mold-release agent, electrical parts, polishes.
Urethane (Foam)	Flexible, tear resistant, absorbs sound and vibration, good electrical insulator, chemical and heat resistance, lightweight.	Mattresses, insulated clothing, padding, coating.

Fabrics are available in numerous forms, weights, weaves, and sizes. They are made from natural or man-made (synthetic) material. The properties and uses of a few types of fabrics are shown in Tables 5 and 6.

Table 5
Qualities and Uses of Natural Fabrics

Name	Qualities	Uses
Cotton	Adaptable, durable, inexpensive, withstands hard laundering.	Clothing, household, canvas, tents, ropes, belting.
Linen	Resists linting, dye stains, and wrinkles, more expensive than cotton, natural luster.	Clothing, tablecloths, household.
Silk	Strong, dyes well, expensive, natural luster.	Upholstery, drapery, clothing accessories.
Wool	Retains shape, versatile, high insulating capacity, dry cleaning or hand laundry, will shrink, needs protection from moths.	Clothing, blankets, carpets, upholstery.

Table 6
Qualities and Uses of Man-Made Fabrics

Name	Qualities	Uses
Acetate	Dries quickly, drapes well, inexpensive, fades when exposed to fumes, low temperature ironing.	Clothing, drapery, upholstery, fiberfill.
Rayon	Absorbent, inexpensive, fair durability, wrinkles easily, flammable.	Clothing, drapery, upholstery, blankets, household, carpets, curtains.
Spandex	High stretch and recovery, resists abrasion, resists baby oils.	Swimwear, ski pants, underwear, surgical hose.
Acrylic	Resists wrinkling, high bulk, soft, lustrous.	Clothing, knitwear, blankets, carpets.
Nylon	Very strong, elastic, shape retention, warm, easily washed.	Clothing, tents, carpets, hoisery, underwear, belting, ropes.
Polyester	Resists wrinkling, retains creases, high bulk.	Clothing, curtains, fiberfill.

Paper is increasingly used to develop new products. Paper products have long been used to package and protect other products. Storage cabinets, furniture, decorative items, toys, clothing and many other useful items are made from paper. Paper and card stock are available in roll and sheet form in various qualities, sizes, and colors. It is an economical and serviceable material to use. Refer to catalogs and distributors for desired technical information.

Connecting and Finishing Material

Adhesives are sticky materials used for holding parts together. They are available in liquid, powder, or sheet form. The powder form is mixed with a liquid for use. Sheet forms of adhesives require the application of heat and pressure to hold the parts and the glue together until the adhesive is activated. Common adhesives with their qualities and uses are shown in Table 7. Adhesives are used to connect wood, plastic, paper, metal, fabric and other surfaces. Various joints are used when connecting wood surfaces. The design of the joint often adds strength when adhesives are used.

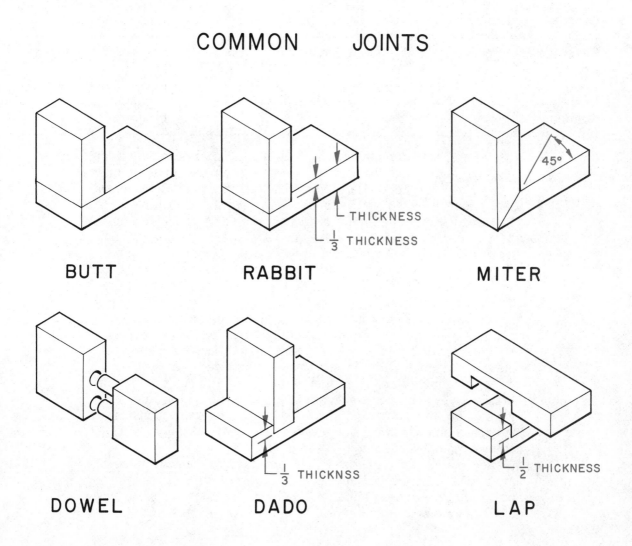

COMMON   JOINTS

BUTT   RABBIT   MITER

DOWEL   DADO   LAP

Table 7
Properties and Uses of Adhesives

Adhesive	Uses	Durability	Strength 100 lbs/sq. foot	Form	Cost
Casein	Laminating, stain tendency	Water resistant	60–80	Powder	Low
Contact Cement	Laminating (sets on contact)	Water resistant	60–95	Liquid	Moderate
Epoxy Resin	Metal to metal or wood	Waterproof	Heavy	Liquid with liquid	High
Polyvinyl (White)	Assembly, laminating edge	Interior	35–50	Liquid	Moderate
Resorcinol Resin	Structures and plywood	Waterproof	50–70	Liquid	High
Urea Powder	Lumber and plywood	Water resistant	35–45	Powder	Low

Metal connecting materials such as solder, brazing and welding materials require heat for melting them and chemicals to assist them in forming a good bond. Plastic materials are also used. Qualities and uses of common metal connecting materials are shown in Table 8.

Abrasives are materials made of grains mounted on a backing material and are used to cut away surfaces by sanding, sharpening, grinding, or polishing. Common materials used in making grains for abrasives are flint, garnet, emery, aluminum oxide, silicon carbide, crocus, and steel wool. A standard index of sizes has been established for grading abrasive grains. Grain sizes range from 12 (very coarse) to 600 (super-fine). In producing a smooth surface, a suitably coarse abrasive is used first. It is followed by finer materials until the desired finish is achieved. On a drawing, the desired finish for a part may be specified in the general notes by designating the finest abrasive to be used. Remember, fine finishes cost more to produce than those made with coarse abrasives. Abrasive types and uses are shown in Table 9. The speeds refer to the rate of movement for the abrasive material. Abrasive machines are high speed and hand use is slow speed. Recommended grain sizes for common materials are shown in Table 10.

Paper, cloth, and rubberized fiber are used as backing materials for abrasives. They are available in the form of sheets, discs, belts, and rolls. Abrasive sheets are 9″ X 11″ in size. Other forms are available in many sizes.

Table 8
Qualities and Uses of Metal-Connecting Materials

Process	Material	Strength	Melting	Uses
Soft Solder	Tin, lead	Light	360°–420°	Copper, brass and tin plated steel — containers and ornaments.
Hard Solder (Silver)	Silver, copper and zinc or brass	Medium	1325°–1400°	Copper, brass and silver — jewelry, tableware, ornaments.
Brazing	Copper, zinc	Medium high	1000°	Copper, brass, ferrous metals — assembly of pipes or bar structures and repair of castings.
Welding Gas	Steel-aluminum	High	High	Steel plates and structures (can be done under water).
Spot	Base metal	High	High	Steel, aluminum — sheet materials.
Arc	Steel-aluminum	High	High	Steel, aluminum, copper, bronze — structure (most commonly used).
Gas-Arc (TIG)	Steel-aluminum	High	High	Stainless steel, aluminum — air and spacecraft (best fatigue properties).

Table 9
Abrasive Types and Uses

Materials to be Removed	ALUMINUM OXIDE		GARNET		SILICON CARBIDE		
	Low Speed	High Speed	Low Speed	High Speed	Low Speed	High Speed	Finish
Enamel					●	●	●
Lacquer					●	●	●
Metal	●					●	●
Plastic					●	●	●
Varnish					●	●	●
Woods	●	●	●				●

Table 10
Abrasive Grains and Uses

	VERY FINE		FINE	MEDIUM	COARSE
Symbol Numbers	10/0 9/0 8/0 7/0 6/0		5/0 4/0 3/0 2/0	1/0 ½ 1	1½ 2 2½
Grain Size	600 500 400 320 280 240 220		180 150 120 100	80 60 50	40 36 30
Grain sizes for fine surfaces in these materials.	Enamel, Lacquer, Metal, Plastics, Varnish		Hard Woods	Soft Woods	

Finish coatings are materials applied to the surfaces of parts to protect them and/or improve their appearance. They are usually applied in paste (wax), liquid (paint), or sheet (paper or plastic) form.

There are many types of finishing coating materials available. A few common finish coating materials with their qualities and uses are shown in Table 11.

Table 11
Qualities and Uses of Finish Coatings

Type	Color	Application	Drying	Uses
Oil	Clear	Cloth or brush	Fast	Furniture (darkens)
Wax	Clear-sheen	Cloth	Fast	Furniture, toys, paint sealer
Lacquer	Clear or colors	Brush, spray, dip	Fast	Furniture, automobiles
Varnish	Clear	Brush, roller, spray, dip	Slow	Furniture, boats
Enamel	Colors	Brush, roller, spray, dip	Slow	Trim, toys, lawn furniture, boats
Latex	Colors	Brush, roller, spray	Medium	Buildings
Polyrethane	Clear	Brush, roller spray	Slow	Floors, tables
Epoxy	Clear or colors	Brush, roller, spray	Medium	Floors, tables, fiberglass

Basic Manufacturing Practices

Manufacturing is processing materials to produce useful products through six basic practices: (1) material handling, (2) quality control, (3) conditioning materials, (4) fabricating parts, (5) assembling parts, and (6) finishing. These are blended in various combinations with a manufacturing plan for making products efficiently. Manufacturing plans are often called production plans and are developed by designers having special abilities with the creative use of basic manufacturing practices.

Man can perform all six basic manufacturing practices by using his own body; that is, by using his senses, brains, and muscles. In his early beginning he produced useful items by changing the forms of various materials to serve different functions. First, he used his hands and feet to break and cut pieces of wood, his hands and fingers to weave grass or vines, and to form clay into bowls. As man learned more about his abilities and the use of materials, he used his manufacturing abilities and the materials of his surroundings to make tools. *The tools were extensions of man's ability to perform basic manufacturing practices.* Man's first tools were sticks, stones, and vines which he used to extend his own ability with his hands and arms to reach, pound, and hold in working with other materials. As time passed, man developed better quality hand tools such as hammers, saws, drills, and wheels. He also learned to harness the power of animals, wind, and water to his tools which became machines such as power saws, grinding mills, and water pumps. Recently, with machines such as motors and engines, man has harnessed the energy of burning wood, coal, oil, and chemicals to provide sources of power. These power sources have been connected to tools with power transmission systems as can be observed in our present-day machines such as drill presses, engine lathes, and milling machines. Thus, you will observe, all tools and machines are extensions of man's own abilities.

In the following pages each of the six basic manufacturing practices are analyzed with several of its component operations. Each operation is described as to how it is performed by man and some of the tools and machines man has developed to extend his ability to perform basic manufacturing practices. These descriptions are intended to give you the concept of each basic manufacturing practice. They provide a means for you to relate the things you know about yourself, tools, and machines with the things you are to learn. As a designer, producer, and/or consumer of products in a technological society, a measure of your success will depend upon how well you develop your ability to deal with basic manufacturing practices.

Material Handling

Material handling is the process of containing masses and carrying them from place to place. Masses include materials, parts and assembled products. There are two operations in material handling: (1) containing and (2) carrying. There are many items used to contain masses such as boxes, cartons, jars, cans, barrels, bins, tanks, and reservoirs. Dollies, trucks, trains, ships, planes, cranes, and conveyors are used to carry items.

335

Table 12 shows material handling *operations* and *man's abilities* to perform each operation. It further shows some of the tools and machines developed by man to extend his ability to perform each operation. The operations, abilities, tools, and machines are pictured in the circular chart on page 337 starting at the 1 o'clock position and proceeding in a clockwise (to the right) direction. In examining the circular chart, start with picture of man in the center circle. Proceed by viewing the man with his hands cupped as he contains materials. In the next larger circle of this segment there are tools such as boxes and bins. In the largest circle are the machines shown as mechanical (cooled or heated) unitized containers and grain elevators. By looking at the pictures around the circular chart and the respective words in the table you can gain a conceptual understanding of material handling.

Each basic manufacturing practice is described in a similar manner. Remember, there are more operations and many, many tools and machines to be included with each basic manufacturing practice; however, the samples shown were selected to give you needed concepts.

Table 12
Material Handling

Operations	Man's Abilities	Tools	Machines
CONTAIN	Hands cupped	Boxes	Unitized mechanical (heated or cooled) containers
		Bins	Grain elevators
	Mouth	Barrels Jars	Storage tanks Reservoirs
	Hands grasping	Sacks Tongs	Mechanical nets Clam shovels
CARRY Wheels	Arms and legs	Hand trucks Dollies	Trucks Trains
Water	Swim	Sailboats Rowboats	Ships Ships
Roll-Chutes	Shoulder and legs	Shovels Conveyors	Chutes Conveyor belts
Lift	Arms and legs	Block and tackles Jacks	Cranes Bucket conveyors
Air	Arms	Pulley line Conveyor-overhead	Rockets Airplanes

MATERIAL HANDLING

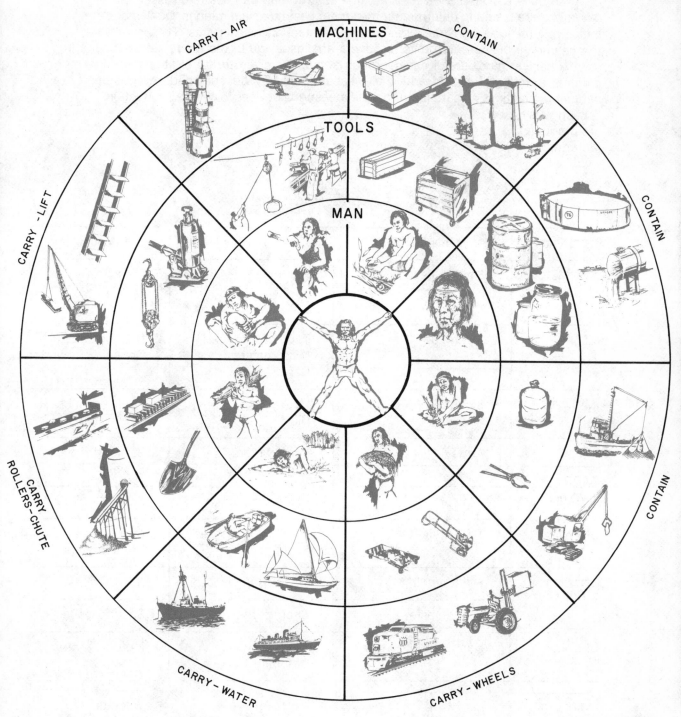

Quality Control

Quality control is measuring and evaluating the properties or characteristics of a mass. In quality control materials, parts or assemblies are tested to determine if they meet desired specifications. Quality control tools and machines serve as detecting instruments. Through the use of measurements, products are made within the limits set by the designer. Careful consideration should be given to the relationship of product function and the measurements to be specified. All basic practices of manufacturing use measuring devices to control production.

Table 13
Quality Control

Operations	Man's Abilities	Tools	Machines
ALIGNMENT	Sight, balance	Plumbs Levels Protractors	Transites Lasers
SIZE	Sight, body	Tape measures Micrometers Gages	Dial indicators Optical comparator
TIME	Sight	Hourglass Clocks	Timing graphs Oscilloscopes
STRENGTH	Arms, legs	Torqometers Torq wrenches	Strength testers Strength testers
WEIGHT	Arms, body	Balances	Scales
SURFACE	Touch, sight	Magnifying glasses Specimens	Microscopes Profilometers
CONTENT	Sight, smell	Magnifying glasses	Microscopes
	Touch, taste	Chemical tests	Spectroscopes
VOLUME	Hands, mouth, arms	Spoons Graduate	Meters Meters

QUALITY CONTROL

Conditioning Materials

Conditioning materials is the modification of the state or content of materials. Materials are conditioned to make them more workable or to improve their functional qualities.

Table 14
Conditioning Materials

Operations	Man's Abilities	Tools	Machines
Wet	Mouth, saliva	Pans	Vats and sprays
Cool	Mouth, breath	Fans	Blowers
Freeze	(Winter)	Ice chests	Refrigerations
Mix	Hands	Spoons	Mixers
Expand	Hands	Beaters	Blenders
Light	(Sun)	Bulbs	Arc lights
Chemical	Body salts, oils	Bowl, spoons	Apparatus
Compress	Hands	Arbor presses	Compressors
Work	Hands	Hammers	Rollers
Heat	Body	Irons	Heat presses
Melt	Body, breath	Torches	Furnaces
Dry	Breath	Dryer	Kiln

CONDITIONING MATERIALS

Fabricating Parts

Fabricating parts is making materials into desired shapes and sizes. The many operations used in shaping and sizing materials can be classified in two groups; (1) cutting and (2) forming. *Cutting* is removing material with a sharp edge tool such as a knife blade or piece of abrasive material. During cutting operations the material is in a solid state. *Forming* is fashioning parts through the action of materials with the surface of tools as pressures are applied. During forming operations the material is in a fluid or flowing state. Dies, molds, and forms are examples of tools used in these operations.

Table 15
Fabricating Parts — Cutting

Operation	Man's Abilities	Tools	Machines
Saw	Hands, feet, teeth	Hand saws Sabre saws Hack saws	Table saws Band saws Power hack saws
Drill	Fingers	Hand drills	Drill presses
Punch	Fingers, teeth	Hand punches	Punch presses
Turn	Teeth	Chisels, knives	Lathes
Plane	Fingers, teeth	Planes	Planers
Shear	Hands, feet, teeth	Snips	Shears
File	Teeth, nails	Files	Filing machines
Mill	Teeth, nails	Routers	Milling machines
Grind	Teeth, nails	Sanders	Grinders
Burn	(Flame)	Torches	Burning machines

FABRICATING PARTS
(CUTTING)

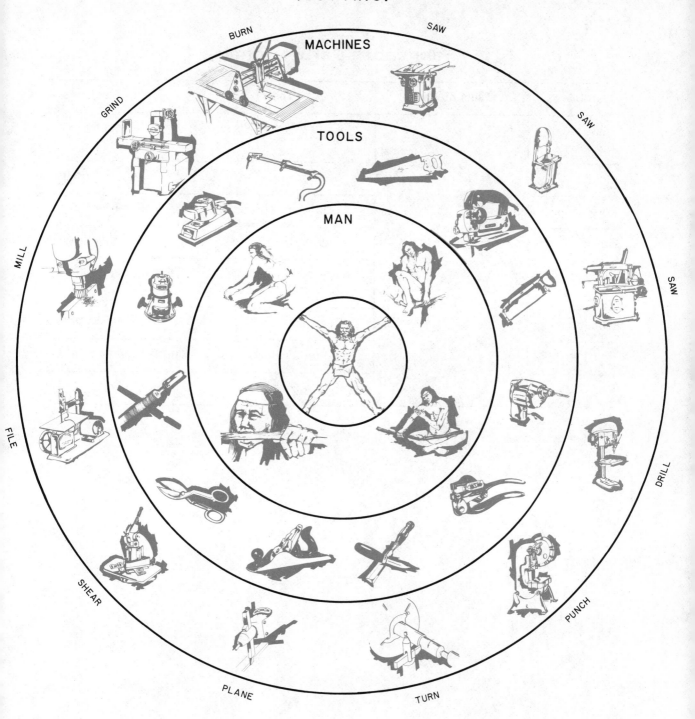

BURN

SAW

MACHINES

GRIND

SAW

TOOLS

MILL

SAW

MAN

FILE

DRILL

SHEAR

PUNCH

PLANE

TURN

Table 16
Fabricating Parts—Forming

Operation	Man's Abilities			Tools	Machines
Cast	H			Flasks	Die casting machines
Mold	A			Vacuum molders	Vacuum presses
Forge	N			Hammers and anvils	Forge presses
Press	D A			Flaring tools	Forming presses
Bend	S N	F		Box and pan brakes	Press brakes
Extrude	D	E		Nozzles	Extrusion presses
Spin		E		Potter's wheels	Spinning lathes
Roll		T		Slip rollers	Rolling machines

FABRICATING PARTS
(FORMING)

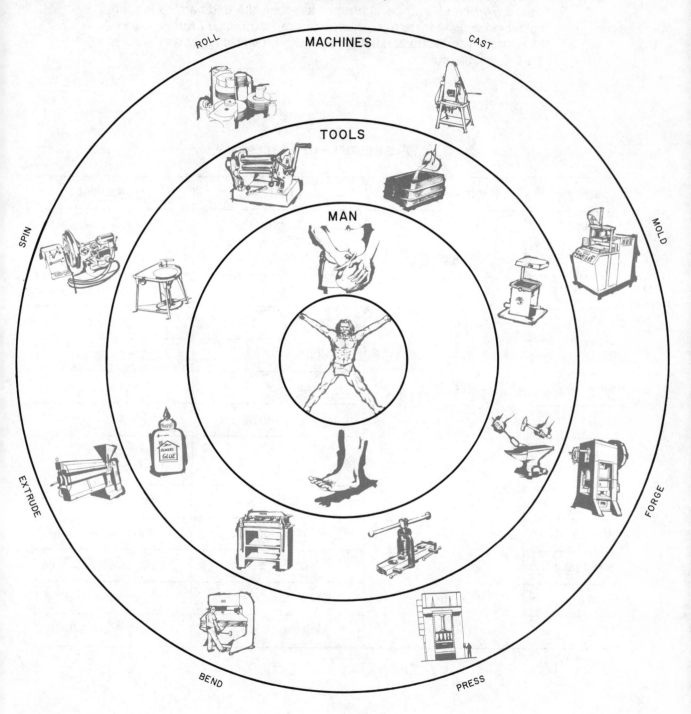

ROLL   MACHINES   CAST

TOOLS

MAN

SPIN   MOLD

EXTRUDE   FORGE

BEND   PRESS

Assembling Parts

Assembling parts is to retain, support, or connect pieces in a desired position. When several parts are put together, the parts are commonly held together with fasterners, glue, wires, tape, thread, or welds. Assembling parts also includes holding parts with clamps or vises as the parts are being fabricated.

Table 17
Assembling Parts

Operation	Man's Abilities	Tools	Machines
Fasten	Mouth,	Rivets, buttons, nails, screws, pins, bolts	Power riveters and drivers
Stitch		Needles	Sewing machines
Weave	Hands,	Looms	Power looms
Clamp		Clamps	Power clamps
Vise	Feet,	Vises	Power vises
Glue		Glue dispensers	Glue guns
Adhere	Legs,	Brushes	Electronic glue welders
Solder		Soldering irons	Solder guns
Weld	and	Welding torches	Welding machines
Strap-tape		Dispensers	Strapping machines
Staple	Arms	Staplers	Stitchers
Magnet		Magnets	Magnetic chucks

ASSEMBLING PARTS

Finishing

Finishing is the application of a coating to the surface of an object. The coating is used to protect and/or beautify the product. Finishing involves applying materials in the form of liquids, powders, pastes, films, or sheets to surfaces.

Table 18
Finishing

Operation	Man's Abilities	Tools	Machines
Brush-spray	Hands,	Brushes	Air brushes and spray guns
Roll		Rollers	Coating machines
Dip		Pans	Vats and conveyors
Wipe-tumble		Cloths	Tumblers
Laminate	Mouth,	Adhesive tiles	Laminating presses
Plate		Dip tanks	Plating machines
Stencil	and	Stencil sheets	Screen printing presses
Print		Rubber stamps	Printing presses
Type		Pens	Typewriter
Copy	Feet	Exposure frames	Reproducers
Photograph		Hand camera	Copy camera
Record			Television camera

FINISHING

Application of Design Fundamentals

In developing your ability to design products, you will find it easier to start improving or altering an existing design. This is done by changing the use of the product or altering its capacity. Of the many factors to be considered in the improvement of a design, these are basic:

1. *Performance* of the product. How can it be made to work better or satisfy additional needs?
2. *Conservation* of parts, materials and manufacturing operations. Can it be made more simply?
3. *Contact* of the item with people. Does it please the senses?

These design problems provide you with the opportunity to develop your ability to design.

Problem 89

Change your orthographic projection drawing of the SANDING BLOCK so the product will be more comfortable (pleasing to the sense of touch) for the user to hold.

Problem 90

Review the drawing problems in Chapter 7, *Drawing Orthographic Projections,* and Chapter 10, *Drawing Developments,* to find a product that can be made with fewer parts, materials or manufacturing operations. Make a drawing of one of your improved design ideas.

Problem 91

Adapt one or more of the product designs in Chapter 7, *Drawing Orthographic Projections,* and Chapter 10, *Drawing Developments,* to a larger or smaller capacity. For example:

1. A sanding block to hold ¼ of a 9″ X 11″ sheet of abrasive paper,
2. Larger mallet head,
3. Picture frame,
4. Book rack,
5. Screen printing frame,
6. Parts drawer, or
7. Card file box.

You should, if practical, use standard parts and materials in developing the design.

Summary

Through study of this chapter you have had the opportunity to learn basic procedures and information required in drafting design. You have learned how *man creates* new products through the use of his unique human abilities and the resources about him. The six steps of the *creative process* were explained for your understanding: (1) identifying problems, (2) applying resources, (3) formulating ideas, (4) recording ideas, (5) refining the product, and (6) presenting the product. *Standard parts and materials* were defined as to their types, qualities, uses, shapes and sizes so you can begin using them in designing product. The six *basic manufacturing practices* illustrated and briefly described for you: (1) material handling, (2) quality control, (3) conditioning materials, (4) fabricating parts, (5) assembling parts, and (6) finishing. The organization and information presented in all of these concepts provide you with a basic foundation for unlimited development of your ability to design and build fine useful products for the improvement of life.

How to Divide Your Classroom Time

CLASS HOURS

Note: The number of hours of study time is noted for each chapter and problem in the vertical columns.

30	45	60	Semester (90)	Year 180
1	1	2	2	4
1	1	1	1	1
1	1	1	1	1
1	1	1	1	1
1	1	1	1	1
			1	1
		1		
			1	1
—	1			1
		1	2	
				2

CLASS HOURS

	30	45	60	Semester (90)	Year 180
Problem 10 – Practice Pictorial Exercises p. 79 — Rounds, squares, flats, boats, planes, cars.	1	1	2	2	8
Working Drawings — Problem 11 – Line Exercises p. 90 — Lines, angles, arcs, circles, arrowheads, lettering.	1	1	1	1	1
Square Objects — Problem 12 – Practice the Drawing Procedure p. 98 — Sanding block, V-block, drill grinding gauge, tinner's hammer head, checker board.	1	1	1	3	2
Round Objects — Problem 13 – Practice the Drawing Procedure p. 102 — Mallet head, funnel, coaster, gavel head, mallet handle.	1	1	1		2
Assemblies — Problem 14 – Practice Assembly Drawings p. 106 — Kicking tee, picture frame, napkin holder, T-bevel, bookcase.	1	1	1	2	2
General Skill Development	–	–	–		4
Chapter 3 DRAFTING CONVENTIONAL PRACTICES — Study	1/2	1	2	3	3
Reference					3
Chapter 4 DRAFTING TOOLS, BOOKS, SUPPLIES, AND EQUIPMENT — Study	1/2	1	1	1	2
Reference					

CLASS HOURS

CLASS HOURS

CLASS HOURS

	30	45	60	Semester 90	Year 180
Chapter 10 **DRAWING A BUILDING**					
Study					
Problem 74 – Learn to Read an Architect's Scale p. 275					
Problem 75 – Design Shelter for Pets p. 280	1	4	5	10	20
Problem 76 – Design Small Storage or Play Area p. 281					
Problem 77 – Design Small Building or Room p. 281					
Problem 78 – Design Large Building Plan p. 281					
Chapter 11 **DRAWING SYSTEMS**					
Study					
Problem 79 – Draw a Map p. 284					
Problem 80 – Draw a Personnel Chart p. 285					
Problem 81 – Draw a Simple Production Plan p. 286					
Problem 82 – Draw a PERT Plan p. 290					
Problem 83 – Draw a Block Diagram and a Schematic of an Electronic Circuit p. 295	1½	3	5	10	20
Problem 84 – Identify Hydraulic Symbols p. 298					
Problem 85 – Draw a Schematic of a Hydraulic Circuit p. 298					
Problem 86 – Draw a Simple Data Processing System p. 299					
Problem 87 – Draw Athletic Plays p. 303					
Problem 88 – Draw a Graph p. 305					
Chapter 12 **REPRODUCTION AND CARE OF DRAWINGS**	1/2	1	1	1	3
Study					
Practice					

CLASS HOURS

<table>
<tr><th></th><th>30</th><th>45</th><th>60</th><th>Semester
90</th><th>Year
180</th></tr>
<tr><td>Chapter 13 DRAFTING DESIGN
Study</td><td rowspan="2">1</td><td rowspan="2">2</td><td rowspan="2">2</td><td rowspan="2">2</td><td>2</td></tr>
<tr><td>Reference
Problem 89—Change Sanding Block Design p. 350
Problem 90—Improve Design of Product p. 350
Problem 91—Reduce or Enlarge Design p. 351</td><td>8</td></tr>
</table>

DECIMAL EQUIVALENT CHART

1/64 __ .015625	33/64 __ .515625
1/32 _____ .03125	17/32 _____ .53125
3/64 __ .046875	35/64 __ .546875
1/16 _____ .0625	9/16 _____ .5625
5/64 __ .078125	37/64 __ .578125
3/32 _____ .09375	19/32 _____ .59375
7/64 __ .109375	39/64 __ .609375
1/8 _____ .125	5/8 _____ .625
9/64 __ .140625	41/64 __ .640625
5/32 _____ .15625	21/32 _____ .65625
11/64 __ .171875	43/64 __ .671875
3/16 _____ .1875	11/16 _____ .6875
13/64 __ .203125	45/64 __ .703125
7/32 _____ .21875	23/32 _____ .71875
15/64 __ .234375	47/64 __ .734375
1/4 _____ .250	3/4 _____ .750
17/64 __ .265625	49/64 __ .765625
9/32 _____ .28125	25/32 _____ .78125
19/64 __ .296875	51/64 __ .796875
5/16 _____ .3125	13/16 _____ .8125
21/64 __ .328125	53/64 __ .828125
11/32 _____ .34375	27/32 _____ .84375
23/64 __ .359375	55/64 __ .859375
3/8 _____ .375	7/8 _____ .875
25/64 __ .39065	57/64 __ .890625
13/32 _____ .40625	29/32 _____ .90625
27/64 __ .421875	59/64 __ .921875
7/16 _____ .4375	15/16 _____ .9375
29/64 __ .453125	61/64 __ .953125
15/32 _____ .46875	31/32 _____ .96875
31/64 __ .484375	63/64 __ .984375
1/2 _____ .500	1 _____ 1.000

DRILL SIZES

SIZE	DECIMAL EQUIV.	SIZE	DECIMAL EQUIV.	SIZE	DECIMAL EQUIV.	SIZE	DECIMAL EQUIV.
1/2	.5000	G	.2610	23	.1540	1/16	.0625
31/64	.4844	F	.2570	24	.1520	53	.0595
15/32	.4687	E 1/4	.2500	25	.1495	54	.055
29/64	.4531	D	.2460	26	.1470	55	.0520
7/16	.4375	C	.2420	27	.1440	3/64	.0469
27/64	.4219	B	.2380	9/64	.1406	56	.0465
Z	.4130	15/64	.2344	28	.1405	57	.0430
13/32	.4062	A	.2340	29	.1360	58	.0420
Y	.4040	1	.2280	30	.1285	59	.0410
X	.3970	2	.2210	1/8	.1250	60	.0400
25/64	.3906	7/32	.2187	31	.1200	61	.0390
W	.3860	3	.2130	32	.1160	62	.0380
V	.3770	4	.2090	33	.1130	63	.0370
3/8	.3750	5	.2055	34	.1110	64	.0360
U	.3680	6	.2040	35	.1100	65	.0350
23/64	.3594	13/64	.2031	7/64	.1094	66	.0330
T	.3580	7	.2010	36	.1065	67	.0320
S	.3480	8	.1990	37	.1040	1/32	.0313
11/32	.3437	9	.1960	38	.1015	68	.0310
R	.3390	10	.1935	39	.0995	69	.0292
Q	.3320	11	.1910	40	.0980	70	.0280
21/64	.3281	12	.1890	41	.0960	71	.0260
P	.3230	3/16	.1875	3/32	.0937	72	.0250
O	.3160	13	.1850	42	.0935	73	.0240
5/16	.3125	14	.1820	43	.0890	74	.0225
N	.3020	15	.1800	44	.0860	75	.0210
19/64	.2969	16	.1770	45	.0820	76	.0200
M	.2950	17	.1730	46	.0810	77	.0180
L	.2900	11/64	.1719	47	.0785	78	.0160
9/32	.2812	18	.1695	5/64	.0781	1/64	.0156
K	.2810	19	.1660	48	.0760	79	.0145
J	.2770	20	.1610	49	.0730	80	.0135
I	.2720	21	.1590	50	.0700		
H	.2660	22	.1570	51	.0670		
17/64	.2656	5/32	.1562	52	.0635		

DIRECTORY OF DRAFTING TOOLS, SUPPLIES, AND EQUIPMENT SALES AND MANUFACTURING COMPANIES

NAME OF COMPANY	PRODUCT
Altender, Theo and Sons 1225 Spring Garden Philadelphia, Pennsylvania	Drafting tools
Alvin and Co., Inc. 607 Palisade Avenue Windsor, Connecticut 06095	Drafting tools, supplies, and equipment
Arthur Brown and Brother, Inc. 2 West 46th Street New York, New York 10038	Pressure-sensitive sheets
Berger, C. L. & Sons, Inc. 43-A Williams Boston, Massachusetts	Drafting protractors and scales
Blu-Ray, Inc. 5362 Westbrook Road Essex, Connecticut 06426	Diazo printing machines
Bruning, Charles Co. 1800 West Central Road Mount Prospect, Illinois 60058	Drafting tools, supplies, and equipment
Cardinell Corporation 13 Label Montclair, New Jersey	Drafting parallel straightedges and supplies
Chartpak-Rotex 2620 South Susan Santa Ana, California	Pressure-sensitive tape and sheets
Clearprint Paper Company 1482 Sixty-seventh Street Emeryville, California 94608	Drafting papers
Dazor Manufacturing Corporation 4455 Duncan Avenue St. Louis, Missouri 63110	Drafting lamps
Dieterich-Post Co. 540 Barneveld Avenue San Francisco, California	Drafting tools, supplies, and equipment
Dietzgen, Eugene Co. 2425 North Sheffield Avenue Chicago, Illinois 60614	Drafting tools, supplies, and equipment
Draftette Company P. O. Box 895 Hemet, California	Drafting kits

Eagle Pencil Company Danbury, Connecticut	Drafting pencils
Faber-Castell Pencil Co., Inc. 41 Dickerson Street Newark, New Jersey 07103	Drafting pencils, erasers
Fullerton Sales Company 811 Milford Street Glendale, California 91203	Drafting tools, supplies, and equipment
Graphic Products Corporation 3810 Industrial Avenue Rolling Meadows, Illinois 60008	Pressure-sensitive sheets
Hamilton Manufacturing Company Two Rivers, Wisconsin 54241	Drafting furniture
The Huey Company 19 South Wabash Avenue Chicago, Illinois 60603	Drafting tools, supplies, and equipment
Keuffel Esser, Inc. 303 Adams Street Hoboken, New Jersey 07030	Drafting tools, supplies, and equipment
Eastman Kodak Rochester, New York 14650	Drafting copy supplies and equipment
KOH-I-NOOR, Inc. 100 North Street Bloomsbury, New Jersey 08804	Pencils and pens
Letraset, Inc. 2379 Charleston Road Mountain View, California 94040	Pressure-sensitive sheets
Lietz Company 840 Post Street San Francisco, California 94119	Drafting tools, supplies, and equipment
Lyon Metal Products 1933 Montgomery Avenue Aurora, Illinois	Drafting furniture
Mayline Co., Inc. 627 North Commerce Sheboygan, Wisconsin 53081	Drafting tools and equipment
Michaels Artists and Engineering Supplies, Inc. 7005 Tujunga Avenue North Hollywood, California 91605	Drafting tools, supplies, and equipment
Para-Tone, Inc. 512 West Burlington Avenue LaGrange, Illinois 60525	Pressure-sensitive tape and sheets

Parent Metal Products, Inc. 6803 State Road Philadelphia, Pennsylvania	Drafting furniture
Plant Layout Materials, Inc. 24 Eastview Road Latham, New York 12110	Architectural models
Post Frederick Company 3646 North Avondale Avenue Chicago, Illinois	Drafting tools, supplies, and equipment
Prestype, Inc. 138 West 21st Street New York, New York 10011	Pressure-sensitive tape and sheets
Rapidesign, Inc. 2601 North San Fernando Burbank, California	Templates
Stacor Corporation 335 Emmet Street Newark, New Jersey 07114	Drafting furniture
Staedtler, J. S., Inc. Montville, New Jersey 07045	Drafting pencils and pens
Technifax 200 Appleton Street Holyoke, Massachusetts 01040	Diazo materials and equipment
Timely Products Company Baltimore, Ohio	Drafting templates
Tolerton Company 269 North Freedom Avenue Alliance, Ohio	Drafting furniture
Universal Drafting Machine Corp. 5200 Richmond Road Bedford Heights, Ohio 44146	Drafting machines and scales
V and E Manufacturing Co. Fair Oaks and Filmore Streets Pasadena, California	Drafting machines and instruments
Varigraph, Inc. 1480 Martin Madison, Wisconsin	Drafting lettering templates
X-Acto Precision Tools, Inc. 48 Van Dam Street L. I. C., New York 11101	Knives and modelmaking tools

DIRECTORY OF DRAFTING AND ENGINEERING ORGANIZATIONS

American Institute of Aeronautics
and Astronautics (AIAA)
1290 Avenue of the Americas
New York, New York 10019

American Institute of Architects (AIA)
1735 New York Avenue, North West
Washington, D. C. 20006

Society of Automotive Engineers (SAE)
485 Lexington Avenue
New York, New York 10017

International Association of Blueprint
and Allied Industries, Inc.
33 I. Congress Parkway
Chicago, Illinois 60605

Society of Die Casting Engineers (SDCE)
19382 James Couzens Freeway
Detroit 35, Michigan

National Institute of Ceramic
Engineers (NICE)
4055 North High Street
Columbus, Ohio 43214

American Society of Civil Engineers (ASCE)
345 East 47th Street
New York, New York 10017

American Institute of Design and
Drafting (AIDD)
18465 James Couzens Freeway
Detriot 35, Michigan

Engineers Joint Council (EJC)
345 East 47th Street
New York, New York 10017

National Society of Professional
Engineers (NSPE)
2029 K Street, North West
Washington, D. C. 20006

Industrial Designers Society of America (IDSA)
60 West 55th Street
New York, New York 10019

National Society of Interior Designers (NSID)
157 West 57th Street
New York 19, New York

Association of Iron and Steel
Engineers (AISE)
1010 Empire Building
Pittsburgh 22, Pennsylvania

Society of Naval Architects and
Marine Engineers (SNAME)
74 Trinity Place
New York 6, New York

Society Packaging and Handling
Engineers (SPHE)
14 East Jackson Boulevard
Chicago 4, Illinois

Society of Plastics Engineers (SPE)
65 Prospect Street
Stamford, Connecticut 06902

National Association of Power
Engineers (NAPE)
176 West Adams Street, Suite 1411
Chicago, Illinois 60603

Fluid Power Society (FPS)
Box 49
Thienaville, Wisconsin

American Society for Quality
Control (ASQC)
161 West Wisconsin Avenue
Milwaukee 3, Wisconsin

Society of Reproduction Engineers (SRE)
18307 James Couzens Highway
Detroit, Michigan 48235

American Society of Safety Engineers (ASSE)
5 North Wabash Avenue
Chicago, Illinois 60602

National Tool, Die and Precision
Machining Association (NTDPMA)
1411 K Street
Washington, D. C. 20005

Society of Manufacturing
Engineers (SME)
20501 Ford Road
Dearborn, Michigan 48128

Areas of Plane Figures

Nomenclature

a, b, c, d — Lengths of Sides
A — Area
d, d_1, d_2 — Diameters
e, f — Lengths of Diagonals
h — Vertical Height or Altitude
l, l_1, l_2 — Length of Arc
L — Lateral Length or Slant Height
n — Number of Sides
θ — Number of Degrees of Arc
p — Perimeter
r, r_1, r_2, R — Radii

CIRCLE

$p = 2\pi r = \pi d = 3.1416d$

$A = \pi r^2 = \dfrac{\pi d^2}{4} = .7854d^2$

$\quad = \dfrac{p^2}{4\pi} = .07958p^2$

SQUARE

$a = b$

$p = 4a$

$A = a^2 = .5e^2$

$e = a\sqrt{2} = 1.414\,a$

RECTANGLE

$p = 2(a + b)$

$e = \sqrt{a^2 + b^2}$

$b = \sqrt{e^2 - a^2}$

$A = ab$

RIGHT TRIANGLE

$p = a + b + c$

$c^2 = a^2 + b^2$

$b = \sqrt{c^2 - a^2}$

$A = \dfrac{ab}{2}$

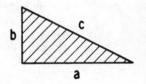

GENERAL TRIANGLE

Let $s = \dfrac{a + b + c}{2}$

$p = a + b + c$

$h = \dfrac{2}{a}\sqrt{s(s-a)(s-b)(s-c)}$

$A = \dfrac{ah}{2}$

$A = \sqrt{s(s-a)(s-b)(s-c)}$

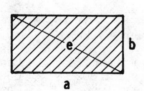

EQUILATERAL TRIANGLE

$p = 3a$

$h = \dfrac{a}{2}\sqrt{3} = .866\,a$

$A = a^2\dfrac{\sqrt{3}}{4} = .433\,a^2$

Index

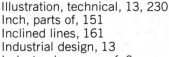